Jane
Austen
Sings
the
Blues

Jane Austen Sings the Blues

Nora Foster Stovel
editor

Graham Guest and
Grant Stovel
producers

Gutteridge
BOOKS
An Imprint of The University of Alberta Press

Published by

The University of Alberta Press
Ring House 2
Edmonton, Alberta, Canada T6G 2E1

LIBRARY AND ARCHIVES CANADA CATALOGUING IN PUBLICATION

Jane Austen sings the blues / editor, Nora Foster Stovel ; with Graham Guest & Grant Foster Stovel.

Essays in honour of Bruce Stovel, with companion CD featuring blues performers. Includes index.

ISBN 978-0-88864-510-4

1. Austen, Jane, 1775–1817—Criticism and interpretation. 2. Blues (Music)—Texts. 3. Blues
(Music). 4. Stovel, Bruce. 5. Teachers—Canada—Biography. I. Stovel, Nora Foster II. Guest,
Graham III. Stovel, Grant Foster IV. Stovel, Bruce

PR4037.J334 2009   823'.7   C2009-900063-6

The University of Alberta Press is committed to protecting our natural environment. As part of our
efforts, this book is printed on Enviro Paper: it contains 100% post-consumer recycled fibres and is acid-
and chlorine-free.

The University of Alberta Press gratefully acknowledges the support received for its publishing program
from The Canada Council for the Arts. The University of Alberta Press also gratefully acknowledges the
financial support of the Government of Canada through the Book Publishing Industry Development
Program (BPIDP) and from the Alberta Foundation for the Arts for its publishing activities.

For my friend Bruce

The Vessel

> *I the flask*
> *Blues, sweet nectar, flow*
> *From my soul*

DAVID "CRAWDAD" CANTERA

Contents

The Blues

Prologue

or How Jane Austen Came to Sing the Blues

NORA FOSTER STOVEL

WHEN THIS PROJECT WAS FIRST PROPOSED TO ME, I confess that the prospect gave me pause. Not being a blues aficionado myself, I doubted my ability to edit *Jane Austen Sings the Blues*. When Bruce Stovel died so suddenly and unexpectedly on 12 January 2007 at the age of 65, just six months after retiring as professor emeritus at the University of Alberta, where he had taught English literature for over 20 years, family and friends were in shock. Edmonton's academic and music communities, which Bruce had been a part of, were also shocked: one colleague wrote, "The world is a poorer place today." We all felt the need to commemorate Bruce. Family, friends, colleagues, and students contributed over $14,000 to establish the Bruce Stovel Memorial Scholarship in eighteenth-century British literature, an area in which he frequently taught courses—and now, *Jane Austen Sings the Blues* commemorates his life and passions brilliantly.

At a celebration of Bruce's life held at the University of Alberta Faculty Club the week after his death and attended by over 300 people, our children, Laura and Grant, were mistress and master of ceremonies. Laura read her tribute to her father: lying awake during that first dreadful week, she had decided to focus on the things Bruce loved, including Jane Austen and the blues. That piece concludes this collection. Family, friends, colleagues, and musicians spoke and read excerpts from the numerous messages that had poured in. Isobel Grundy spoke as a colleague, and Tom Faulkner spoke as a neighbour; both have contributed reminiscences to this collection. Patricia Clements, Amy Stafford, and Malcolm Azania (Minister Faust) read tributes from Bruce's colleagues, students, and music associates, respectively. Former colleagues (including Melissa Furrow and Martin Tweedale) and former students (including Amanda Ash, Heidi Jacobs, Heidi Janz, and Kim Solga) have contributed personal reminiscences to this volume.

Music also played a large part in our celebration. Jimmy (Guiboche) and the Sleepers (Chris Brzezicki and David "Crawdad" Cantera) played during the reception. Bruce's nephew, Montreal musician Robb Surridge, played a piece by Villa-Lobos on a guitar crafted by his own hands. Grant played an excerpt from Bruce's last radio show the preceding week, in which he introduced and played "This May Be the Last Time," as performed by Ndidi Onukwulu. Edmonton singer Kat Danser closed the celebration by singing "Carry Me Home," Bruce's favourite song from her album *Somethin' Familiar*. Those who had not been undone by Ndidi Onukwulu's recording were overcome by Kat's heartfelt performance. "(Notes from) The Other Side," the song Kat wrote for Bruce, is recorded on the enclosed compact disc and includes the line "Jane Austen sang the blues"; Kat sang this song on the main stage of the Edmonton Folk Festival on 12 August 2007, the seventh-month anniversary of Bruce's death.

The week after our celebration of Bruce's life, a musical celebration, hosted by Grant Stovel, was held at Edmonton's Yardbird Suite on Tommy Banks Way, where Bruce had volunteered for several years arranging blues acts. Numerous Alberta musicians performed, including Donald Ray Johnson, Dave Babcock, Scott McCrady, Chris Brzezicki, David Bridges, David "Crawdad" Cantera, Jimmy (Guiboche) and the Sleepers, Edmonton keyboard artist Graham Guest, and Bruce's cousin from Calgary, Chris Robb.

Just one week later, Kat Danser launched her new album, *Somethin' Familiar*, at the Yardbird Suite, a launch that Bruce had arranged. She dedicated her moving performance of "Carry Me Home" to Bruce. Linda Cameron, director of the University of Alberta Press and a blues fan herself, approached me during Kat's performance to suggest doing a book for Bruce; I was delighted, because I had wanted to suggest the very same thing to her. When we met a few days later, however, it turned out that we had very different ideas. I planned to edit a collection of Bruce's own essays on Jane Austen and others (and that project, titled *Jane Austen and Company*, is also under way), whereas Linda wanted to publish a collection of pieces by Bruce and others that would span his interests in Jane Austen and the blues. It was to be titled *Jane Austen Sings the Blues*. I told her I thought that was a great idea, and I loved the title, but I didn't think it would be possible: Bruce didn't write formal essays on the blues, and the two interests sprang from very different areas of his life.

Bruce's passion for the blues originated in his childhood. In those days, men climbing the executive ladder were moved from city to city every few years. Bruce's father, Samuel Rodger Stovel, a chemical engineer by training, moved from Niagara Falls to Winnipeg; from Pittsfield, Pennsylvania, to Warwick, New York; and from Toronto to Montreal on his way to becoming president of Cyanamid of Canada—much to the dismay of his wife, Bruce's mother, Elizabeth McLeod Robb Stovel, who was faced with the prospect of redecorating a house and getting to know a new community every other year. As a result, Bruce attended 13 schools in as many years. He seemed to thrive on this nomadic existence. In Warwick, New York, Bruce discovered the blues on his ham radio in his attic bedroom. His mother called him "Blue Boy" when he was young, perhaps because of his love of the colour blue. That proved to be an accurate sobriquet, because he grew up to be a blues man.

In Pittsfield, he had a little friend named Jimmy, who was African American, with whom he used to play. Whether or not Jimmy introduced Bruce to the blues, Bruce developed an interest in African American culture. For example, he enjoyed the Alvin Ailey Dance Company, and we used to drive from New Haven to New York to see them perform at the City Center. We strolled through Harlem on a visit to New York City in 1961: when a panhandler asked Bruce for money and he replied that he had none, turning out his pockets in proof, the man said to me good-humouredly, "Divorce him!" When I first met Bruce at the beginning of my freshman year at McGill—when he was a sophisticated sophomore studying honours philosophy and political science in preparation for a career in law, as well as editor-in-chief of the *McGill Daily* newspaper (a privilege normally reserved for senior students)—he had a collection of blues long-playing records featuring artists like Blind Lemon Jefferson and Big Bill Broonzy. We went to a nightclub near McGill to hear Sonny Terry and Brownie McGhee perform, but I never heard him play those records. The blues entered a hiatus.

The saga of Bruce's love of the blues resurfaced in an unexpected way many years later. He rented the 1983 movie *Risky Business*, starring Tom Cruise. He explained to our children that the background music was by the great blues musician Muddy Waters. Laura, accompanied by Grant, decided to buy Bruce a recording of Muddy Waters for his birthday. That was 1989. The rest, as they say, is blues history. Bruce went on to write a blues column, "Long-Distance Call," for blues magazines overseas. He also did media coverage of the Edmonton Folk Music Festival for several years and for the Edmonton Blues Festival during its early years; he contributed to CKUA, Canada's oldest independent radio station, and he booked blues artists for Edmonton's Yardbird Suite—all on a volunteer basis.[1] He taught a course on The Blues as Poetry. Essays and reminiscences from students in that course—including Megan Evans and Amanda Lim—are included in this collection. The article that Bruce co-wrote with Tracy Chao, about teaching the blues, which focussed on his innovative use of the webboard, is included in *Jane Austen Sings the Blues*. One of the students in his blues course, Josh Nodelman, has contributed to this collection an assignment that he wrote on Willie Dixon's "Evil" as performed by Howlin' Wolf to illustrate the dynamics of the course.

By moving to Edmonton in 1985 to take up an appointment teaching English at the University of Alberta, Bruce, unbeknownst to himself, landed in a blues brier-patch. Edmonton, known for its richness in theatre, was also a city rich in music, including the blues. Clubs such as the Yardbird Suite were revered institutions. CKUA, Canada's oldest public broadcaster, featured Canada's longest-running blues program, *Natch'l Blues*, hosted by Holger Peterson. CJSR, the University of Alberta volunteer radio station, boasted a blues program called *Off the Wall*, hosted by Doug Langille. After listening to Doug's show, Bruce got in touch with Doug, and the two became good friends. Occasionally, Bruce assisted Doug in his weekly Wednesday-night show. When Langille moved away to San Francisco, Bruce took over the show and hosted *Calling All Blues*, assisted by our son Grant, for a decade.

The week after Bruce's death, while the University of Alberta flag flew at half-mast from the Administration Building, Grant heroically hosted *Calling All Blues*. He was joined by the remaining members of the family—our daughter Laura, her husband Rod, and myself. Indeed, Laura, Rod, and I made our radio debut that night. Grant was also joined by Edmonton musicians Graham Guest, David "Crawdad" Cantera, Jim Guiboche, and Mark Sterling, some of whom performed live on the show. Crawdad remarked, "God needed Bruce to organize things in heaven." Graham commented, "I can see Bruce hosting a dinner party with Jane Austen, Muddy Waters, and Howling Wolf. Muddy is saying, 'Miss Austen, I have to thank Bruce for introducing me to your novels. Now I have eternity to read them.'" The tiny cement studio, formerly the vault of the Canadian Imperial Bank of Commerce, was so full of love that night that you could have cut it with a knife. Grant continued to host *Calling All Blues*, assisted by his friend Graham Guest, and followed that initial tribute with two more memorial programs.

Jane Austen Sings the Blues includes blues poems by our colleagues Elaine Bander, Doug Barbour, Jonathan Hart, and Christopher Wiseman, and by my former students Jannie Edwards and David Martin. It also includes reminiscences and tributes by blues artists Ann Rabson and Graham Guest, blues aficionado Martin Tweedale, and blues and jazz journalists Roger Levesque and Peter North, as well as an essay on the blues poetry of Langston Hughes by Nadia Rushdy, which was inspired by a guest lecture on the Harlem Renaissance that Bruce gave in my modernist poetry course a few years ago.

The origin of Bruce's interest in Jane Austen was very different. Always a voracious reader (in fact, he introduced me at McGill to Canadian literature), Bruce had read Austen at an early age. I had attempted at the age of nine to take out *Pride and Prejudice* from my local library in High Park, Toronto, but the librarian refused to sign it out to me, objecting that I was too young to read it. Offended by having my reading censored, and inferring that the novel was too risqué for my young years, I did not read it until I was in university. Bruce was, of course, vastly amused by this story.

His interest in Austen did not become serious, however, until some years later. While pursuing his doctorate at Harvard, Bruce was specializing in the Renaissance. We developed a system whereby he would read aloud while I washed the dishes after dinner. We soon found that no writer was as delightful read aloud as Jane Austen. Her balanced syntax, precise diction, and ironic wit were unmatched. (After our daughter was born in New Haven, we bought an automatic dishwasher from Sears, but, because it interfered with our after-dinner reading of Austen, we sent it back.) At Harvard, Bruce had been planning a dissertation in the Renaissance and was attempting to decide among Spenser, Sidney, Shakespeare, and Milton, when he realized that he could not fight it any longer: he had to write his thesis on Jane Austen. He had been working with distinguished Milton scholar Herschel Baker as his supervisor, assisting Baker in his Milton course, and so, of course, he had to change areas and find a new supervisor — Robert Kiely.

After completing his PHD magna cum laude at Harvard, Bruce taught as assistant professor at Yale University. One of his ideal teaching assignments was a course on comedy, which allowed him to teach Austen, among other favourite authors of comic fiction, including Henry Fielding, Evelyn Waugh, and Kingsley Amis. When he came to the University of Alberta, his interest in Austen was raised to new heights by our colleague Juliet McMaster. Together, they founded the Edmonton chapter of the Jane Austen Society of North America in 1992 and convened the following year a JASNA conference at the Chateau Lake Louise that was, simply put, a triumph. The text of the meeting was Austen's novel *Persuasion*, and the 600 delegates were treated to a musical version, *An*

Accident at Lyme, written by Paula Schwartz, with music by Neil Moyer. Headliners Elaine Showalter, Jan Fergus, and Isobel Grundy were joined by British novelist Margaret Drabble, who wrote an original fiction inspired by *Persuasion*. Maggie, as she is known, has contributed a delightful essay to this collection. *Jane Austen Sings the Blues* includes two of Bruce's own essays on Austen, as well as essays by his distinguished colleagues Isobel Grundy, Juliet McMaster, and Peter Sabor.

Bruce frequently taught undergraduate and graduate courses on Jane Austen at the University of Alberta. Some of the students in his Austen courses—including Mary Chan, Kelsey Everton, Amy Stafford, Kerry Taillefer, Kari Trogen, and Jessica Wallace—have contributed their course papers to this collection, and Laura Cappello Bromling and Natasha Duquette have also contributed essays. Teaching was very important to Bruce, and he was awarded the Students' Union Award for Leadership in Undergraduate Teaching (SALUTE), the Faculty of Arts Teaching Award, and the Rutherford Teaching Award, all at the University of Alberta. The University of Alberta's Bruce Peel Special Collections Library dedicated to his memory a first edition of Jane Austen's *Pride and Prejudice*, with a handcrafted case commissioned by the Friends of the University of Alberta, a charitable organization to which Bruce contributed, as Jeannine Green, director of the Bruce Peel Special Collections Library, describes in her contribution to this volume.

To return to the fateful meeting with Linda Cameron, Grant argued that, different as Austen was from the blues, and different as the origins of those interests were in Bruce's life, both Austen and the blues have a common love of life, a profound understanding of human nature, and a wicked sense of humour—all things that Bruce admired and, indeed, shared. I told Linda Cameron that, although I thought that it was a great idea, I didn't think that I could do it because I didn't have the expertise in the blues to edit such a volume. My son Grant, who was present at the meeting, gamely volunteered to help. With the guidance of Linda Cameron and the assistance of his *Calling All Blues* co-host Graham Guest, Grant organized the recording of music by local and international artists, such as Kat Danser and Ann Rabson, for the enclosed CD.

I have to thank many people who assisted in the compilation of this collection, including, of course, the contributors. In addition, I wish to thank my daughter Laura and son-in-law Rod; my son Grant, who prepared the CD with his colleague Graham Guest; Bruce's and my colleague Juliet McMaster, who contributed in valuable ways, especially in co-editing the Jane Austen student essays; and, of course, Linda Cameron, who first suggested the brilliant idea of publishing *Jane Austen Sings the Blues* and who oversaw the entire project.

NORA FOSTER STOVEL
6 June 2008
Edmonton

NOTE

1. Cam Hayden and Carrol Deen commemorated Bruce in the 2008 Edmonton Labatt Blues Festival program with these words: "Media Crew Coordinator and long-time blues booster Bruce Stovel was a true blues lover who hosted *Calling All Blues* on CJSR Radio, booked blues acts into the Yardbird Suite and did everything he could to bring his love of the blues to all Edmontonians" (7).

Tribute

OVERLEAF: *The week after Bruce's death, while the University of Alberta flag flew at half-mast from the Administration Building. Photo: Krystina Sulatycki.*

1 Bruce Stovel, 1941–2007

NORA FOSTER STOVEL

JOSEPH BRUCE STOVEL was born 21 February 1941, in Montreal, to Samuel Rodger Stovel and Elizabeth McLeod Robb Stovel. After graduating as Gold Medalist with his BA in honours English at Sir George Williams University (now Concordia) in Montreal in 1964, his MA with first-class honours in English at the University of Cambridge in 1966, and his PHD magna cum laude in English at Harvard University in 1970, Bruce served as assistant professor at Yale University 1970–1975, associate professor at Dalhousie University 1975–1985 (where he also served as department chair), and professor of English at the University of Alberta, where he twice served as associate chair and supervisor of graduate teaching assistants. He retired on 30 June 2006, as professor emeritus, to become, in his own words, a patron of the arts.

His special area was literature of the eighteenth century, particularly fiction and comedy. He published essays on Samuel Richardson, Laurence Sterne, Tobias Smollett, Fanny Burney, Jane Austen, Charlotte Lennox, Walter Scott, George Eliot, Kingsley Amis, Margaret Drabble, Brian Moore, Mordecai Richler, and Margaret Laurence, but his special love was Jane Austen. He co-edited two collections of essays on Austen and contributed to *The Cambridge Companion to Jane Austen*. He co-founded the Edmonton chapter of the Jane Austen Society in 1992, co-hosted the Jane Austen Society of North America (JASNA) Annual

3

General Meeting at the Chateau Lake Louise in 1993, and contributed to many JASNA AGMS and local chapters in Edmonton and elsewhere.

Bruce was a dedicated teacher, and was awarded the Students' Union Teaching Award, the Faculty of Arts Teaching Award, and the Rutherford Teaching Award at the University of Alberta. As much as he achieved academically, his greatest impact was felt at a personal level. He was a beloved husband and father, teacher and colleague, music man and friend. Bruce was an enthusiastic presence on campus and on the local arts scene, and he was a generous volunteer in academic, artistic, and humanitarian causes.

Bruce loved blues music as well as literature, and he worked as a volunteer at the Yardbird Suite, where he organized blues events. Beginning in the mid-1990s, he co-hosted with his son Grant *Calling All Blues*, a weekly blues program on CJSR, the University of Alberta radio station, as well as contributing to CKUA. Following his early career in journalism as editor-in-chief of the *McGill Daily* and as reporter for the *Montreal Star* and the Canadian Press in the early sixties in Montreal, he wrote a blues column titled "Long-Distance Call" and reported on the Edmonton Folkfest, the Edmonton Bluesfest, and the Chicago Bluesfest.

He died suddenly on 12 January 2007. He will be much missed and deeply mourned by his loving wife of 42 years, Nora Foster Stovel, his son Grant Foster Stovel, and his daughter Laura Elizabeth Stovel and son-in-law Rod Girard, as well as his brother Robb Stovel and his sister Margaret Surridge and their families and the Foster family.

The Bruce Stovel Memorial Prize in eighteenth-century studies has been endowed in his honour through the generosity of family, friends, colleagues, and students.

2 Walking Blues

DAVID MARTIN

Robert Johnson is playing to an empty
corner in the Gunter Hotel.
A long-fingered Faust, his third arm
made of suspended strings, he measures
the distance of each song by tapping
his foot against swamp maple floorboards:
stationary steps that score the path of a
twenty-seven-year-old voice, leading
deeper into the earth. Only forty-eight paces
to build the blues: another circle behind us
but the needle outruns the guitar trail
and a spinning hiss dissolves his footprints.

3 In Honour of Bruce Stovel

TOM FAULKNER

*Tom Faulkner gave this talk at the celebration for Bruce Stovel, the
week after Bruce's death.*

I HAVE KNOWN BRUCE and Nora Stovel ever since my wife and I
moved into the house next to theirs over 30 years ago in Halifax, just
a few metres away from the Halifax Commons. It's very kind of Nora
to ask me to write in honour of Bruce. He was an extraordinary neighbour and a dear friend from whom I learned so much.

I write with some trepidation because I do want to get this right, to
do justice to Bruce, who is so well known to so many. In doing so, I take
some comfort from the words of a lady to whom Bruce introduced me:
"Seldom, very seldom, does complete truth belong to any human disclosure; seldom can it happen that something is not a little disguised,
or a little mistaken; but where, as in this case, though the conduct is
mistaken, the feelings are not" (Austen, *Emma* 431).[1] Bruce, of course,
would have been quick to recognize the words of Jane Austen. If my
words here are clumsy, please accept that my feelings are firm and
unambiguous.

Bruce was simply one of the most gentle and thoughtful men I
have ever known. Although I am a bit simple-minded as a Christian,
I am usually reluctant to imagine the afterlife. After all, until one has

managed to live well in this life, it seems frivolous to try to envision the next one. Bruce did live this life well, and so I don't hesitate to say that one of the pleasures that I look forward to without reservation is someday to watch and to listen as Miss Jane Austen meets Bruce for the first time, and discovers how delightful he truly is.

That lies in the realm of speculative hope. What lies in factual memory is the day when my wife and I decided to renew our marriage vows while altering our surname to reflect both our families. We invited three couples to the ceremony: Patricia's nearest relatives, my friends Wilfred Cantwell Smith and his wife Muriel, and Bruce and Nora.

Bruce and Nora did more than merely live next door. They shared our moments of joy and of sadness; their children cared for and played with our children. While every home in the city of Halifax is neatly divided from its neighbour by a well-maintained fence, Bruce remembered Robert Frost's scorn for what conventional wisdom tells us about good neighbours. He reminded us of Frost's secretly held opinion:

> Before I built a wall I'd ask to know
> What I was walling in or walling out,
> And to whom I was like to give offense.
> Something there is that doesn't love a wall,
> That wants it down. (33–37)

The four of us tore down the fence that divided our private backyards and created a sort of "commons" where both families enjoyed themselves and each other. There was never any offense to give, and always a great deal of love to share among us and our children.

I've never known a good neighbour to match Bruce. Long may his memory remain among us, and may he rest peacefully.

NOTE

1.   All quotations from Jane Austen's published works are taken from *The Oxford Illustrated Jane Austen*, 3rd ed., ed. R.W. Chapman (Oxford: Oxford UP, 1988), and are documented by short title and page number in the body of the chapter.

WORK CITED

Frost, Robert. "Mending Wall." *The New Pocket Anthology of American Verse from Colonial Days to the Present*. Ed. Oscar Williams. New York: Washington Square, 1961. 200.

4 Remembering Bruce

ISOBEL GRUNDY

Isobel Grundy gave this talk at the celebration for Bruce Stovel, the week after Bruce's death.

THIS IS SOMETHING I NEVER THOUGHT TO DO. Bruce died far too early, and the reaction has been very strong among his colleagues and the whole community where he worked. I've had emails and phone calls from people on campus, or formerly on campus, who have sounded shattered or even outraged. Even people not really close to Bruce have been having a terrible week, exhibiting all the symptoms of loss: misplacing things, forgetting to do things, feeling unable all of a sudden to cope with the day-to-day. Bruce was someone that everybody liked, that everybody trusted, that everybody was always glad to see—and that everybody had banked on seeing around for a whole lot longer.

Bruce was very reticent, never one to talk about himself. I heard a bit about his time at Dalhousie, probably rather less about his time at Cambridge or Harvard or Yale. One of the few things that everybody knew about him was his devotion to his family. I have heard him tell the story of how he and Nora met, and also how he took on the role of the father-at-home while Nora was holding a post-doctoral fellowship at the University of Calgary, and about the letters and phone calls that sustained them during that time. Bruce's role as a father was actually one of the earliest things I learned about him, when the Stovels' daughter Laura was a young thing going backpacking 'round Europe, and my house in London, U.K., was her first port of call. Laura asked if she might lighten the backpack by leaving a whole mound of stuff behind in my house to pick up at the end of her trip. She said that while she was doing her packing a whole lot of things were added by mum and dad that they thought she couldn't do without.

That was before I moved to the University of Alberta, so my friendship with Bruce goes back a long way. He was the person who called me transatlantic to say that the English department was hoping to persuade me to apply for the Tory Professorship—that was because he was on the relevant committee at the time, but of course no one would have done that phone call better. Bruce inspired confidence. He was endlessly patient about consulting and answering questions. When I actually came to the University of Alberta, he and I team-taught my first course in the department: a graduate course, the Eighteenth-Century Novel: Women Novelists. Once again, he consulted and saved me from potential blunders that make me shiver to look back on: first, as to what constituted (just) an acceptable reading load, and second, by communicating a clear and accurate sense of marking levels. We did set a heavy workload, but it became, as it were, part of the mythology of the course, so the students' complaints became ritualized and good-humoured. If I had drawn up that reading list myself, fresh from a completely different system and without Bruce's gentle but firmly restraining hand, the teacher-student relationship might have been totally shot.

We did have terrific students in that class. Several of them produced term papers that I thought publishable, and several are now in the profession. Of course the material we were teaching is wonderful, and had, in 1990–1991, all the excitement of new discovery about it. But the chief thing about the course was the class atmosphere of camaraderie and enjoyment. Bruce did something astonishing to me in suggesting at the first meeting that everyone might like to take turns in producing treats or goodies for the break midway in the class. The students did something astonishing in not only agreeing to this suggestion but deciding that they would prepare both goodies and class presentations on the same day, thereby getting it all over at once. Bruce and I slotted into the cooking rota somehow without doing class presentations. The most astonishing thing of all was the way this system worked to increase good cheer without, apparently, any extra stress. (Though I well remember the outrage of Dan Coleman when someone asked if his wife had been involved in producing something especially yummy that he brought.)

That course meant that it was no surprise to me that Bruce won teaching awards. Toward the end of his career, he was chosen for two of these, completely independently, in the same year; but I think probably the one that meant the most to him was the Students' Union's own award, SALUTE, in 1996–1997. He had the gift of providing what students need, which involves the perceptiveness first to figure out what that is for each individual. He was probably the best interpreter that Heidi Janz had in the department, and that would be just the most striking of the various kinds of interpreting that he did as well.

During my first year here, Bruce was one of three people who helped me to move house from a condo I'd been renting to a condo I'd bought. It was typical of him to do a really valuable friendly service, and to do it with plenty of purposeful energy but with absolute, total freedom from flap. He had great organizing capacity and was a master of detail. Juliet McMaster, who collaborated with him in the running of two conferences, said he was "a wonderful guy to work with," not only because he "got on with everyone" but also because of this ability to make complicated arrangements come out right.

Bruce's scholarly interests were a marvellous blend of the mainstream and the surprising: Kingsley Amis and Brian Moore, as well as Jane Austen and blues songwriters. It was appropriate for him, with his own intense perceptiveness, good sense, irony, and reticence, to be an Austen scholar. He functioned particularly well and was immensely popular in the warm and closely-knit communities made up by Austen enthusiasts on the one hand and blues lovers on the other. I think the article of his that I admire the most is the one about Jane Austen's prayers, and I think that he may be most remembered for his encyclopedic and critically astute command of Austen filmography. His finest moment with the Austenites came at the end of a very interesting lecture he gave on *Emma*, when someone confided that he was exactly her idea of Mr Knightley.

"Interesting" is a word that makes me think of Bruce. He would turn up at the office door to communicate something interesting that he had just learned, and whereas with most people you know pretty well what their interests extend to, and what topic they're going to report about, with Bruce it could be absolutely anything under the sun, but always, sure enough, something to make you really think. Then he would say, "Well, just thought you might find that interesting," and go on his way.

I was particularly glad that Bruce and Nora met my parents when they were in Edmonton, and that the last time I saw him was just before Christmas, when my brother and all his family were here, and we ran into the Stovels in the interval of Handel's *Messiah* at the Winspear Centre. The warmth and regard was instant, and my relations (ranging from a Handel fan to someone hearing him for the very first time) were delighted by Bruce's characteristically energetic comments on the energetic style of the symphony's new conductor. His enjoyment and his critical delight were infectious. I shall miss him more than I can say, and I am very glad to have been his colleague and friend.

5 Neighbours and Good Friends

MELISSA FURROW

MY ANECDOTE ABOUT BRUCE STOVEL touches on both Jane Austen and the blues. It recalls an occasion that was for me for many years a source of the blues and a source of doubt about the profession that Bruce helped welcome me into at Dalhousie in 1980. We were office neighbours and good friends, and I missed his daily presence as a raconteur and purveyor of the latest bit of nonsense or mischief when he moved with Nora to Alberta in 1985. We met again at the Learneds at Queen's in 1991. That year, the plenary was given by a rising American star; it was a reprise of a paper she had recently given at the Modern Languages Association, to great scandal in the press and a frisson of excitement in the academy, on the masturbation scene in *Sense and Sensibility*. (For those not familiar with the scholarship in question and unable to identify the scene in the book, I should add that it is the scene that is very often understood to be about Marianne agitatedly writing a letter to Willoughby after he rejects her.)

As I recall the event, the performance was scheduled for Sunday morning, but unfortunately there was a glitch in the booking: the hall was regularly used by a Christian group on campus for Sunday service, and there was half an hour of learned philologers' milling about outside in baffled uncertainty while the sacred service went on within. At last we heard that we were to be let into the room for the plenary, which Bruce was looking forward to with gloomy foreboding. As a Jane Austen scholar himself, and one much given to the old-fashioned practices of reading closely and basing interpretation on evidence, he did not expect much enlightenment from the talk. (Nor was he to receive it: as I recall the question period afterwards, the first very mildly phrased but richly deserved question about the speaker's methodology was met with a dressing down and the robust assertion *ex cathedra* that if the questioner was not willing to accept the speaker's project, then, as she persuasively phrased her reasoning, "Fuck you.")

Now, Bruce's appreciation of the absurd was always for me the most characteristic of his traits: his lips would tighten, the air escape in a miniature explosion of laughter, then would come the quip, then the roar of merriment at his own or another's folly. That Sunday morning, as we thronged toward the doorway that was letting the Christians out and the scholars in, "Ah," cried Mr Stovel, "from mass to masturbation in half an hour." I shall miss that sensibility, and the good sense that accompanied it.

6 Phantasmagoric

AMANDA ASH

I TWIST AND TURN THE TINY GOLD PACKAGE with clammy fingers as if it's a Rubik's cube. Or a crinkling, enigmatic new addition to my English vocabulary. "Phantasmagoric," one of my English professors said in a previous class. *Oh dear God, I'm going to fail.* I slouch further in my plastic seat.

"I can't eat candy. If I can't eat it, someone's got to. That's your job this semester. To eat the candy I can't. I will bring some to every class, so make sure you don't eat any dessert with lunch."

I pick up the Werther's Original and allow it to untie itself, examining the hard, waxy lozenge at arm's length before popping it into my mouth. I find it odd to be receiving candy in a second-year university course. It makes me feel like I should be lugging bright fingerpaints in my backpack instead of cheap plastic Bic pens. I lift my fingers to my nose and sniff. They smell like tinfoil, sweat, and butterscotch.

"So this class is English 347, Restoration and Eighteenth-Century Drama. We'll spend our Tuesday classes engaging with the text as it is on the page, but then, come Thursdays, I'll ask you to get into your assigned groups and act out a key scene. Dramatic literature isn't meant to be read; it's meant to be performed, to come alive. Only when you're up here, standing in front of the class, will you truly understand and feel what the text is attempting to do."

I reach for the small paperback book in front of me, its glossy blue cover gliding beneath my fingertips. Mindlessly, I flick through the pages. They have that new, meaty smell to them, the kind that warm photocopy paper gives off. I flip it around, tracing its rounded corners, my fingers dragging over the sharp edges of paper just enough to give me goosebumps but not enough to inflict any serious skin-shearing damage.

My professor stands in the centre of the classroom, oscillating the textbook slightly above his head. He's a sophisticated man adorned with silver-rimmed glasses and a wrinkle-free suit. His sloping shoulders and lanky stature suggest he's spent years poring over library books.

He stands, before all his shy students, belting out the passages from plays we've never heard of, his excitement visible at the corners of his mouth. My mind continues to wander, and I begin to doubt whether I can exist as an English student. I look at him. I can't imagine myself ever being in his place, someone of importance, a university professor who's incredibly in love with every hoity-toity eighteenth-century word that flutters off the page. With a sigh, I sink lower into my chair, my butt becoming one with its knobby texture.

For the most part, my first class of English 347 with Professor Bruce Stovel was a blur, but those feelings of fear, anxiety, and impending failure I remember quite vividly. It was the beginning of my second year in university and the start of my undergraduate career in English honours. Having been in sciences the previous year, I had no idea what to expect. I wanted to do well. I wanted to talk to my professors after class about this image or that comparison. I wanted to fit in. I was a nervous wreck. Every. Single. Day. During my first week, Professor Stovel was just another professor, and I was just another name on the list; but as the term scurried along, each and every one of us was forced to reveal ourselves through the disguises we wore on Thursdays.

At first, I was known as the girl with the cool scarf. Then I was the girl who read passages aloud well. Then I became that girl who sat beside that other girl with a cool scarf. Then I became Amanda. "We'll start the candy bag with Amanda today." "Amanda's group can choose which scene they want to act out." "Oh, what character are you going to play, Amanda?" Professor Stovel soon discovered my love for drama and my knack for playing ditzy country girls or unfaithful wives. I would sit with my group, blue textbook in hand, poking at the pages, turning them upside down, sideways, rightways, allowing the words to untie themselves into something much larger, always striving to portray my allotted character to perfection. My left pocket would contain the wrapper from the day's candy ration, and I'd crunch it or squish it as I concentrated on the page.

During one of my first performances, I played a character that was forced to say the words "sea men" multiple times. Professor Stovel was a grandpa to the class, one who would read us plays and send us home on a sugar high, and so, naturally, my cheeks flushed with rouge before I went on stage. When it finally came time for me to speak those unholy words, my eyes darted over at Professor Stovel. I expected a loud gasp, a "how dare you," or a "clean your mouth out with soap, young lady," but instead, his head gave a little bow. He started to quiver, then shake, and soon his head was thrown back with laughter.

There was something about his sense of humour, his openness, and the way he pushed me to keep plugging away at school that gave me confidence. After every essay, after every mark I got from him, he always wrote, "This is an excellent paper, Amanda, but I can see through you; I know you can do better. Keep going." At the time, Professor Stovel's class was the only one I was doing well in. The rest of my classes were weighing me down.

Professor Stovel wanted to get to know us outside of class, so he made it mandatory that we schedule a meeting with him in his office. I remember stumbling up to the fourth floor of the Humanities Building and approaching his door. It had been left open a foot, and I could see him absorbed in a dusty old book as the daylight peeked over his shoulder.

"Hi."

"Well, hello, Amanda. Come in. Sit down."

I clumsily removed my backpack and took a seat. He sat there, hands clasped, looking like he was ready to talk politics.

"Tell me a bit about yourself."

We chatted for a while. I learned he had written a book with a teacher I knew in high school, that he was in love with Jane Austen, and that he had graduated from Harvard. All I had to offer in exchange were my worries.

Silence.

"You're too hard on yourself. You're a smart girl, and I know it. Just keep pushing, and you'll get there. It won't be easy, but I know you'll do fine."

A smile.

"Here, have a candy."

From that day on, I always knew Professor Stovel's door was open a foot or two for me. I would wander by while on break and dump my problems on his desk, or we'd pass each other in the stairwells and discuss recent plays.

To most of the class—and heck, even myself—he was known as "the professor who gave his classes candy every day." When he passed away, I realized he gave me something much more. He could've spoken empty words and dismissed my anxieties, but instead he became a friend and confidant who taught me to keep twisting and turning life until I'd experienced it from all angles.

7 "The mere habit of learning to love is the thing"

Notes on Being a Student of Bruce and Nora Stovel

HEIDI L.M. JACOBS

FOR CHRISTMAS LAST YEAR, a friend who knows me very well gave me a little cardboard Virginia Woolf and a little cardboard Jane Austen. Virginia Woolf is dressed in a tasteful purple print dress, and she stares wistfully at her wristwatch. Jane Austen is dancing in a white empire-waist dress that she coquettishly lifts to reveal her bare feet with toenails painted a daring red. Together, they occupy the space over my computer monitor at work, and many times in my workday I find myself gazing at them. Like the proverbial angels over one's shoulders, Woolf and her wristwatch implore me to work while Miss Austen and her toenails tempt me to step away from my desk and do something fun.

As I sat down to write this piece on Professor Bruce Stovel, I found myself unusually wordless. My gaze wandered between the cardboard figures of Virginia Woolf and Jane Austen. I looked over to my bookshelf and saw one of the two complete sets of Jane Austen's novels I own and the copy of Woolf's *Night and Day* that I am currently reading on lunch hours. By the time my eyes wandered back to my blank screen,

I smiled. I realized that it was through Bruce and Nora Stovel that I became so attached to these two writers: Nora Stovel introduced me to Virginia Woolf in her British Modernism class, and Bruce Stovel nurtured and honed my love for Jane Austen in his stellar Austen graduate seminar.

As a former teacher of English literature and a fledgling gardener, I have come to think of teaching as planting seeds. As any gardener will tell you, seeds can do miraculous things: sometimes they sprout almost overnight, other times they take weeks or months to peek through the soil, and sometimes they never sprout at all. Occasionally, seeds will lie dormant for years and then flourish in entirely unexpected places. As a gardener, one usually sees which seeds flourish and which don't. What is difficult about teaching is that we rarely get to see what becomes of the seeds we sow. In this way, teaching is an act of faith that, somewhere along the way, we're making a difference.

From the moment I met them, the Stovels planted seeds that grew to make a huge difference in my career and my life. Perhaps they might have guessed that they inspired me to continue in an academic career, but I'm not sure they would have known how much they influenced how I live my life within the academic world. For example, I doubt that Bruce Stovel would have known how distinctively I remember his seemingly bottomless delight in finding new nuances or elements in Jane Austen's novels, even though he'd clearly read them over and over again. In a profession built on endless reading and rereading, it's easy to become blasé about the incredible literary works we study. When I felt ennui slipping into my rereadings, I would remind myself of Bruce Stovel's exhilaration at seeing something new in Mr Bingley or his sheer delight in Austen's careful use of an adjective. From him I also learned the necessity of bringing to our work freshness, joy, and awe at the literary works we often take for granted. There were many days when his example not only revivified my work but also reminded me why I was doing what I was doing. When I began teaching the literature I loved, I felt emboldened by his example to express joy and delight at the works we read. I am certain that he would not have known that his Austen seminar inspired me so fully that every time I read *Pride and Prejudice* I mentally add Bruce Stovel as a character in the novel. Sometimes he's at Rosings repressing a smile at Lady Catherine de Bourgh or he's laughing with Mr Bingley at the Meryton Ball, but most often he's dancing with one of the Bennet sisters at Netherfield. Whenever I picture the wedding of Bingley and Jane, he's always in the background joyously throwing rice.

Similarly, I doubt whether Nora Stovel knows that she was the first of my professors to notice that, though I was quiet, I had things to say. I do not know if she knows how grateful I was when she would say, "Heidi, it looks like you're thinking something. Would you like to add something to our discussion?" After a few such invitations, it became much easier for me to contribute to class discussions. I doubt she knew how much those invitations mattered to me or that when I taught I would remember those moments and would always try to find ways to invite quiet students into conversations. I am also sure that she does not know I remember that she had written "Ezra Pound joins me in wishing you a very fine summer" at the bottom of her British Modernism final almost 20 years ago. Nor do I expect she knows that I would include a variation of that sentence on every final exam I wrote for my students as a small tribute to her. I remembered the small smile I had when I saw that tiny bit of humour in the otherwise humourless process of writing final exams, and I liked seeing that small smile on my students' faces when Nathaniel Hawthorne or Nellie McClung joined me in wishing them a very pleasant summer.

Perhaps the ultimate tribute to one's teachers is to carry on in their scholarly footsteps. As students and young academic professionals, we often articulate our professional identities by saying, "I was a student of _____." Statements such as these reveal not only one's area of scholarly inquiry and critical mode but also one's way of being in the academic world. Although I did not become a Woolf scholar or an Austen scholar and have recently left teaching English for a career in academic librarianship, I would very much say that I was a student of Bruce and Nora Stovel, since they taught me many things about how to live in the academic world.

As with most of Bruce and Nora Stovel's students, I first got to know them as professors and scholars. Slowly, I learned that they were people too. While I am undoubtedly a better reader, writer, scholar, and teacher for having had them as professors, their most powerful lessons to me related to the importance of the personal in the professional. I got to know their daughter Laura in my classes, and I remember being surprised to hear her talking about her parents as if they were just regular people not unlike my own parents. I remember my brother Paul being really impressed at having seen them bobbing their heads at their son Grant's band's show just as my parents did at Paul's shows. Eventually, I was fascinated to learn that Bruce Stovel had a tremendous passion for and encyclopedic knowledge of the blues and that Nora Stovel had a lifelong love of ballet. I remember being very impressed that they found the time to have and nurture interests that seemed slightly incongruous with novels and literature classrooms.

It now seems odd to me that I was surprised by the revelation that the Stovels were real people; yet I regularly see this same incredulity in our undergraduate English majors who also struggle to comprehend that their professors are people with lives and interests outside of books and classrooms. I remember being amused by one of my former students asking me with all sincerity, "Are professors allowed to be out this late?" when she saw us at a late-night event at a pub. While I smile at my own undergraduate naïveté and that of some of our students, I am also reminded of some of my peers and colleagues who have told me—sometimes with regret, sometimes with pride—"If I don't talk about work, I have nothing to talk about" or "I have not seen a movie for seven years" or "I do not have time to read fiction outside of my area." When I was troubled to find myself only talking about work or only reading nineteenth-century fiction, I reminded myself of Bruce Stovel's passion for the blues and Nora Stovel's love for ballet, and set about to revive the interests I'd let atrophy over the years. At difficult moments, the Stovels reminded me through example that maintaining personal interests and passions was not incongruous with success within the academic world but rather imperative to surviving it.

Finally, I am not certain that Bruce and Nora Stovel would have known how inspirational they were to young academic couples. My husband Dale and I met in undergraduate English classes 16 years ago. When we first realized we were meant to be together, he said, "We could be like the Stovels," and I said, "Yes, I would like that very much." To us, then and now, the Stovels represented a true partnership of minds, hearts, and intellects. We liked their kindness and commitment to their students and to each other. We liked that they were a strong unit but also that they were strong individuals. We liked how they made their individual professional journeys together. Above all, we liked how they were passionate about their work and yet made time for other passions and interests. I am also not certain they would have known how many times Dale and I would turn to their strong example in moments of doubt, confusion, disappointment, and frustration as we negotiated a bleak job market made even more complicated by our being an academic couple. When we despaired that it might never work out, we remembered the Stovels. Their example allowed us to dust ourselves off and forge ahead more times than I'd like to remember. When we finally secured two very good tenure-track jobs, I thought of writing and thanking them for all they had done. Last January, I deeply regretted that I had not written to thank them for the various seeds they'd given me many years ago.

Like the cardboard Woolf and Austen "angels" over my computer screen who collectively implore me to work yet also to live life fully, Bruce and Nora Stovel have shown me through their example that loving one's work is vitally important, but so is doing what one loves and being with and present for those whom one loves. In this way I am proud and grateful to be able to say, "I am a student of Bruce and Nora Stovel," and that they, like Jane Austen and Virginia Woolf, are never far from my mind.

8 Remembering (How) to Teach

KIM SOLGA

I MET BRUCE AND NORA STOVEL by accident in the fall of 1994. I was an honours-level student in the Department of English at the University of Alberta, and I had a problem with my schedule. I'd signed up for all my courses far in advance, as was my habit, but now, during the first week of classes in the third year of my degree, I was sitting in our comfy student lounge across from my friend Andrew Taylor, listening to him tell me why I had to ditch my modern novel course and take Nora Stovel's later modern drama course instead. Nora was, Andrew told me, an amazing teacher, and her course was not just inspiring, but genuinely fun. Suddenly I was overwhelmed by need edged with panic: I had to get into that course.

Get into it I did, with far-reaching effects my 20-year-old self could never have anticipated. Over the course of the next two years (my final three terms at the U of A), I would take Nora Stovel's later modern drama class, her Victorian drama class, and Bruce Stovel's memorable Restoration drama class, and the experience not just of learning from the Stovels but of watching them teach would change the trajectory of my adult life.

Both Bruce and Nora Stovel taught their undergraduate drama courses as workshops in theatre making. We would read approximately a play per week, and, after offering lectures on context and discussions of the material in conventional English-class fashion, Bruce and Nora would turn the final period of the week over to us, the students, as a forum in which to play with the texts before us. We were divided into groups: one group would put on a brief scene from the play under discussion, another group would interview the performers, still "in character," in order to learn more about those characters' motives and the consequences of their choices, and the third group would use the text as fodder for a kind of performance-art riff, a third perspective used to illuminate what had been, at the beginning of the week, no more than words on a page. It was thanks to this novel method of teaching drama that I suddenly began to appreciate not just that plays were meant to be performed, but that text and performance, rather than modelling a straightforward page-to-stage trajectory, could sometimes have an awkward, even difficult, relationship to one another. In other words, the Stovels introduced me to the notion that performance has a life of its own, and is a generative rather than derivative practice that can shed light on any number of contexts and situations, from the purely artistic to the violently political. In Bruce and Nora's classes, we learned to play with text and to use words, our own bodies, and the power of imagination to demonstrate the civic, public potential of performance.

I went from the U of A to Dalhousie University in the fall of 1996 to pursue my master's degree. By then, thanks to Bruce and Nora, I had already decided that I would make my life in and around performance, whether inside or outside the academy. The intervening few years found me in England, where I studied the practice of actor training at the Royal Academy of Dramatic Art and King's College London, then home to Canada and the University of Toronto's Graduate Centre for the Study of Drama, where I earned my PHD, and finally on to the University of Texas at Austin, where, thanks to Jill Dolan, Charlotte Canning, Deborah Paredez, Stacy Wolf, and the other bright lights in the Department of Theatre and Dance, I discovered an entire subdiscipline within North American performance studies dedicated to what I had begun to learn from the Stovels: Performance as Public Practice.[1] When I returned to Canada and to a position in the University of Western Ontario's Department of English in the summer of 2005, I was ready to put everything I had learned from the Stovels into practice in my very own classroom.

My undergraduate courses in contemporary theatre (Canadian, American, and Modern) at Western are modelled on the structures I learned more than ten years ago from Bruce and Nora. At the beginning of every semester, I divide my students into four groups; the groups are large, but I have learned that size matters in making theatre. The more bodies in a group, the more chances of finding a friend over the course of the term; the more chances of getting to do a range of different jobs, trading off with peers; the better to hang back when feeling shy; and the more comrades to offer those gentle nudges when shyness (or fatigue, or the end-of-term blues) begins to take over. My students stay with their groups throughout the year, and over the course of that year, they are assigned three scene studies per term. It is their job to pick a scene from the play they are assigned in any given week, to get up a poor-theatre version of that scene during the final hour of class, and then to field questions from their peers during a formal classroom "talk back" after the performance. This might seem like a pretty elaborate process, but let me stress—as I do to my students on the very first day of class—that nobody is expected to be a star actor, or a flawless prop-master, or to spend any money on this task. It is about effort, it's about invention, and it's about pushing yourself to your limits—and beyond. It's about discovering the power of performance to change your mind and our minds, to introduce us to new perspectives and new ideas, to help us think 360 degrees around a topic that seemed entirely unidimensional just moments ago. The students are, of course, terrified of the prospect of this performance work early in the term, but they soon embrace it as an essential part of what our coursework is about. I am astonished every year to see students make discoveries in performance, staging aspects of a play that even I had not considered before; I am also thoroughly impressed with their ability to handle—and not to shy away from—the kinds of tough questions that arise in a tangible, often terrifying way in performance. How do we stage a rape? How can we perform a story about slavery with no black members in our group? How do we tell other people's stories without overtaking them, put our bodies where their bodies should be without erasing the stories of those bodies? The text becomes infinitely more complex—and more uncomfortably, dangerously, thrillingly public—when it gets up and walks around the classroom, and when my students walk out of my classroom at the end of the year, there is no question that they have been changed, irrevocably, by what they have seen and done with both body and text.

When I look back at my drama courses with Bruce and Nora, and then forward to my own American and Canadian drama courses, I can see how different the latter are from the former. Of course they would be: teaching does not happen in a vacuum, and ten years of experiences have helped shape the work I do with students. That work, however, has its roots in a place and time thousands of kilometres from where I now teach, and I have learned to shape my classroom around the power, the potential, and the activism of performance because Bruce and Nora taught me how to understand the complexities of the relationship between page and stage, the intricate web that is the making of theatre. I could not have imagined, when I walked into Nora's classroom for the first time, that she and Bruce would teach me not just about drama, and not just about theatre, but about teaching, about the public acts that shape our world and make our children its citizens—but that is exactly what they did.

NOTE

1. Performance as Public Practice is one of the PHD program streams in the Department of Theatre and Dance at the University of Texas at Austin.

9 Sense and Sense-Ability

The Education of Bruce Stovel

HEIDI L. JANZ

IT WAS SUCH AN INAUSPICIOUS BEGINNING to a friendship that would span over two decades. In fact, I have a strong hunch that, if, on that first day I wheeled into Bruce Stovel's English 210 class, someone had come along and given us a sneak preview of some of the things that lay in store for us over the next 20 years, it would have sent one or both of us bolting from that classroom in terror. Such, I believe, is the nature of Divine Providence.

Both Bruce and I were new arrivals at the University of Alberta in September 1985. Of course, I was considerably *newer* than he was; while Bruce had just come from being chair of the English department at Dalhousie University to join the faculty of the U of A's English department, I was an unclassified student taking my first-ever university course while I finished off my remaining high school courses at Alberta College and Glenrose School Hospital. Having had most of my K–12 education in a "special" school for students with disabilities, I was, to say the least, less than certain about whether or not I would be able to cope with the demands of going to university. My first thought when I saw six-foot-something Bruce walk into the classroom was, "Oh, great! I'm going to have to get a hydraulic lift installed in my wheelchair just so this guy will be able to see me!" The 50 minutes of class that followed passed quite smoothly, but then came the moment of truth. After class, I had to go up to him and get a class outline that had been distributed. So I went up to Bruce, introduced myself, and asked for an outline. He gave me the class outline, so I figured either he could understand my impaired speech, or he was a good guesser. He also sat down while I talked to him. Now there was a good sign. I left class that day with an undefined good feeling. Still, if someone had come up to me that day and told me that this new professor would turn out to be, not only a good friend, but also one of my most reliable aides and even, eventually, my PHD supervisor, I would have said they were *nuts*! Perhaps it's just as well that it wasn't until years later that I heard the other side of this story from Bruce and Nora's daughter, Laura. Apparently, Bruce sat down to dinner with his family that night and declared, "Boy, did I get a shock in my last section of 210 today!" Well, if Bruce was thrown into a state of shock by my sudden entrance into his life, he certainly got over it in record time. Within a matter of weeks, not only was I thoroughly immersed in an introductory course in university English, but Bruce was thoroughly immersed in a crash course in life with Heidi. Among his first lessons was that DATS, which ostensibly stands for "Disabled Adult Transportation System," actually stands for "Doesn't Arrive Till Sundown." I knew he had mastered that lesson the day DATS got me to university about five minutes before class ended. I wheeled into class just as Bruce was giving the homework assignments for next class. After dismissing the class, Bruce walked up and asked me where I'd been. I replied, "Would you believe riding around the city on a DATS bus?!" With a little chuckle, Bruce responded, "I see, sounds like fun! Well, since you finally did make it, I might as well give you your reading test!" That's when I realized, almost to my chagrin, that Bruce was adjusting quite well to having me as a student.

It was, to a large extent, my overwhelmingly positive experience in Bruce's first-year course and the personal encouragement I received from him that prompted my decision to go into the honours English program—another endeavour that many other people thought to be far beyond my physical abilities. I subsequently went on to take several undergraduate courses and one graduate course from him. As an instructor, he not only had a firm command of the course material, but also a genuine and infectious enthusiasm for his subject matter. He had an exceptional talent for getting students to engage with even the most daunting and difficult texts (such as Samuel Richardson's 2,100-page novel *Clarissa*) through the skilful combination of lecture, class discussion, student presentations, and, in more recent years, Internet conferencing. Bruce had a truly unique gift for fostering students' desire and ability to learn.

On a personal level, two things that always struck me about Bruce were how easily trainable he was as a prof, and how genuinely excited he got about my daily accomplishments. From the beginning, Bruce approached my disability-related needs, not as some onerous drain on him or the rest of the class, but as an opportunity to create a genuine sense of community within the classroom. By the end of my first semester, he had decided that we really didn't need to go through Disabled Student Services to make arrangements for me to write my exams at home. Instead, he simply instituted his "99 Street run" and started dropping off and picking up my exams himself. Bruce thus set a precedent that came in awfully handy when I had to train subsequent professors. His pragmatic approach in working with me to find ways to accommodate my disability-related needs also helped me develop a sense of self-confidence and independence that served me well throughout my undergraduate and graduate career.

Another way in which Bruce continually bolstered my self-confidence was by insisting on publicizing my little daily victories over obstacles of various shapes and sizes. For example, when we first got a phone in the Honours Lounge, I discovered that you had to dial the number within ten seconds in order to be connected. For a while, this seemed like an insurmountable challenge for me. Hence, Bruce saw the phone call he got from me one day saying I was stuck alone in the lounge and needed him to come pick up the books I had dropped on the floor as a red-letter event. As he was leaving the lounge, Bruce ran into one of his colleagues and gleefully announced, "Guess what! Heidi just called me on the phone all by herself!" Unaware of the background to this situation, the professor just smiled vaguely and said, "Oh, that's... that's nice."

One of my all-time favourite bits of free publicity from Bruce came the day my wheelchair got a flat and I had to call my dad to come in to the university and fix it. By the time Dad got to the Humanities Building, I was about 20 minutes late for Bruce's class. Since the class was just down the hall, I got Dad to walk me into class minus the chair. Later that day, Bruce was helping me with the elevator when another prof walked by and greeted us. Bruce immediately said to the other prof, "Would you believe Heidi literally walked into class this morning?!" That was the first time I'd ever seen an English prof speechless!

My decision to ask Bruce to supervise my PHD dissertation was, without a doubt, one of the best decisions I have ever made—professionally as well as personally. As a supervisor, he was unfailingly supportive and encouraging, while at the same time constantly spurring me on to strive for academic excellence in my own research. Just as he had from the beginning of my undergrad, Bruce continued to encourage me to challenge the boundaries of my perceived ability. For example, when, three years into my PHD program, I lamented the fact that my peers were getting teaching experience that seemed, even to me, to be beyond my reach, his response was, "What makes you think you can't teach?" I was, frankly, quite flummoxed by the apparent naïveté of this response. Had this question come from *anyone but Bruce*, I would have dismissed it out of hand as being entirely uninformed and/or outright foolish. This question was coming from Bruce, however —the same person whose assistance I'd had to enlist several times over the years to help educate new professors about the fact that my severe speech, motor, and visual impairments *were not* insurmountable barriers to my full participation in any class as a student. Now he was using the very same lines of argument to convince *me* that my various significant disabilities did not constitute an insurmountable barrier to my being an effective instructor either! It was his support (not to mention his persistent prodding!) that gave me the courage to apply to the English department for a Graduate Teaching Assistantship; this ultimately led to my co-teaching a section of English 101 in 2000–2001, and a section of English 105 in the fall of 2001. There were many times when, as a rookie instructor confronted with a difficult situation in the classroom, I would think about how I had seen Bruce handle similar situations, and act accordingly. The results were almost always positive. One of the most rewarding moments in my academic career came when I had asked Bruce to come and echo for me in my English 105 class, as my regular co-teacher was away; following the class, Bruce took me aside and told me how gratifying it was for him to see that I had truly become a good and capable instructor. Considering the source, I could not wish for a better or more meaningful endorsement of my ability as a teacher. Bruce has taught me, in both word and deed, the kind of intellectual integrity, caring for students, and striving for excellence that it takes to be a truly good teacher.

My ultimate realization of just how incredibly blessed I was to have Bruce as my mentor and friend came in the month preceding my PHD defence. A sudden attack of appendicitis had landed me in the hospital for emergency surgery just four weeks before my defence. My medical condition was significantly complicated by my pre-existing respiratory weakness and susceptibility to pneumonia. Immediately upon learning of my hospitalization, Bruce began making daily trips to the hospital to check on me. During one of these visits a couple of days after my surgery, I asked Bruce (via the use of a letterboard because the insertion of an NG tube had made oral communication impossible), "*What is the absolute deadline?*" Bruce vehemently insisted that I was not to worry about my defence for the time being; I was to focus on my recovery. His parting words to me that day were "You've got too much time to lie here and fret—that *can't* be good for you. I'm going to do something about that." Not half an hour after Bruce left, a hospital maintenance worker came up to my room to install a television set. When I indicated that I hadn't ordered a TV, the man asked, "Do you know someone named Bruce Stovel?"

I nodded.

"Well, he rented this TV for you...said something about it being 'Pre-Defence Relaxation Therapy'—whatever *that* means!"

I knew *exactly* what that meant: Bruce had decided that I *was* going to have a defence, and that, regardless of whether that defence took place next month or next year, his primary goal was to do everything in his power to make sure that I went into that defence at full strength. Because he was my friend and not just my supervisor, concern for my well-being totally eclipsed any worries about academic schedules or faculty deadlines. This also meant that, before I could even entertain thoughts of proceeding with the defence as scheduled, I would have to convince Bruce, beyond any reasonable doubt, that I was indeed physically strong enough to go through with it. This I eventually managed to do only through a series of daily visits, phone calls, and email correspondence in the days immediately following my return home from the hospital. Nice guy though he was, Bruce was no pushover!

My PHD defence *did* proceed as scheduled, and as planned—*almost*. The original plan had been for my best friend since high school, Michelle, who was now a faculty member in the Education department at the University of British Columbia, to fly out to Edmonton to echo for me at my defence. That plan, though, changed abruptly when Michelle called me at 8:00 A.M. the day of my defence, to tearfully tell me that she had gotten sick at the airport, and so they wouldn't let her fly because of the SARS scare, which was at its peak just at that time. Although Bruce was my obvious first choice as a backup echo, I knew that this wasn't really a viable option, given that he would be one of my examiners! Consequently, my friend and then pastor Shafer Parker was quickly pressed into service as my backup echo for the defence. Bruce still turned out to be invaluable as a backup for my backup echo for those excruciatingly complex "academese" words and phrases that Shafer sometimes didn't pick up on right away. Thanks largely to Bruce's calming influence, both my echo and I survived my defence.

Following the successful completion of my defence, and the subsequent nomination of my dissertation for the Governor General's Gold Medal, Bruce promptly morphed from supervisor to publicity agent. It was a role that he took on with obvious relish, and a zeal that I found *almost* overwhelming. One of the fruits of his efforts was a feature article written by Larry Johnsrude for the *Edmonton Journal*. Part of the introduction to this article reads, "'I think the reason I like writing is that it is a way for me to express ideas without being impaired by my body,' she says, slowly and painstakingly, while mentor and friend Bruce Stovel acts as an 'echo,' repeating her words for easier comprehension."

Mentor and friend, Bruce Stovel...I'll never know what I did to deserve such a tremendous blessing in my life for over 20 years. I do know that I'll remain forever grateful.

10 Respect for What I Do

ANN RABSON

I'M THE ONLY MEMBER OF MY FAMILY WITHOUT A PHD. In fact, I never made it to college, and my high school years pretty much happened without me. Not really an academic. My mom has really tried to be tolerant and accept this, but I know that, deep down in her heart, she wasn't thinking of my career in blues as being valid as a life's work.

One year, I invited her to come to the Chicago Blues Festival with me. I had the weekend off, and I thought it might be nice if she could enjoy the music and meet some of my mentors and just generally have a good time.

She had a *ball*. Everyone treated her like a queen, and she got to meet many wonderful people, including Sunnyland Slim, Erwin Helfer, and Yank Rachell. I think she was beginning to see the light about my nonacademic career.

Her change of heart was clinched by meeting Bruce. We had stopped by Legends so she could hear some music in a club setting. As it happened, Bruce was sitting next to us, and they got to talking. My mother is a huge Jane Austen fan—reads her books once a year. She was very impressed by Bruce, his intellect, his love of Jane Austen, and his love for and understanding of the blues. I think when we walked out of there, my mom had a new appreciation of my obsession with the blues.

I always enjoyed spending time with Bruce. He was a wonderful, patient, funny, warm human being. I will always remember his dedication to the music I love, and also that he helped my family gain respect for what I do.

II First Edition of *Pride and Prejudice*

JEANNINE GREEN

FOR THE PAST SEVERAL DECADES, the Friends of the University of Alberta have generously supported the Bruce Peel Special Collections Library by donating funds for the purchase of books dedicated to retiring faculty. Early this year, the academic community and blues aficionados were shocked and much saddened to hear of the death of Bruce Stovel. Dr Stovel, among his many other activities, had been an active member of the Friends and of the Jane Austen Society of North America, and a staunch advocate for the university libraries.

Ronald Betty, the secretary-treasurer of the Friends, contacted us early in the spring to ask for suggestions for an appropriate book that would honour Professor Stovel's memory. It seemed obvious to all of us that our copy of *Pride and Prejudice* was the perfect choice.

The Peel Library has owned the very rare first editions of *Sense and Sensibility* and *Pride and Prejudice* since the early sixties. These three-decker novels are in very good condition, and to preserve and protect them in the future, custom-made conservation slipcases and chemises were commissioned from a local bookbinder, Alex McGuckin, in 2006. The Friends offered to donate funds to pay for the case for *Pride and Prejudice*.

Jane Austen began to write what would become *Pride and Prejudice* when she was the same age as her most famous protagonist, Elizabeth Bennet. Her father offered the manuscript to the publisher Thomas Cadell in 1797, but it was turned down sight unseen. *Sense and Sensibility: A Novel by a Lady* was published to great success in 1811. Capitalizing on its popularity, Austen extensively rewrote her first manuscript, dropping the title *First Impressions*, which had been used by a novelist in 1800. *Pride and Prejudice: A Novel by the Author of Sense and Sensibility* was published to loud acclaim in 1813, and sold out almost immediately. It is not certain how many copies of this printing were issued, but of the approximate 1,500 or so, the Peel copy is one of only two in Canada.

In September, Nora and Grant Stovel were joined by Ronald Betty; Dr Peter Savaryn, chairman of the Friends and chancellor emeritus of the university; Dr Juliet McMaster, former university professor in the Department of English and renowned Austen specialist; Karen Adams, director of Libraries and Information Resources; Jeannine Green, special collections librarian; and reporters from the university student newspaper. The occasion marked the formal dedication of *Pride and Prejudice* in the Peel Library. The bookplates read, "Presented in memory of Professor Bruce Stovel, 1941–2007." The event was duly reported in the *Gateway*, the University of Alberta student newspaper, and resulted in an unexpected but greatly appreciated flurry of media interest. Literally dozens of students have since asked to see the first edition of their "favourite novel of all time." We are delighted that the continuing interest in Austen will be associated with Dr Stovel for many years to come.

12 Blues World Loses a Faithful Booster

Professor, Author, and Broadcaster Also Became an International Authority on Jane Austen

ROGER LEVESQUE

MEMBERS OF THE MUSIC AND ACADEMIC communities are mourning the sudden death of Bruce Stovel. The University of Alberta literature professor, author, broadcaster, and untiring promoter of the blues suffered a massive coronary following a swim on Friday, 12 January. He was 65.

To mark his passing, the flag on the University of Alberta Administration Building was lowered to half-mast Tuesday and Wednesday (an official obituary ran in Tuesday's *Edmonton Journal*).

Joseph Bruce Stovel was born in Montreal. During his youth, his father became the chief executive of a major manufacturing company and the family moved frequently, even settling in New York state for a time, an experience that undoubtedly expanded his world view and inspired his interest in culture generally. He married Nora Stovel (also a professor at the U of A) 42 years ago, and the couple moved to Edmonton in 1985 with their two children, Laura and Grant.

It's typical of Bruce's modest character that few people outside academia knew he had gained his PHD in English magna cum laude at Harvard University, that he subsequently taught at Yale University in the early 1970s, or that he was awarded several of the highest honours for teaching at the U of A before he retired last year. Following his specialty in eighteenth-century English literature and numerous published essays, he became an authority of international stature on Jane Austen in particular, co-editing two volumes of essays on Austen and co-founding the Edmonton chapter of the Jane Austen Society; he co-organized an international conference on the novelist here in 2003.

While Bruce was an avid fan of music generally, the blues was his particular passion. From the mid-1990s, his volunteer efforts included co-hosting the weekly program *Calling All Blues* on CJSR-FM with his son Grant, seeking out many lesser-known blues artists for the Yardbird Suite club, and working some five years as media liaison for Edmonton's Labatt Blues Festival. His passions even intermingled when he hosted a 400-level class at the U of A on The Blues as Lyric Poetry and invited various musicians to perform for the class.

If Austen's novels and blues music seem like incongruous interests, then you have to credit Bruce's continual curiosity and an acute analytical sense that drove him to explore the subtext and social context of both spheres. In doing so, he offered an admirable example to the rest of us, by approaching the artifacts of culture with such a balanced and broad perspective.

He will be remembered for treating everyone as a respected individual, bringing a positive attitude to meeting new people, and exhibiting a natural enthusiasm for art and life that he couldn't help instilling in others. His vast knowledge was appreciated by many, and, with his tall stature, Bruce was always easy to track down at music events, his hat bobbing up out of the crowd. There's an image and a person who won't be forgotten.

AUTHOR'S NOTE

This article was originally published in the *Edmonton Journal* on 17 January 2007, in the Culture Section, and is reproduced here with minor changes. ©2007 *The Edmonton Journal*.

13   I Sing the Blues

GRAHAM GUEST

LIFE IS BOOKENDED WITH CATACLYSMS. Our routines collapse when we are rocked by the unforgiving and basic realities of life and death. Birth provides hope, passion, and love incarnate; death remains always a humourless equalizer. We are unflinching statues without dimension if we are not moved, confused, humbled, and saddened by the passing of time, each moment a diminishing percentage of the whole. We stand as witnesses to this erosion, while the future, like a perfectly balanced jury, remains resolutely uncertain.

Still, we persevere and hopefully experience something of the world. Family, friends, acquaintances, and strangers mould our common human experience into individualized dramas with beginnings, middles, and ends. These stories, our lives, can become convoluted, and we are aided greatly by people who give us our regular bearings.

For me, on levels too personal to expand upon fully, the death of Dr Bruce Stovel was a loss of one of those key individuals.

Stovel was a mentor of mine, and his passing highlighted for me the importance of such relationships. Emotional health hopefully includes an understanding of loss, and I'll admit to not being the best at following the steps of grieving, but this loss continues to upset me, move me, and advise me. I was shocked and saddened by his death; but I lay no unique claim to this reaction and emotion. Perhaps my unique perspective was my proximity to him during my formative years.

Clawing my way down the back alleys of manhood, I found Bruce a comforting presence in my life. I was without uncle figures during this time, and a questioning young man growing mistrustful of parental guidance can subconsciously look to others as role models. Bruce was one I saw as a role model, and for that I'm thankful. Luckily, when the clouds finally clear, those above the fray are evident to all.

I wonder who his role models were. I imagine they were remarkable human beings.

When people pass away we are left with defining moments, no matter what the trajectory of the life being remembered was. I wish to share a single anecdote about Bruce. It concerns a blues singer who shall remain nameless. After a performance in Edmonton that Bruce had arranged, a guitar was brought backstage for this singer to sign. This was a normal occurrence, and Bruce and I were there taking stock of the night. The backstage was relaxed as it normally would be, but there was a slight heaviness in the air. The elderly singer was seated and looked up at Bruce with a silent request.

In an exchange that spanned a generation, a massive difference in upbringing, or, at least, formal education, Bruce picked up the supplied pen and signed the guitar on the artist's behalf. Bruce didn't say anything, nor did the artist, and I've mentioned this sparingly.

A few of us involved in the show had already gathered that the singer couldn't read or write—even his own name. I hadn't been sure whether Bruce knew that his artist's expression of lyrics and, in fact, his life skills in general were the result of memory work, but his action proved the answer in gentle form. This moment remains suspended in time for me. The singer trusted Bruce, and Bruce understood what was happening and lived up to the high standard he had established for himself. There is a guitar collector with a famous signature on one of his prizes, but he doesn't know how special it is.

Bruce Stovel is missed, and I hope his esteemed example lives on in those he mentored. He enjoyed good food and company, and I suspect he more than tolerated earthly cuisine and lively characters as well! He was a social man, and he measured his different worlds with a common scale. One can imagine in a further realm that Jane Austen and Muddy Waters are invited guests to a dinner party of his, and that they are in animated discussion. No longer are they without a bond.

Bruce taught by example and was guided by inclusion. He had a soft touch for a man with such intelligence and conviction. He's missed, and I hope his esteemed example lives on in those he mentored.

I sing the blues indeed.

14 Tacet

DAVID MARTIN

a concert-hall stage littered with used notes
first plucked from strings, given life
upsetting the air like bees
drunk as they slip from ear to ear
repeating their names as proud children
    until
they fall, exhausted,
breathless against the wooden stage,
covered over by other spent music,
waiting in silence until they are swept up
    collected
in a waste-bin by the night janitor
and scattered in the alley: a diaspora
of second-hand notes drifting unheard,
some finding homes in women's tangled hair
others hugging a chain-link fence
    or else
huddled at the trunks of trees
pleading to be given a second chance with
a new instrument—
    maybe this time a cello

Jane Austen

PRIDE & PREJUDICE.

CHAPTER I.

It is a truth universally acknowledged, that a single man in possession of a good fortune, must be in want of a wife.

However little known the feelings or views of such a man may be on his first entering a neighbourhood, this truth is so well fixed in the minds of the surrounding families, that he is considered as the rightful property of some one or other of their daughters.

"My dear Mr. Bennet," said his lady to him one day, "have you heard

VOL. I.   B

15 Jane Sings the Blues

JONATHAN LOCKE HART

In memory of Bruce Stovel and for him

How can Jane sing the blues
But in your mind? How could
You resolve the young woman
Of the manse with the delta heat
Pushing up the Mississippi
To Chicago? The delicate roses
By the church, house, manor bending
In the English drizzle are not
The bayou or the tenements, the smoke
And fast buzz of jazz? The rifts
Heavy in the night air have their own
Scent, sense, care. Each keeps
Its own sensibility, and elegance
Finds rest, gives pause, in variation.
And in the park they stroll
Regardless of the music they make

16　A Day Out in Kew

MARGARET DRABBLE

EVERY READER OF JANE AUSTEN will have noticed the reference to an early jigsaw in *Mansfield Park*, though some of us may have paid more attention to it than others. Early in this novel, we discover Maria and Julia Bertram looking down on their poor little cousin Fanny Price because she is not acquainted with the dissected map of Europe. In the first weeks of Fanny's residence at Mansfield Park, evidence of her prodigious ignorance is brought regularly in fresh reports to Lady Bertram in the drawing room: "Dear Mamma, only think, my cousin cannot put the map of Europe together—or my cousin cannot tell the principal rivers in Russia—or she never heard of Asia Minor—or she does not know the difference between water-colours and crayons! How strange!—Did you ever hear of any thing so stupid?" (*Mansfield Park* [MP] 18).[1]

I cannot claim that this casual reference caught my attention when I first encountered it, and I came back to it through a circuitous route. Two or three years ago, I came up with the project of writing a short illustrated history of the jigsaw puzzle. It would be a pleasant little Christmas cracker of a book, brightly coloured, neatly packaged, which would sell in museum and gallery shops. As a child, I enjoyed doing jigsaws, and I thought it would be fun to devote a few months to the topic. I found a publisher who seemed interested, and embarked on my research; but I found the subject so many-branched, so complex, so suggestive that my plans changed almost beyond recognition, and my book grew and grew, into a mixture of family memoir, pedagogical theory, travel writing, sociology, literary criticism, and art history. As I write these words, the book is still evolving, and I am still searching for missing pieces to complete my pattern. So I take the opportunity to pause here, and to take a diversionary tour of Kew Gardens, and to visit Kew Palace, where one of the earliest jigsaws ever made now resides.

The first jigsaw puzzle was a dissected map, and it was made in London in 1766, or thereabouts, by a printer and engraver called John Spilsbury. Spilsbury's idea was dazzlingly simple. He mounted maps on thin mahogany board and cut them along country or county boundaries with a fine marquetry saw, then boxed them up for children to reassemble. In retrospect, it seems astonishing that nobody had hit on this concept before. Dissected maps were both educational and entertaining, and they soon became popular in the schoolroom and the drawing-room, at a period when the market for children's books and games was rapidly expanding. Writers as diverse as Maria Edgeworth and Mrs Sherwood (Mary Butt) endorsed them, and before long puzzles were devised to teach subjects other than geography. Delicate, hand-tinted, dissected illustrations enlivened lessons in historical chronology, Bible stories, and natural history, and booksellers soon began to produce puzzles that had little or no educational purpose. They made them just for fun.

The word "jigsaw" is a late nineteenth-century coinage, so it is anachronistic to refer to the Spilsbury maps as jigsaws, but the term has been so widely adopted that everybody now knows what it means. It has become part of our daily vocabulary, both as object and as metaphor. How did we manage without it?

Maria and Julia despise Fanny for her ignorance, but it is not surprising that dissected puzzles were unknown in her Portsmouth home. They were, at this period, fairly expensive items, handmade for the children of the upper classes and the aristocracy. Spilsbury's prices ranged from 9 shillings to 1 pound 1 shilling, though you could buy a model more cheaply without the sea. The maps that I went to see in

Kew had been acquired by Lady Charlotte Finch, enlightened governess of the many children of George III (and mother of four children of her own), and they were used to instruct the royal infants. The maps were housed in two handsome little mahogany cabinets, one with three deep drawers, the other with thirteen shallow drawers, furnished with brass locks and handles, perhaps for travelling between the royal residences. These cabinets contained several Spilsbury maps, of which thirteen engraved puzzles, three manuscript puzzles, and two manuscript maps survive. Across a vast tract of the Northwest of the Spilsbury map of North America are inscribed the words "*Partie Inconnue*."

Canadian scholar of children's literature Jill Shefrin has written a beautifully produced and entertaining monograph on these cabinets, their contents, and Lady Charlotte's teaching methods. Charmingly entitled *Such Constant Affectionate Care*, it gives due prominence to Spilsbury's invention. It is not known (or not yet known) whether the maps and cabinets were commissioned directly from Spilsbury by Lady Charlotte. In 2000, they were offered for sale by a private owner, and they spent some years in limbo in England with a dealer awaiting an export licence before a successful appeal to save them for the nation was made through the Department for Culture, Media and Sport. The appeal, as reported by the press, slightly overstated Lady Charlotte's accomplishments, for it claimed that she herself was the inventor of dissected maps, which has been dismissed for some time as false. The price paid, I believe, was £120,000. In 2007, they were put on display at Kew Palace, and I am told they will in future travel between Kew and the newly renovated Museum of Childhood at Bethnal Green, spending six months of the year at each address.

It was in Kew that I went to see them, having made an appointment with members of staff from the Historic Royal Palaces, an organization that looks after Kew Palace, the Tower of London, Hampton Court, the Banqueting House, and Kensington Palace. It was a delightful outing. Kew Gardens have long been a favourite tourist attraction, providing a day out for Londoners and a destination for botanists and gardeners from all over the world, and I have visited them many times. The first time I went was with my aunt, on my first visit to London when I was

11 or 12 years old. My aunt used to intone an old song to us to whet our appetite: "Go down to Kew in lilac-time,...It isn't far from London."[2] (Like George III's oldest daughter, she couldn't sing.) We also liked the famous couplet "I am his Highness' Dog at Kew, / Pray tell me Sir, whose Dog are you?" (Pope 826). I don't think we knew then that it was by Alexander Pope, but we liked it. The entrance price was one old copper penny, which would then have borne the head of George VI. It costs a lot more now, even with a senior citizen's reduction, but it is worth the increase.

Kew became a royal retreat in Jane Austen's period, so it was a good place to stroll about, thinking of old friends, and of Austen, and of Austen's contemporary Fanny Burney, who spent much time there not wholly happily as second keeper of the robes in attendance on Queen Charlotte. The gardens of Kew, beautifully situated by the River Thames, are spacious, and in the time of George III, Kew provided a summer residence for his growing family, who were scattered around the grounds in various houses, palaces, and cottages. As Flora Fraser comments in her gripping account of the lives of George III's daughters, *Princesses*, it became "a full-blown royal campus, which the royal children rarely left during the summer months, where servants intrigued against each other, and where tradesmen in the village that had grown up around the church on the Green vied for preferment" (34).

Kew Palace, which was formerly known as the Dutch House, then as the Prince of Wales's House, was originally built as a merchant's residence in 1631, and it has now been renovated to give a sense of royal family life of George III, Queen Charlotte, and their many children. It is a handsome building, with delightfully detailed brickwork painted in a bright red ochre wash. I was greeted there by the curators, who complimented me on having chosen to wear a turquoise T-shirt for my outing: this was a lucky omen, they said, for I would match the renovated green verditer wallpaper. The palace is an appropriate home for the puzzles, for the royal family used Kew as a retreat for many years, and in various houses, palaces, lodgings, and gardens, the princes and princesses enjoyed fresh air, picnics, games, and botanizing. In the palace, as well as the Spilsbury map cabinets, visitors may see cut-paper silhouettes, a silver rattle, a silver ink stand, globes, musical and scientific instruments, examples of George III's architectural drawings, and a "baby house" (a doll's house) complete with furnishings embroidered by the princesses.

The wallpaper of the doll's house is striking. It is what I call turquoise, and what the experts call verditer, and it shows an overall pattern of irregular amoeba-like blobs outlined in white, floating against a background dotted with tiny spots. This colour scheme has been picked up in the house itself. In the queen's boudoir, on the first floor, the walls are a strong clear verditer, with a Greek key border of black and green, recreated from an early nineteenth-century fragment uncovered during restoration. The curtains are black and yellow chintz, and there are two little tables, one a green baize card table, the other a sewing table with a work basket, at which the queen and the princesses would spend hours on their needlework and knotting and netting. It is not a room of excessive grandeur. Austen and her family would not have been overawed by its appointments.

The message of the house is mixed: it was a place of domesticity and safety, but it was also a place of suffering and frustration, eventually contaminated for the king by memories of attacks of illness and the menaces of doctors pursuing him with straitjackets. Life at court, even in this rustic outpost of the court, could be difficult, and at times, for the captive princesses, insufferably tedious. The constraints on the lives of upper-middle-class women of this period were portrayed by Austen with both sympathy and satire, and the royal women present an extreme case of what had to be endured by dutiful daughters subject to a father who was also their monarch. Princess Elizabeth, born in 1770, pining for a husband and feeling her beauty fade, wrote in despair in 1802 from the regular family holiday in Weymouth to her confidante Lady Harcourt: "Read to the Queen the whole evening till cards, when I play at whist till my eyes know not hearts from diamonds and spades from clubs. And when that is over, turn over cards to amuse the King, till I literally get the rheumatism in every joint of my hand....News there is none, but who bathes and who can't, and who won't and who will, whether warm bathing is better than cold, who likes wind and who don't, and all these very silly questions and answers which bore one to death and provoke one's understanding" (qtd. in Fraser 200). Austen's lot was more fortunate than this, and so was Fanny Price's.

My search for the origins of the jigsaw has allowed me time to think about family life in Jane Austen's time and in particular about the concept of child-centred education, newly adopted in the eighteenth century. Family portraits with small children, celebrating the companionate marriage, are a good hunting ground for images of toys — musical instruments, pull-along carriages and wooden animals, playing cards, little windmills, and even the occasional jigsaw. We may see Masters Thomas and John Quicke at work on a dissected map of Europe in a pastel portrait by Bath-based artist William Hoare, dated c. 1770, which may be the earliest image of a jigsaw ever portrayed. Hoare shows the younger brother holding the shape of Italy in his hand and looking up to his brother for approval or affirmation. Family groups of this period often show informal educational scenes, with parents reading to children, or children holding books, or books strewn casually (but not carelessly) upon the nursery or drawing-room floor. Little dogs remained the most favoured accessory, but the portrayal of pursuits that illustrated parental concern and interaction also became very popular. Some of these ostentatiously affectionate groupings may protest a little too much, but the Quicke children playing quietly with their map, without visible adult interference, seem happy with their task. The painter shows them as they are, without condescension or sly adult moralizing. He shows them with respect.

We don't know what Jane Austen thought of dissected maps, for her reference in *Mansfield Park* is coloured by Fanny Price's sense of inferiority and the arrogant complacency of her cousins. I imagine that, like Maria Edgeworth, she would have approved of them as rational educational aids, but we can't be sure. The little princes and princesses who learned geography with Lady Charlotte Finch from the Spilsbury maps have left no record of what they thought of them either, unless there is some as yet untranscribed comment to be found in the vast surviving and not always legible mass of royal correspondence through which Flora Fraser has trawled so assiduously.

We can make a better guess at what she would have thought of the private theatricals that went on at Windsor and at Kew, involving vast expense of fancy dress and scenery, and no doubt on occasion some anguish and tedium for the younger participants. Zoffany's sumptuous portrait of *Queen Charlotte with Her Two Eldest Sons* (c. 1764–1765) shows the elegantly robed and jewelled young queen in her dressing room, with the two-year-old Prince of Wales and his one-year-old brother Frederick grouped around her in colourful fancy dress, both somewhat dwarfed by an enormous but docile boar-hound. The Prince of Wales is dressed, warrior-like, as Telemachus, son of Ulysses and Penelope, and Frederick as a tiny Turk with a pretty silvery turban and a diminutive gown of blue and gold. These trappings cannot have been very comfortable, but the Prince of Wales, as we know, grew up with a taste for exotic "oriental" display, so maybe he enjoyed his appearance in juvenile pageants. (He also, or so a court physician claimed, grew up to admire Jane Austen, a more refined and home-grown taste. This claim prompted Austen's dedication of *Emma* to "His Royal Highness the Prince Regent," but we do not know if he ever read it. We do know that she disapproved of him.)

Many fond parents at this period commissioned portraits of their children in fancy dress and historical costume. Reynolds's child portraits immortalized little boys in the garb of Jupiter, Hannibal, Bacchus, and Henry VIII, images that curiously combine playfulness with pathos and an ominous sense of destiny. Caroline Lennox (later Lady Holland) was painted at the age of nine as she appeared in a performance of Dryden's *Indian Emperor*. Amateur theatricals were also a thriving tradition, in country houses as well as at court, and could make severe demands on their participants. Fanny Burney's nephew Charles gives a lively account in a letter to his mother (10 January 1802) of a Christmas visit to Crewe Hall in Cheshire, "and the exertions expected by the guests of the Lady of the Hall. The lad of sixteen, having had to fag himself until two in the morning getting the lines for two parts, found himself, on the drawing of the famous green curtain, 'all cover'd with Mrs Crewe's Jewels seated on my Throne as King John; we had the first scene,...and the famous scene between King John and Hubert, after which we had Chrononhotonthologos; and I assure you, what with the trouble of Learning nearly 200 lines, the dressing, the speaking them, the battle...the fright, and the *tout ensemble*, I hardly ever was more tired in my life'" (Burney 5:144).

The theatricals at Mansfield Park, in contrast, seem quite modest.

These intriguing glimpses into the educational pursuits and entertainments of late eighteenth- and early nineteenth-century society seem to come to life at Kew, which, like Versailles, provides a setting well suited to ghosts and revenants, with few disturbing intrusions from the twenty-first century. The gardens and grounds have been in a constant process of renewal and renovation, and some of the most famous buildings (such as the Decimus Burton Palm House) were built after Jane Austen's time, but the prevailing spirit of the place is Georgian rather than Victorian. The gardens were landscaped by (amongst others) Charles Bridgeman, William Kent, and Capability Brown, and the great botanical collections were assembled under the aegis of Joseph Banks. The Pagoda, a sublimely fantastic example of chinoiserie by William Chambers, was built in 1761, and Queen Charlotte's homely timber-framed and thatched *cottage ornée*, which she is said to have designed herself, dates from 1772. These two buildings represent two extremes of architectural invention of the period, and between them and around them stretch timeless lawns and walks and woodlands, dotted with temples and picturesque ruined arches and little lakes. Here a visitor can wander, or sit on a bench with a book, or botanize, or picnic, and breathe the freshness of the air, and think of the past.

The Spilsbury dissected maps provided me with an excuse for my day's outing, and it was curiously touching to see them in their eighteenth-century cabinets and their twenty-first-century display case, newly returned to their original home. Maria Edgeworth wrote at some length about the use of puzzles in her *Practical Education*, but the casual reference to the "map of Europe" in *Mansfield Park* is suggestive in its very brevity. There is room for more scholarship on the subject of the puzzles, games, and educational devices and theories of Austen's day. The Spilsbury cabinets are eloquent, and the questions they pose are testimony to the way in which everything Austen touched upon expands on investigation. She never travelled through the map of Europe herself, nor did she penetrate the *Partie Inconnue* of North America, but her readers have colonized the globe, and her books have fostered friendships across continents.

NOTES

1.   All quotations from Jane Austen's published works are taken from *The Oxford Illustrated Jane Austen*, 3rd ed., ed. R.W. Chapman (Oxford: Oxford UP, 1988), and are documented by short title and page number in the body of the chapter.

2.   The complete stanza, from Alfred Noyes's "Barrel Organ," reads as follows: "Go down to Kew in lilac-time, in lilac-time, in lilac-time; / Go down to Kew in lilac-time (it isn't far from London!) / And you shall wander hand in hand with love in summer's wonderland; / Go down to Kew in lilac-time (it isn't far from London!)" (Noyes 365).

WORKS CITED

Burney, Fanny. *The Journals and Letters of Fanny Burney (Madame d'Arblay)*. Ed. Joyce Hemlow. 12 vols. Oxford: Clarendon, 1872–84.

Fraser, Flora. *Princesses: The Six Daughters of George III*. London: John Murray, 2004.

Noyes, Alfred. "Barrel Organ." *The Oxford Dictionary of Quotations*. London: Oxford UP, 1956. 365.

Pope, Alexander. *The Poems of Alexander Pope*. Ed. John Butt. London: Methuen, 1965.

Shefrin, Jill. *Such Constant Affectionate Care: Lady Charlotte Finch, Royal Governess, and the Children of George III*. Los Angeles: Cotsen Occasional, 2003.

Zoffany, Johan. *Queen Charlottte with Her Two Eldest Sons*. c. 1764–1765. RCIN 400146. Royal Collection, U.K. *The Royal Collection: e-Gallery*. 2008. 15 October 2008 <http://www.royalcollection.org.uk/eGallery/>.

17 Two or Three Prayers
Possibly by Jane Austen

PETER SABOR

THERE ARE MANY FAMOUS PUZZLES in Jane Austen's life and writings that her modern biographers have been unable to solve. Was she the subject of the *Rice Portrait*? Did she contribute the letter by "Sophia Sentiment" to her brothers' periodical the *Loiterer*? Was she the author of the comic adaptation of Samuel Richardson's novel *Sir Charles Grandison*? When did she write *Lady Susan*? Was she unhappy at Bath? Why did she abandon *The Watsons*? How would she have completed *Sanditon*?

Another difficult puzzle is furnished by a manuscript first described in the *Times Literary Supplement* by R.W. Chapman in 1926, first published in an expensive, limited edition in 1940 by Colt Press as *Three Evening Prayers*, and now housed in the Olin Library of Mills College, Oakland, California. In their forthcoming edition of Austen's *Later Manuscripts*, Janet Todd and Linda Bree outline what we know, and don't know, about the authorship and date of composition of the prayers. They are written on two sheets of paper, the first bearing a watermark of 1818. This sheet contains a single prayer, entitled "Evening Prayer"; the second contains two untitled prayers. On the first sheet is an inscription, "Prayers Composed by my ever dear Sister Jane," and beneath this is a pencilled inscription, in another unknown hand, "Charles Austen." If the anonymous inscription can be trusted, Charles Austen is attributing the prayer on the first sheet and some other prayers to his sister Jane, but we cannot be sure that the second and third prayers, on a different sheet, are the other prayers in question. The hand in which the first and second prayers, and part of the third, are written is probably that of Austen's brother James, while that of the latter part of the third prayer is probably that of her sister Cassandra. Since James died in December 1819, all but the last part of the third prayer must have been copied before that date, while the part in Cassandra's hand was probably added either at the same time, in 1818–1819, or else well before her death in 1845. Todd and Bree also record the interesting suggestion that the first and third prayers are more likely to be by Jane Austen than the second, for two reasons. First, the second prayer contains "far more ejaculations and more Latinate words," such as "mediation" and "devotion," than the others. Second, it uses the standard form for exclamation marks in phrases such as "Oh God!" whereas the other prayers both prefer the form "Oh! God," a usage found in Austen's manuscripts from the juvenilia through to *Sanditon*. A further mystery concerns the date when Jane Austen might have composed the prayers. There would have been no reason for her to do so before her clergyman father's death in 1805. Deirdre Le Faye conjectures that they might have been written in Southampton in January 1809, when rainy weather kept the Austen sisters, Jane and Cassandra, and their mother from church (171),[1] but, as Todd and Bree note, they could also have been written in the last few months of Austen's life, during her final illness, when, from March 1817, she could no longer attend church services.

In the sparkling collection that he co-edited with Juliet McMaster, *Jane Austen's Business: Her World and her Profession* (1996), Bruce Stovel published what is still the finest essay on Austen's prayers. Although he was unable to identify the hands in which the prayers were written, he was aware that they were not Jane Austen's and suggested that the prayers "were copied out, at two different times, by a combination of the Austen brothers and sisters" (194). He rightly noted that because the prayers "raise some very puzzling questions," Austen's biographers "have by and large left them alone" (199). Significantly, the two major lives of Austen by Claire Tomalin and David Nokes, both published a year after Bruce Stovel's essay, have nothing to say about the prayers at all. Undated works of uncertain authorship, written in indeterminate hands, are enough to make any biographer sing the blues.

Bruce Stovel, however, approached the prayers primarily as literary texts that "speak in a shared voice of a generic predicament (unlike the very personal *Prayers and Meditations* of [Austen's] mentor Samuel Johnson)" (194). Intriguingly, he illustrated their characteristic tone, diction, and rhythms through lengthy quotations from both the first and third prayers, while avoiding close reading of the second. I suspect that, with his ear so finely attuned to Austen's prose style, Bruce had sensed that the second of the prayers was somewhat different from the others. He was surely right in stating that the prayers "are meant to be read as the work of the common, generic believer, not the idiosyncratic individual—the first-person plural rather than the first-person singular," yet this observation is less true of the second prayer than of the others (198). In the first prayer, the one most clearly identified as Austen's, the author writes, with moving simplicity: "Be Gracious to our Necessities, and guard us, and all we love, from Evil this night." In the second, a similar wish is expressed in more ornate fashion, and with a greater apparent effort at fine writing: "To Thy Goodness we commend ourselves this night beseeching thy protection of us through its darkness & dangers."[2] The inverted syntax and the alliteration make this rather more an individual plea, and less the expression of what Stovel terms the "common, generic believer."

One of the few critics since Bruce Stovel to make a close study of the prayers is Brian Southam. He pays particular attention to their style, pointing out its characteristic simplicity and suggesting that "sometimes we seem to overhear an unritualised near-speaking voice" (Southam 86). Of the three quotations provided by Southam to illustrate his point, two are taken from the first prayer, none from the second, and one from the third. It is not, I believe, a coincidence that neither Stovel nor Southam found examples in the second prayer of what they felt to be Austen's characteristic manner: it is less colloquial, more embellished than the others. Southam suggests that Austen's aim in composing prayers was "to ensure that the household, including the servants and any visiting nephews and nieces, was not lulled by familiar sonorities but kept wide awake with language more emphatic and down to earth" (87). There remains, however, the possibility that none of the prayers are by Jane Austen. As Todd and Bree observe, "if it had not been for the scribbled annotation by her brother Charles—an annotation itself unsupported by any other family evidence through to the 1920s—we would not be considering any of these prayers as even possibly by Jane Austen" (cxxv). In their 2008 edition of Austen's *Later Manuscripts*, they print the prayers as an appendix, indicating that the attribution remains open to question.

Unlike Todd and Bree, Bruce Stovel saw no reason to doubt Jane Austen's authorship of all three prayers, taking the inscription said to be by Charles Austen at face value. He did acknowledge the many difficulties that they pose to Austen's critics, including the obvious question of consistency: "they seem so different from her letters—chatty and observant, gossipy and often malicious—and from her novels—so worldly in tone, so seemingly silent on spiritual matters" (200-201). Stovel, however, remained undaunted, finding ways in which the prayers illuminated what he termed the "moral and spiritual terrain" (205) of Austen's fiction.

Among the difficulties that Bruce Stovel encountered in writing on the prayers was that no accurate edition was yet available. As he noted wryly, the text of the first published edition, prepared by their then owner William Matson Roth for publication in 1940, was "a little strange" (Stovel 193); it was printed in capital letters throughout, and the punctuation was frequently modernized. When Chapman printed the prayers in his edition of Austen's *Minor Works* (1954), he simply reversed Roth's system, printing everything in lower case (453-57). In *Catharine and Other Writings* (1993), edited by Margaret Anne Doody and Douglas Murray, a typed transcription by Roth, rather than the manuscripts, formed the basis for the text (Austen 283). Dissatisfied with these editions, Bruce sought out the original manuscripts and used them as the basis for his essay. He would have been still less satisfied with a recent edition of the prayers published by the Friends of

Godmersham Church. It is an attractive publication, with illustrations by John Ward, but textually it is fatally flawed: Prayer I is printed as Prayer II; Prayer II as Prayer III; and Prayer III as Prayer I. In 2007, a reliable text of the prayers, taken from the manuscripts and not from the Roth edition, was published in Brian Southam's *Jane Austen: A Students' Guide to the Later Manuscript Works*; and in 2008, a definitive text was printed in the *Later Manuscripts* volume of The Cambridge Edition of the Works of Jane Austen. Both of these works were, sadly, published too late for Bruce Stovel to use; but he would have been glad to see the long-neglected prayers receiving sustained scholarly attention at last.

NOTES

1. Elsewhere, Le Faye writes that Cassandra, after her sister's death, "cherished her memories, copying out the 'Prayers composed by my ever dear sister Jane'" (267). This suggests, misleadingly, that the inscription attributed to Charles Austen was in fact written by Cassandra.

2. Quotations from Austen's prayers are taken from an appendix in *Later Manuscripts* (Todd and Bree 573, 574).

WORKS CITED

Austen, Jane. *Catharine and Other Writings*. Ed. Margaret Anne Doody and Douglas Murray. Oxford: Oxford World's Classics, 1993.

———. *Three Evening Prayers, written by Jane Austen*. Intro. William Matson Roth. San Francisco: Colt, 1940.

———. *Three Prayers and a Poem by Jane Austen*. Godmersham, Kent: Friends of Godmersham Church, 2007.

Chapman, R.W. "A Jane Austen Collection." *Times Literary Supplement* 14 January 1926: 27.

Le Faye, Deirdre. *Jane Austen: A Family Record*. 2nd ed. Cambridge: Cambridge UP, 2004.

Nokes, David. *Jane Austen: A Life*. London: Fourth Estate, 1997.

Southam, Brian. *Jane Austen: A Students' Guide to the Later Manuscript Works*. London: Concord, 2007.

Stovel, Bruce. "'The Sentient Target of Death': Jane Austen's Prayers." *Jane Austen's Business: Her World and her Profession*. Ed. Juliet McMaster and Bruce Stovel. London: Macmillan, 1996. 192–205.

Todd, Janet, and Linda Bree. Introduction. *Later Manuscripts*. The Cambridge Edition of the Works of Jane Austen. Cambridge: Cambridge UP, 2008. cxviii–cxxvi.

——, eds. *Later Manuscripts*. The Cambridge Edition of the Works of Jane Austen. Cambridge: Cambridge UP, 2008.

Tomalin, Claire. *Jane Austen: A Life*. London: Viking, 1997.

18 Insignificant Dwarves and Scotch Giants

Height, Perception, and Power in Jane Austen

MARY M. CHAN

I had the pleasure of being in Bruce Stovel's graduate course on Jane Austen in the fall of 2003. The following essay is based on the term paper that I wrote for his course, a paper that Bruce encouraged me to revise and submit to Persuasions, the journal of the Jane Austen Society of North America. After some repeated encouragement (prodding), I did. The day I received the acceptance email for what would be my first scholarly publication, Bruce was the first person I told. I still fondly remember his reaction — a big "Yes!"

IN ONE OF JANE AUSTEN'S INCOMPLETE PIECES of juvenilia, "Lesley Castle," the tall Margaret Lesley writes to a friend about her new stepmother: "She has not a bad face, but there is something so extremely unmajestic in her little diminutive figure, as to render her in comparison with the elegant height of Matilda and Myself, an insignificant Dwarf" (*Minor Works* [MW] 122).[1] The new stepmother, Lady Lesley, returns the favour in a letter to the same friend, referring to the "two great, tall, out of the way, overgrown Girls" as "Scotch Giants" (123). Evidently, Austen understood from an early point in her career the absurdity of juxtaposing something big with something small. However, beneath the broad humour of this comic juxtaposition runs an undercurrent of animosity. Margaret Lesley and her new stepmother are engaged in a battle for power, one that manifests in their disdain for each other's height. Criticizing a person's height becomes a means of criticizing the person him- or herself, even though no one can control his or her height. In fact, the irrationality of the criticism indicates the speaker's frustration at the lack of control. Margaret, after all, cannot control whether her father remarries and therefore whether she and her sister are displaced in status in their own home. Height, then, and particularly the perception of height, can function in Austen's fiction as a means of rationalizing a difficult and sometimes subconscious power struggle and transform it into a physical, yet uncontrollable, characteristic.

The emphasis on height is more subdued in Austen's complete novels, but its significance is not diminished. Physical description in Austen resembles a guessing game in which the enterprising reader is left to fill in many blanks. Austen informs us, for example, that Elizabeth Bennet possesses fine eyes, but withholds the eye colour. Anne Elliot, who is described as a "nobody" at the beginning of *Persuasion* (5), literally has no body that is described for the reader. Even exact height can be withheld in favour of the more nuanced, yet less specific, terms "figure" or "air." Mrs Weston praises Emma's "firm and upright figure" and her "pretty height and size" (*Emma* [E] 39) but Emma's actual height is not given. In an 1814 letter to her niece Anna, an aspiring novelist, Jane Austen warns against providing too much detail when writing: "You describe a sweet place, but your descriptions are often more minute than will be liked," she advises. "You give too many particulars of right hand & left" (*Letters* 275). A writer noted for her scant physical descriptions, Austen herself could not be accused of giving "too many particulars."

Austen's sparse descriptors emphasize the importance of the physical references that do appear. Of all the physical descriptors, height is particularly significant. In their notes to "Lesley Castle," Margaret Anne Doody and Douglas Murray point out that the question of the proper size for beauty was "a running joke in Jane Austen's family"

(327n), and in their notes to "Love and Freindship [sic]," they observe that in her later fiction, Austen "always concerns herself with height" (315n).

Austen's concern with height extends beyond the empirical. There is no set code that distinguishes a potential hero from a potential villain. Mr Darcy, Mr Knightley, and Henry Tilney are all tall, but it does not follow that all tall men are heroes (consider Willoughby, for example). In fact, with the exception of five-feet-eight-inch-tall Henry Crawford, exact heights are never provided. Instead, height is expressed comparatively. For example, the narrator in *Persuasion* notes that, of the three captains in Lyme, "Captain Benwick looked and was the youngest of the three, and, compared with either of them, a little man" (97). Actual heights are not provided because they are immaterial. More crucial is how one person's height relates to another's, which in this case suggests that the captains' relative height indicates their comparative moral value. Captain Wentworth is indeed a worthy sailor, who fights bravely in battle, but who also breaks the news of Fanny Harville's death to her fiancé, Benwick, and stays to nurse his friend through his grief. Captain Harville remains loyal to the memory of his sister, insisting that she would not have forgotten Benwick as quickly as he has forgotten her. In fact, even though Benwick's diminished stature initially elicits sympathy from the party at Lyme, as well as from the reader, the esteem is temporary. He is inconstant in a novel that celebrates and depends upon constancy, and thus his diminutive physical appearance parallels his diminishing worth.

Difference in height often indicates a difference in influence, or in the power to influence. Lady Catherine de Bourgh, one of the most thorough meddlers in Austen's fiction, is "a tall, large woman, with strongly-marked features" (*Pride and Prejudice* [PP] 162). This tallness becomes a physical indicator of power, for "Elizabeth found that nothing was beneath this great Lady's attention, which could furnish her with an occasion of dictating to others" (163). Indeed, Lady Catherine's attentions range from advising on the proper way to pack trunks (213–14) to determining "what weather they were to have on the morrow" (166). Comic as it can be, the source of Lady Catherine's power is a serious one: rank. As an aristocrat she can extend her influence as far as she sees fit. Her authority rests upon the value of a titled name, and her height reflects that power.

Lady Catherine's authority, however, is compromised by the height of her daughter, Anne de Bourgh. Comparing the daughter to the mother, Elizabeth marvels at Miss de Bourgh as "being so thin, and so small. There was neither in figure nor face, any likeness between the ladies. Miss de Bourgh was pale and sickly; her features, though not plain, were insignificant; and she spoke very little" (162). Anne de Bourgh's quiet personality makes sense, given the mother she has grown up with, yet her sickly nature suggests that the power of the de Bourgh line is in jeopardy. The mother's height and physical vigour have not been passed down to the daughter, and neither, therefore, has her power to influence.

When height is mentioned in dialogue, the perception of height contributes to the way we understand power in Austen's novels. Factual height ceases to be the focus; rather, it is the speaker's perception of this height that is significant. The theme of perception and the subjectivity of "facts" pervade all of Austen's works, as critics such as Mark Hennelly Jr, Tara Ghoshal Wallace, Juliet McMaster, Martha Satz, Susan Morgan, and Isobel Armstrong have noted. *Pride and Prejudice*, for example, can be interpreted as a novel about biased perception and the process of attaining knowledge free from prejudice. Elizabeth, she of the fine eyes, becomes the novel's epistemological centre, who filters various accounts of Darcy with varying degrees of success.

While Jean Graham notes in "Austen and 'The Advantage of Height'" (1999) that "Descriptions of height also serve as guides to characterization" in Austen (par. 2), this is not entirely the case. Descriptions of height reveal aspects of the speaker's character more than they do the character of the person described. What a character perceives frequently reveals more about the perceiver than the perceived. For example, Mr Rushworth notes that Henry Crawford is "not above five feet eight" (*Mansfield Park* [*MP*] 186) and declares to a puzzled Sir Thomas Bertram, "Nobody can call such an under-sized man handsome. He is not five foot nine. I should not wonder if he was not more than five foot eight. I think he is an ill-looking fellow" (102). While this interestingly draws attention to Henry Crawford's diminished stature (both physical and moral, as Graham notes [par. 10]), it also indicates Mr Rushworth's subconscious awareness that his fiancée is attracted to Mr Crawford, and that he himself cannot seriously compete for her affections. That he can criticize Henry Crawford only for his height reflects poorly on Rushworth's own attractiveness and intelligence.

Since height can be a physical indicator of power, and perception of height reveals character, it follows that the way characters perceive height illuminates how they perceive power. Speaking of height and speaking of power are not unrelated. In *Pride and Prejudice*, for example, Bingley facetiously claims that possessing an advantage in height and size is crucial to winning an argument:

> "By all means," cried Bingley; "let us hear all the particulars, not forgetting their comparative height and size; for that will have more weight in the argument, Miss Bennet, than you may be aware of. I assure you that if Darcy were not such a great tall fellow, in comparison with myself, I should not pay him half so much deference." (50)

Bingley jokes, yet he still acknowledges the influence that Darcy exerts over him. Bingley certainly has a more pliant personality than Darcy, yet one wonders how much of this pliancy stems from the difference in the rank and fortune of the two men. Bingley reduces the power hierarchies he encounters with Darcy to a difference in height, which is an unchangeable and therefore uncontrollable fact of nature. Bingley rationalizes his frustration or insecurity about social advancement into a more acceptable discussion about one man being taller than another. Though he is joking, to a certain extent Bingley does perceive height to be the reason he defers to Darcy, a misperception that suggests Bingley's own subconscious awareness of the disparity in class and status between himself and his friend.

Like Mr Bingley, Emma Woodhouse is a character who notices height. Unlike Mr Bingley, Emma, "handsome, clever, and rich" (*E* 5), suffers no anxieties about her self-worth and her own height. A heroine more used to influencing than being influenced, Emma is occupied with other people's height. Her attempts to exert power over others extend to how tall they are, as demonstrated in an intriguing passage in which the height of the newly engaged, absent Mr Elton is debated. When Miss Bates says that Jane Fairfax is curious to see him, Jane herself needs to respond quickly: "'No—I have never seen Mr Elton,' she replied, starting on this appeal; 'is he—is he a tall man?'" (174). Clearly, Jane has been thinking of other things (likely her own, more uncertain, wedding date), and this is the first topic she lights on. Emma's response is characteristic: "'Who shall answer that question?' cried Emma. 'My father would say 'yes,' Mr Knightley, 'no;' and Miss Bates and I that he is just the happy medium. When you have been here a little longer, Miss Fairfax, you will understand that Mr Elton is the standard of perfection in Highbury, both in person and mind'" (174). When Emma asks who shall answer that question, she of course means it rhetorically, for she then scripts and performs the ensuing discussion. Based on this conversation, one can conjecture that Mr Elton is a medium-sized man who is taller than Mr Woodhouse but shorter than the tall Mr Knightley. Emma echoes the theme of misperception by purposely making contradictory (though she would think witty) comparisons that draw attention to the fallibility of perception and the vulnerability of facts. After all, Mr Elton cannot be both a tall and a short man. Emma then falsely resolves the contradiction by declaring that Mr Elton is the "standard of perfection." Mr Elton is hardly perfect, especially given Emma's failed attempt to match him with Harriet, and Emma knows it. To gloss over truth politely requires a little reshaping of malleable fact. Emma is aware that what she is saying is ironic, but she does not possess sufficient perspicacity to apply the same principles to herself. She fails to realize that she, too, is capable of misperceiving.

Emma understands the worth associated with the proper height, recognizing that Jane Fairfax's height is "just such as almost everybody would think tall, and nobody could think very tall," which indeed makes her size a "most becoming medium" (167). What Emma does not understand is that she cannot alter height as she tries to do with the portrait she draws of Harriet. Realizing that Harriet, who is "short, plump and fair" (23), is hardly tall enough to be considered quite beautiful, Emma uses the portrait to make her taller and thus more desirable to Mr Elton: "as she meant to throw in a little improvement to the figure, to give a little more height, and considerably more elegance, she had great confidence of its being in every way a pretty drawing at last" (47). In her 1999 article about Emma and the portrait scene, Annette Leclair notes that the picture fails both as a portrait of the real Harriet and as an original creation of Emma's. Instead, the subject of the portrait is society's image of what a gentleman's potential wife should look like. Emma, Leclair argues, simply reproduces the shapes that society has already drawn for her (117). Emma's attempt to give Harriet a little more height cannot succeed. The question of Harriet's height is striking, considering how frequently other characters refer to her as "little." Emma considers Harriet "my dear little modest Harriet" (56) and "her own particular little friend" (219). Mrs Elton calls Harriet "poor little Miss Smith!" at the Crown Inn ball (328), Mr Knightley refers to her as "a pretty little creature" (58), Frank Churchill calls her "Miss Woodhouse's beautiful little friend" (266), and even Mr Woodhouse refers to Harriet as "Our little friend" (104). The list continues, almost ad nauseam. Even Fanny Price, who is short compared to her tall Bertram cousins, is referred to as "little" only twice. The frequent references not only constantly emphasize Harriet's height, but also indicate her immaturity, for children in *Emma* are also referred to in the diminutive. Isabella's new baby is "little Emma" (99), Emma worries that Mr Knightley's marrying Jane Fairfax will cheat "little Henry" Knightley out of his Donwell inheritance (228), and Mrs Weston gives birth to "little Anna Weston" (462). Harriet, like the children of the novel, is still growing.

Harriet's growth is explicitly revealed during her awkward social call on the Martin ladies at Abbey Mill farm. The insultingly short 15-minute visit is Harriet's first return to the farm after she rejects Robert Martin's marriage proposal:

They had received her doubtingly, if not coolly; and nothing beyond the merest common-place had been talked almost all the time—till just at last, when Mrs Martin's saying, all of a sudden, that she thought Miss Smith was grown, had brought on a more interesting subject, and a warmer manner. In that very room she had been measured last September, with her two friends. There were the pencilled marks and memorandums on the wainscot by the window. He had done it. They all seemed to remember the day, the hour, the party, the occasion—to feel the same consciousness, the same regrets—to be ready to return to the same good understanding; and they were just growing again like themselves...when the carriage re-appeared, and all was over. (186–87)

Here, Emma's thwarted attempts to artificially give Harriet more height in a portrait are replaced by Mrs Martin's perception that Harriet has actually grown. Recognition of increased height also indicates recognition of increased social standing, for Harriet has indeed acquired a little status by virtue of being Emma's particular friend. As Mr Knightley tells Emma, another Martin (Robert), initially had qualms about proposing to Harriet, "having some apprehension perhaps of her being considered (especially since *your* making so much of her) as in a line of society above him" (59). During the visit at Abbey Mill farm, however, there is no latent anxiety over Harriet's increased status. Rather, the reverse occurs. The anxiety is overt, and the tension relieved only when a previous, more comfortable situation is mentioned. Increased height is discernible and therefore can be a natural, spontaneous topic of conversation.

Harriet's growth is signalled by a second usage of "little" in *Emma*, a usage associated with Isabella Knightley. Isabella is Harriet's counterpart in diminutiveness, as she is referred to as "little" several times in the novel. As Emma uncovers her portrait of her sister, for example, she praises the likeness: "There is my sister; and really quite her own little elegant figure!" (45). The narrator also describes "Mrs John Knightley" as "a pretty, elegant little woman of gentle, quiet manners, and disposition remarkably amiable and affectionate" (92). Isabella's main characteristic is her maternal concern for her family. She is "wrapt up in her family; a devoted wife, a doating mother" (92). "Little," in Isabella's case, means motherly. To be maternal certainly suggests a progression from being childish, and if others do continue to refer to Harriet as "little," it at least does not fix her in a permanent state of immaturity. Paradoxically, then, the continuous references to "little" Harriet Smith suggest her potential for growth and for the possession of a narrative that occurs after *Emma* ends. Harriet eludes the power of a closing narrative, and by leaving the Hartfield circle, also leaves its narrative authority. There is hope, then, for Harriet Smith after all.

Height in Austen develops from being a source of comedy in "Lesley Castle" to being a means of elaborating on major themes in *Emma*. The perception of comparative height reveals a character's attitude toward his or her own empowered or powerless position, often betraying a subconscious frustration over loss of control. Thus, height demonstrates how a character consolidates and rationalizes, subconsciously or not, complex forces into a seemingly straightforward fact. Conversely, for the reader, height in Austen is hardly factual or simple. The vulnerability of fact to subjective interpretation speaks to the intricate moral, economic, psychological, and even narrative forces working within and upon characters. To understand height is to understand how these forces operate and to see that, in Austen, small details are actually matters of great importance.

AUTHOR'S NOTE
A version of this essay was originally published in *Persuasions: The Jane Austen Journal* 26 (2004): 89–97, and is reprinted by kind permission of the editor.

NOTE

1. All quotations from Jane Austen's published works are taken from *The Oxford Illustrated Jane Austen*, 3rd ed., ed. R.W. Chapman (Oxford: Oxford UP, 1988) and from *Jane Austen's Letters*, 3rd ed., ed. Deirdre Le Faye (Oxford: Oxford UP, 1995), and are documented by short title and page number in the body of the chapter.

WORKS CITED

Armstrong, Isobel. Introduction. *Pride and Prejudice*. By Jane Austen. Ed. James Kinsley. Oxford: Oxford UP, 1998. vii–xxvi.

Doody, Margaret Anne, and Douglas Murray. Notes. *Catharine and Other Writings*. By Jane Austen. Ed. Margaret Anne Doody and Douglas Murray. Oxford: Oxford UP, 1998.

Graham, Jean E. "Austen and 'The Advantage of Height.'" *Persuasions On-line* 20.1 (1999): 11 pars. 15 November 2003 < http://www.jasna.org/pol01/graham.html>.

Hennelly, Mark, Jr. "*Pride and Prejudice*: The Eyes Have It." *Women and Literature* 3 (1983): 187–207.

Leclair, Annette. "Owning Her Work: Austen, the Artist, and the Audience in *Emma*." *Persuasions* 21 (1999): 115–27.

McMaster, Juliet. "The Watchers of Sanditon." *Persuasions* 19 (1997): 149–59.

Morgan, Susan. *In the Meantime: Character and Perception in Jane Austen's Fiction*. Chicago: U of Chicago P, 1980.

Satz, Martha. "An Epistemological Understanding of *Pride and Prejudice*: Humility and Objectivity." *Women and Literature* 3 (1983): 171–86.

Shields, Carol. *Jane Austen: A Penguin Life*. New York: Penguin, 2001.

Wallace, Tara Ghoshal. *Jane Austen and Narrative Authority*. New York: St. Martin's, 1995.

19 The Novel Reader's Blues

Northanger Abbey *and the Tradition of the Female Quixote*

LAURA CAPPELLO BROMLING

Although I completed my BA in English at the University of Alberta, I didn't actually meet Bruce until the day I defended my master's thesis at the University of Lethbridge, with him in the role of external examiner. From that time onwards, he was an inspiring mentor to me: warm, enthusiastic, and strikingly generous with his time and insight. The following essay is based on material from my thesis—which I also adapted, at Bruce's suggestion, into a presentation for a meeting of the Jane Austen Society of North America several years ago.

IN A FAMOUS PASSAGE near the beginning of *Northanger Abbey*, the narrator laments the unjust treatment of novels and novel readers. Her tirade against society's apparent "general wish of decrying the capacity and undervaluing the labour of the novelist, and of slighting the performances which have only genius, wit, and taste to recommend them" (37) targets, in particular, those novelists who denigrate the very craft they practise. There is, however, something peculiar about the venue Austen has chosen for singing these particular blues—for *Northanger*

Abbey itself belongs to a tradition of stories whose chief purpose is to disparage novel reading: the female quixote narrative.

Female quixote novels are characterized by plots that hinge on credulous readers' absurd and literal confusion of fact with fantasy, and the eighteenth and early nineteenth centuries saw an explosion of such stories. Beginning in 1752 with Charlotte Lennox's *The Female Quixote* and concluding with Sarah Green's *Scotch Novel Reading* in 1824, these books focussed on the miseducation of the central character, almost always a young lady, through her reading of romances or sentimental novels. In general, the female quixote novels had two basic purposes: to educate women about the moral and intellectual dangers of reading and to mock the conventions of romantic fiction. While every quixote novel demonstrates both of these purposes to some degree, most of them tend heavily toward one or the other.

These novels are often uninventive in selecting delusions to inflict on their respective heroines, and the same types of incidents and misapprehensions are repeated across the genre. Common follies include the heroine's belief that the truth of her birth has been concealed from her; her insistence on upgrading to a more flamboyant variant of her name; her mistaking of a lowborn servant, often Irish, for a nobleman in disguise; and her exploration of some mysterious (or absurdly mundane) edifice in the hopes of uncovering its dark, Gothic, and—to the knowing reader—palpably non-existent secrets. Catherine Morland's elaborate, novel-inspired fantasies about Northanger Abbey and its residents place her squarely among the ranks of such quixotic heroines.

In many quixote novels, entertaining references to the conventions of romantic fiction provide a vehicle for the serious lessons that the authors of these books intend for their readers to take away with them, and for the opinions of moralists and literary critics of the day. Concerns about the strong influence and possible negative effects of reading fiction, along with the conviction that women were particularly susceptible to such effects, were very strong, and these books are addressed to the female quixote presumed to lurk in the heart of every young girl. Their direct concern is not that novel readers routinely fancy themselves to be displaced heiresses with outrageously embellished names, but that their reading may cause them to lose sight of the everyday truths that society endorses.

Novels were one of the most readily accessible sources of information during this period, and many critics assumed that they must therefore exert considerable influence over their readers. In an 1867 article, one anonymous writer suggests that "Novel-reading, like a classical or scientific education, must have some definite effect upon the age that imbues itself in it....The whole imagination of younger men and women is every day immersed in a vapour-bath of either a useless or useful kind, and it is idle to suppose that nothing on earth will come of it, either for good or evil" ("Novel-Reading" 593). The relatively realistic style of the novel, compared to its forerunners in the realm of fiction, was also a major factor in its perception as an influential genre. With psychologically complex characters, detailed descriptions of social interaction, and logical narrative progression, the novel's brand of verbal photography was a departure from earlier versified and epic modes of fiction.

Particularly in the early part of the century, women were thought to be especially vulnerable to foolish notions contained in novels. The education manual *Practical Education*, written in 1798 by Maria Edgeworth and Richard Lovell Edgeworth, warns,

> With respect to sentimental stories, and books of mere entertainment, we must remark, that they should be sparingly used, especially in the education of girls....We know, from common experience, the effects which are produced upon the female mind by immoderate novel-reading. To those who acquire this taste every object becomes disgusting which is not in an attitude for poetic painting; a species of moral picturesque is sought for in every scene of life, and this is not always compatible with sound sense, or with simple reality....The difference between reality and fiction is so great, that those who copy from any thing but nature are continually disposed to make mistakes in their conduct, which appear ludicrous to the impartial spectator. (332–33)

That these comments read like a road map to the generic female quixote novel attests that the cautionary agenda of these novels was a serious one: the absurd behaviour of the fictional quixotic heroines differed only in degree from the beliefs and actions of which real-world readers were thought capable.

Throughout the nineteenth century, perhaps the most commonly observed and criticized feature of novels is their preoccupation with love. Moralists of the day argued that because of this preoccupation, novel-reading gave women unrealistic expectations about love and endangered their virtue by making them susceptible to seduction. Writing in 1810, Anna Laetitia Aiken Barbauld comments, "Love is a passion particularly exaggerated in novels. It forms the chief interest of, by far, the greater part of them. In order to increase this interest, a false idea is given of the importance of the passion. It occupies the serious hours of life; events all hinge upon it; every thing gives way to its influence, and no length of time wears it out. When a young lady, having imbibed these notions, comes into the world, she finds that this formidable passion acts a very subordinate part on the grand theatre of the world....and is often little consulted even in choosing a partner for life" (182–83). Meanwhile, in her 1798 education manual *The Boarding School*, Hannah Webster Foster writes, "Novels are the favourite, and the most dangerous kind of reading, now adopted by the generality of young ladies. I say dangerous, because the influence, which, with very few exceptions, they must have on the passions of youth, bears an unfavourable aspect on their purity and virtue" (280). Hannah More's *Strictures on the Modern System of Female Education* similarly claims that novels "take off wholesome restraints, diminish sober mindedness, impair the general powers of resistance, and at best feed habits of improper indulgence, and nourish a vain and visionary indolence, which lays the mind open to error and the heart to seduction" (216). Given, then, that female quixote novels are the very books that Austen's narrator accuses of "degrading by their contemptuous censure the very performances, to the number of which they are themselves adding" (*Northanger Abbey* [NA] 37),[1] how do we reconcile Austen's pronovel message with the perplexing vehicle she has chosen for it?

The answer lies chiefly in the purpose and style with which Austen has approached her own version of the quixote narrative. Like the didactic novelists, she uses the standard quixote narrative to illustrate the disparity between fiction and reality, but to a different end. Her concerns are far more aesthetic than moral; warnings about the intellectual and moral danger of unwise reading are mostly replaced in *Northanger Abbey* with a good-humoured and constructive critique of the aesthetic conventions of the gothic romance. Thus, her real point is less that readers should avoid patterning their lives after fictions than that fictions should aim to be more true to life. As Linda Hutcheon has noted, parody "marks the interaction of creation and re-creation, of invention and critique" (101), and Austen is clearly endorsing an alternative aesthetic to the one that drives the fiction *she* critiques, however sympathetically.

The key to this more realistic ideal of fiction lies in the characterization of its heroine. Catherine Morland is more believable as a person than virtually any other example of the female quixote figure. While many of her quixotic counterparts comment outrageously on their own slavish adherence to the conventions of gothic fiction, the ironic self-consciousness in *Northanger Abbey* belongs entirely to the narrator, freeing Catherine herself to behave in the relatively natural manner characteristic of Austen's later fiction. In the first volume of the novel, Catherine is pointedly depicted as being essentially practical and unromantic, responding to people and situations as any normal individual might be expected to do. When she leaves her home and family, for example, her departure is conducted, the narrator informs us, "with a degree of moderation and composure, which seem[s] rather consistent with the common feelings of common life, than with the refined susceptibilities, the tender emotions which the first separation of a heroine from her family ought always to excite" (NA 19). Later in the novel, Austen describes a scene in which the hero, Henry Tilney, is "talking with interest to a fashionable and pleasing-looking young woman, who lean[s] on his arm, and whom Catherine immediately guesse[s] to be his sister; thus unthinkingly throwing away a fair opportunity of considering him lost to her for ever, by being married already" (53).

Catherine's behaviour in the second volume, when she visits Northanger Abbey and falls victim to a number of far-fetched gothic fancies, does border on the forehead-slappingly silly; however, she at least has the sense to be aware of and embarrassed by the absurdity of her notions, even as she embraces them in order to satisfy her "craving to be frightened" (200). Her credulousness is more moderate than the typical quixote figure's wholesale abandonment to her delusions. Though she searches a mysterious cabinet for hidden secrets, she does so while telling herself that she "never from the first had the smallest idea of finding any thing in any part of the cabinet" (169), and when the roll of papers that she discovers in the cabinet turns out to be a collection of bills, rather than a mysterious manuscript, she is ashamed of "the absurdity of her recent fancies" (173). Her paranoia may be extreme by real-world standards, but the very fact that we are tempted to judge her by such standards attests to the unusual degree of realism that Austen has introduced to the conventional quixote story. Catherine is an essentially lifelike character, contained in, and controlled by, a self-consciously fabricated text.

From the outset of the novel, Austen uses the voice of the narrator to draw attention to the alliance of a realistic style with pointedly unrealistic fictional conventions. She opens by describing Catherine as overwhelmingly average and consequently ill-suited to the traditional role of heroine, then asserts her own power, as the author of the story, to contrive for her credibly middle-of-the-road heroine an improbably romantic narrative context—a love story. The narrator informs us that there are no suitable love interests in Catherine's neighbourhood, "But when a young lady is to be a heroine, the perverseness of forty surrounding families cannot prevent her. Something must and will happen to throw a hero in her way" (17). This self-conscious narrator surfaces repeatedly throughout the story to disrupt the illusion of an unmediated relation of events, reminding us that the "pen of the contriver" (232) governs all that occurs. She frequently alludes to "the rules of composition" (251) that dictate the progress of her novel, mocking their disregard for the demands of realism even as she adheres to them. In order to achieve an appropriate ending of "perfect felicity" (250), for instance, Austen must provide both of her deserving female characters with conventional, happy marriages. To this end, she contrives to introduce a suitable husband for Eleanor Tilney on the second-to-last page, legitimating his presence in the story by identifying him as the man whose laundry bills Catherine has discovered in the mysterious cabinet—and cheerfully pointing out the dishonesty of her own device.

This juxtaposition of the realistic and parodic modes in *Northanger Abbey* strikes many readers as incongruous. Frank Kearful suggests that "at times the fiction presented seems purely (i.e., structurally) satiric and at other times purely novelistic, with the result that our expectations are made to work at cross-purposes" (514). Catherine's early pragmatism conflicts with her delusional actions in the second volume, and the conventional progression and resolution of the plot are at odds with the narrator's ironic commentary on these very conventions.

In order to understand this contradiction in the text, according to George Levine, we must accept "a separation of plot from the primary concerns of the novel" (71). Though the action of the story is structured around the traditional female quixote storyline, Austen's main purpose in *Northanger Abbey* is neither to condemn romantic fiction as hopelessly absurd, nor to offer her readers solemn warnings against confusing fiction and reality. As Levine writes, "In the bracing sanity of Austen's world, we could hardly expect her to be unaware of the illusoriness of all fictions (or for that matter to think it worth her trouble to write novels to prove it)" (66). Rather, her aim is to provide a humorous illustration of the artifice inherent in all fiction, her own relatively realistic brand included. The novel is offered not in the spirit of didactic revelation, but rather in the same tone of complicity with her readers that underpins all her novels' laughing commentary on the various absurdities of life.

NOTE

1.   All quotations from Jane Austen's published works are taken from *The Oxford Illustrated Jane Austen*, 3rd ed., ed. R.W. Chapman (Oxford: Oxford UP, 1988), and are documented by short title and page number in the body of the chapter.

WORKS CITED

Barbauld, Anna Laetitia Aiken. "On the Origin and Progress of Novel-Writing." 1810. *Women Critics, 1660–1820: An Anthology*. Ed. The Folger Collective on Early Women Critics. Bloomington: Indiana UP, 1995. 175–86.

Edgeworth, Maria, and Richard Lovell Edgeworth. *Practical Education*. 1798. New York: Garland, 1974.

Foster, Hannah Webster. *The Boarding School*. 1798. *Women Critics, 1660–1820: An Anthology*. Ed. The Folger Collective on Early Women Critics. Bloomington: Indiana UP, 1995. 279–83.

Hutcheon, Linda. *A Theory of Parody: The Teachings of Twentieth-Century Art Forms*. London: Methuen, 1985.

Kearful, Frank. "Satire and the Form of the Novel: The Problem of Aesthetic Unity in *Northanger Abbey*." *English Literary History* 32.4 (1965): 511–27.

Levine, George. *The Realistic Imagination: English Fiction from Frankenstein to Lady Chatterly*. Chicago: U of Chicago P, 1981.

More, Hannah. *Strictures on the Modern System of Female Education; With a View of the Principles and Conduct Prevalent Among Women of Rank and Fortune*. London: T. Cadell and W. Davies, 1811.

"Novel-Reading." 1867. *The Victorian Art of Fiction: Essays on the Novel in British Periodicals, 1851–1869*. Ed. John Charles Olmsted. New York: Garland, 1979. 593–96.

20 "Sublime Repose"

The Spiritual Aesthetics of Landscape in Austen

NATASHA DUQUETTE

Conversations with Bruce Stovel in 2006, both at the University of Alberta and by email, reaffirmed my conviction that Austen's novels are deeply engaged in dialogue with eighteenth-century texts. Bruce took special delight in sharing the fact that Austen had played the role of Mrs Candour in an amateur production of Richard Brinsley Sheridan's School for Scandal (1777), a statement that confirmed my resolve to include Sheridan's satirical play in a course titled Jane Austen in Context.

THERE IS A PROGRESSION in Jane Austen's fiction from a satirical deployment of the eighteenth-century sublime in *Sense and Sensibility* (1811), through a flirtation with the picturesque in *Pride and Prejudice* (1813), to the articulation of a more ethically engaged, contemplative sublime in *Mansfield Park* (1814). In *Sense and Sensibility* and *Pride and Prejudice*, Austen successively applies the concepts "sublime" and "picturesque" not only to visual landscapes but also to key characters. In *Sense and Sensibility*, Marianne Dashwood's perception of John Willoughby fits Edmund Burke's sublime, and, in *Pride and Prejudice*, Elizabeth Bennet eventually views Mr Darcy in terms of William Gilpin's picturesque.

In *Mansfield Park* there is a shift: Fanny Price and Edmund Bertram share experiences of contemplative sublimity as they gaze upon natural landscapes together, gaining lasting and substantial connections to nature, God, and community.

In her early novel *Sense and Sensibility*, Austen exposes the dangers of a naïve engagement with the extremes of the eighteenth-century sublime through the character of Marianne Dashwood. Edmund Burke's *Philosophical Enquiry into the Origin of Our Ideas of the Sublime and the Beautiful* (1757) uses a series of binary divisions to define the terrifying and humbling sublime against its foil, the comforting and pleasurable beautiful. These severe binary divisions, with their gendered implications, prompted women writers, including Austen, to question the exclusivity of Burke's categories. The early nineteenth-century aesthetic theorist Mary Anne Schimmelpenninck, for example, envisioned a flexible, "contemplative sublime," which she placed between the "terrible" sublime and the "sentimental" beautiful.[1]

In the years immediately preceding Schimmelpenninck's observation of what she termed Mr Burke's "mistake," Austen was already satirizing the extremes of Burkean horror in *Sense and Sensibility*. Her character John Willoughby enters the narrative twice amidst the stormy landscapes defined by Burke as sublime. Burke emphasizes how the sound of thunder "awakes a great and aweful sensation in the mind" (82), and continues, "In everything sudden and unexpected, we are apt to start; that is, we have a perception of danger" (83). The physical setting of Marianne's first encounter with Willoughby meets Burke's requirements for sublimity. Austen's narrator notes how "suddenly the clouds united" over Marianne and her younger sister Margaret before "a driving rain set full in their face" (*Sense and Sensibility* [*ss*] 41).[2] Adding to the danger of the scene, Willoughby appears as "a gentleman carrying a gun" (42), who turns from hunter to knight in shining armour when he carries Marianne home through the rain. When he arrives in the Dashwood home, Marianne's sister Elinor and mother Mrs Dashwood respond to Willoughby with the "amazement," "wonder," and "admiration" (42) usually triggered by the sublime. Austen's narrator laughs, with gentle Horatian satire, at the impressionability of the Dashwood women. Lorrie Clark notes, "Austen corrects the potentially tragic, idealist excesses of the romantic sublime in the name of the higher ideal of philosophic comedy" (32).

Willoughby's second appearance out of a storm occurs after he has rejected Marianne and she has become severely ill. As she is recuperating at Cleveland, the narrator tells us, "The night was cold and stormy. The wind roared round the house, and the rain beat against the windows" (ss 316). When Willoughby emerges out of this storm, Elinor looks at him with "horror" (317). He has not come to frighten Elinor, however, but to ask for her forgiveness. Contemporary critic Anne Richards notes that within this episode Willoughby "utters the word God four times; the devil, twice; soul, three times; heart six times; guilty, twice; blessed twice; and also diabolical, saint, heaven, faith, temptation, and atonement" (145). Richards then reads Marianne's recovery as a story of Christian rebirth. However, it is Elinor, not Marianne, whom Austen represents as listening to Willoughby's speech full of Christian diction, and it is Elinor who experiences a transformation from judgemental legalism to merciful grace. In one of Austen's printed prayers, Austen asks "Almighty God" to cultivate in us "a benevolent spirit toward every fellow-creature" (*Minor Works* [MW] 454–55). Elinor's interaction with Willoughby generates such a transformation within her.

Austen's final allusion to the eighteenth-century sublime in *Sense and Sensibility* occurs in her description of Edward Ferrars's deliverance from his previous engagement to Lucy Steele, which frees him to marry Elinor. Upon his discovery that Lucy has secretly married his brother Robert, Edward is "half stupified between the wonder, the horror, and the joy of such a deliverance" (ss 365). Within *Sense and Sensibility*'s ultimately comic conclusion, Austen applies the language of sublimity to a seemingly divine intervention into the social circumstances of her characters' lives.

In *Pride and Prejudice*, Austen moves from satirizing the sublime as defined by Edmund Burke to flirting with the picturesque as defined by the Rev. William Gilpin. Henry Austen notes of his sister Jane that "She was a warm and judicious admirer of landscape, both in nature and on canvas. At a very early age she was enamoured of Gilpin on the

FIGURE 20.1: Crossing the Brook, *by J.M.W. Turner. 1815. Tate Gallery, London.*

Picturesque" (7). According to Gilpin, the picturesque is found in a landscape's variety, as opposed to the stark unity of the sublime. For Burke, the vast expanse of the ocean is terrifyingly sublime. For Gilpin, the ocean surface broken by dancing foam and sailing boats would be dynamically picturesque. Gilpin was quite specific in his formula for the picturesque, arguing that three cows in a landscape create a picturesque effect that is destroyed by the addition of a fourth. Austen lightly satirizes this specificity when Elizabeth Bennet refuses to join Mr Darcy and the Bingley sisters on a stroll, remarking, "The picturesque would be spoilt by admitting a fourth" (*Pride and Prejudice* [PP] 53). Whereas the Burkean sublime is wild and untamable, the Gilpean picturesque is more social and reveals evidence of the domestic. J.M.W. Turner's *Crossing the Brook*—painted between 1811 and 1813—provides a version of the picturesque contemporary with Austen (see FIGURE 20.1). The natural landscape is framed and contained by two signs of civilization: the women and their dog in the foreground and the bridge in the background.

In *Pride and Prejudice*, Austen applies Elizabeth's taste for the picturesque to both Darcy and to his estate of Pemberley. Gilpin argues, "The picturesque traveller is seldom disappointed with pure nature, however rude" (56). Mrs Bennet likewise remarks on "the shocking rudeness of Mr Darcy" (PP 13). The picturesque is rough around the edges. Gilpin observes, "Turn the lawn into a piece of broken ground: plant rugged oaks instead of flowering shrubs: break the edges of the walk: give it the rudeness of a road...in a word, instead of making the whole smooth, make it rough; and you make it picturesque" (8). Darcy is also rough around the edges. He often injures others with his blunt honesty, as in his first proposal to Elizabeth. Juliet McMaster observes, "Darcy tells the truth...but there is moderation in all things; and on the occasion of his first proposal Darcy serves up all together too strong a dose of truth" (91). Darcy speaks with passion in this proposal; however, his declaration is contained, or framed, within the walls of Mr Collins's vicarage. This framing creates the balance of the picturesque.

Indeed, it is not Elizabeth's hurried attraction to the sublime, but her reflective musing on the picturesque that leads to her acceptance of Darcy. Darcy's estate also meets many of Gilpin's criteria for the picturesque. As Elizabeth and her aunt and uncle drive toward Pemberley, the narrator observes,

> The park was very large, and contained great variety of ground.... They gradually ascended for half a mile, and then found themselves at the top of a considerable eminence, where the wood ceased, and the eye was instantly caught by Pemberley House,

situated on the opposite side of the valley, into which the road
with some abruptness wound. It was a large, handsome, stone
building, standing well on rising ground, and backed by a ridge
of high woody hills. (PP 245).

Just as Darcy caught Elizabeth's eye at the beginning of the novel with
"his fine, tall person, handsome features, noble mien" (5), despite his
shocking rudeness, so the large, handsome house at Pemberley catches
her eye despite the abruptness of the estate's angular road. Critic
Barbara Britton Wenner notes, "not only is Jane Austen describing the
landscape, she is describing Darcy himself, and Elizabeth recognizes
him for what he is immediately by analogy" (57). After Darcy's second,
accepted proposal, Elizabeth's spirits soon rise "to playfulness again"
(PP 380) as she embraces the enlivening picturesque.

Near the end of Austen's third published novel, *Mansfield Park*,
the heroine Fanny Price has a response to a landscape comparable to
Elizabeth's response to Pemberley, but Fanny's perceptions lean more
toward what Mary Anne Schimmelpenninck would term the "contemplative sublime" than to Gilpin's picturesque. At this point in the
narrative, Fanny has been staying with her family in their crowded
home at Portsmouth and has been missing the countryside around
Mansfield Park. As Fanny rides back to Mansfield with Edmund, the
narrator notes that "when they entered the Park, her perceptions and
her pleasures were of the keenest sort. It was three months, full three
months, since her quitting it; and the change was from winter to
summer. Her eye fell every where on lawns and plantations of the
freshest green" (*Mansfield Park* [MP] 446). Fanny's delight in the landscape is both sensory and spiritual. Britton Wenner writes tentatively,
"Fanny loves the place and feels an almost spiritual connection to it"
(66–67). I would argue that Fanny undoubtedly has a spiritual connection to the landscape of Mansfield Park, a spiritual delight initially
cultivated through her connection to Edmund.

From the novel's beginning, Edmund encourages Fanny to develop
a contemplative life of her own that involves prayer, reading, and
walking in nature. When ten-year-old Fanny first arrives at Mansfield

Park and misses her family terribly, Edmund comforts her, saying, "let us walk out in the park, and you shall tell me all about your brothers and sisters" (MP 15). Edmund teaches Fanny to seek spiritual pleasure and commemorative consolation within green spaces. Austen, through Fanny, emphasizes the natural landscape's function as a source of peace. As Fanny rides in a carriage from Sotherton back to Mansfield Park, the narrator gives us a glimpse into her consciousness, writing, "It was a beautiful evening, mild and still" (106). Here, Austen echoes William Wordsworth's 1802 sonnet "It is a beauteous evening, calm and free," but Fanny prefers comforting stillness to exhilarating freedom. Fanny's preference for what the narrator terms "the serenity of nature" closely parallels what Anne Radcliffe labels "sublime repose" (qtd. in Talfourd lxxxii). Despite her early parody of Radcliffe's style in her mock-gothic novel *Northanger Abbey*, Austen appears to later follow Radcliffe to a degree in *Mansfield Park* in her depictions of the contemplative sublimity shared by Fanny and Edmund.

Austen echoes Radcliffe's idea of "sublime repose" in a small sermon on the "sublimity of nature" voiced by Fanny as she and Edmund gaze on the grounds of Mansfield Park,

> where all that was solemn and soothing, and lovely, appeared in the brilliancy of an unclouded night, and the contrast of the deep shade of the woods. Fanny spoke her feelings. "Here's harmony!" said she, "Here's repose! Here's what may leave all painting and all music behind, and what poetry only can attempt to describe. Here's what may tranquillize every care, and lift the heart to rapture! When I look out on such a night as this, I feel as if there could be neither wickedness nor sorrow in the world; and there certainly would be less of both if the sublimity of Nature were more attended to, and people were more carried out of themselves by contemplating such a scene."
> (MP 113)

The "deep shade" of the woods and the reference to "rapture" are in accord with earlier, eighteenth-century definitions of the sublime, but

Fanny's use of terms like "repose" and "contemplating" is more akin to Radcliffe's idea of "sublime repose" and Schimmelpenninck's category of the "contemplative sublime." With its exclamation marks and poetic diction, this is a remarkably long and bold utterance from Fanny, one of Austen's most silent heroines. Within it, Fanny agrees with Burke's idea that poetry is the best vehicle for the sublime, an idea bolstered by her reading of evangelical poet William Cowper. She asserts that experiences of sublimity discovered in poetry and nature have the potential to "lift the heart" and thus draw human beings away from wickedness. For the habitually silent Fanny, this is a bold theological statement with social implications.

Fanny's contemplation of nature strengthens her moral convictions, which she voices with increasing frequency as the novel progresses. Bruce Stovel notes, "Fanny emerges as the strongest and most heroic of Austen's heroines" (par. 23). Three instances are of particular note: Fanny's vocal admiration of "a whole family assembling regularly for the purpose of prayer" (MP 86), her objection to the staging of a play within her uncle's house, and her later questioning of her uncle regarding his potential involvement in the practices of slavery. These convictions set Fanny apart, and as a result she often retreats into contemplation, finding companionship in the plants and books of her east room. Notably, Fanny also writes in the east room, prompting critic Sarah Emsley to observe, "She is thoughtful, contemplative, and actively engaged in thinking....She is temperate, she engages in serious philosophical contemplation, and she may be Jane Austen's strongest heroine" (108). Emsley is on the right track, but she works with a purely intellectual definition of contemplation as the "life of the mind," and thus neglects Fanny's life of the spirit. For Fanny, contemplation may occur in family chapels and in natural landscapes as well as in a study. It is this spiritual contemplation that gives Fanny her moral strength.

Though Austen explores the dangerous delights of the Burkean sublime in *Sense and Sensibility* and the enlivening pleasures of the Gilpean picturesque in *Pride and Prejudice*, she moves on to a more contemplative and ethically engaged aesthetic in *Mansfield Park*. Fanny's hope that an increased attention to God's immanence in the wonders of nature will lead to a decrease in wickedness and suffering still speaks to us today. Yes, we may catch solitary glimpses of transcendent sublimity, but Austen pushes us to ask ourselves: how then shall we live, as social creatures, in this world?

AUTHOR'S NOTE

I would like to dedicate this essay to the memory of two individuals: Bruce Stovel, who strongly encouraged me while I was crafting my course Jane Austen in Context, and my father, Michael Aleksiuk, a zoologist and writer who shared his reverence for nature with me.

NOTES

1. For a more detailed comparison of Schimmelpenninck's *Theory on the Classification of Beauty and Deformity* (1815) to Burke's *Philosophical Enquiry*, see my article "'Dauntless Faith': Sublimity and Social Action in Mary Anne Schimmelpenninck's Aesthetics" in *Christianity and Literature* (Summer 2006).

2. All quotations from Jane Austen's published works are taken from *The Oxford Illustrated Jane Austen*, 3rd ed., ed. R.W. Chapman (Oxford: Oxford UP, 1988), and are documented by short title and page number in the body of the chapter.

WORKS CITED

Austen, Henry. "Biographical Notice of the Author." *Northanger Abbey and Persuasion*. 3rd ed., ed. R.W. Chapman. Oxford: Oxford UP, 1988. 3–9. Vol. 5 of *The Oxford Illustrated Jane Austen*. 6 vols.

Burke, Edmund. *A Philosophical Enquiry into the Origin of Our Ideas of the Sublime and the Beautiful*. 1757. Ed. J. T. Boulton. London: Routledge, 1958.

Clark, Lorrie. "Transfiguring the Romantic Sublime in *Persuasion*." *Jane Austen's Business: Her World and her Profession*. Ed. Juliet McMaster and Bruce Stovel. New York: St. Martin's, 1996.

Emsley, Sarah. *Jane Austen's Philosophy of the Virtues*. New York: Palgrave Macmillan, 2005.

Gilpin, William. *Three Essays: on Picturesque Beauty; on Picturesque Travel, and on Sketching the Landscape: To Which is Added a Poem on Landscape Painting*. 2nd ed. London: Blamire, 1794.

McMaster, Juliet. "Mrs. Elton and Other Verbal Aggressors." *The Talk in Jane Austen*. Ed. Bruce Stovel and Lynn Weinlos Gregg. Edmonton: U of Alberta P, 2002. 73–90.

Richards, Anne. "The Passion of Marianne Dashwood: Christian Rhetoric in *Sense and Sensibility*." *Persuasions* 25 (2003): 141–54.

Schimmelpenninck, Mary Anne. *Theory on the Classification of Beauty and Deformity*. London: John and Arthur Arch, 1815.

Stovel, Bruce. "Once More with Feeling: The Structure of *Mansfield Park*." *Persuasions On-Line*. 30 May 2007 <http://www.jasna.org/persuasions/on-line/vol27no1/stovel.htm>.

Talfourd, Thomas. "Memoir of the Life and Writings of Mrs. Radcliffe." *Gaston de Blondeville or, The Court of Henry III, Keeping Festival in Ardenne : A romance; St. Alban's Abbey: A metrical tale, with some poetical pieces, to which is prefixed a memoir of the author with extracts from her journals*. London: H. Colburn, 1826. i–cxxxii.

Turner, Joseph Mallord William. *Crossing the Brook*. 1815. Tate Britain, London. *Tate Online*. 14 February 2008 <http://www.tate.org.uk/servlet/ViewWork?cgroupid= 999999996&workid=14757>.

Wenner, Barbara Britton. *Prospect and Refuge in the Landscape of Jane Austen*. Burlington: Ashgate, 2006.

Wordsworth, William. "It is a beauteous evening, calm and free." *Poems in Two Volumes*. London: Longman, 1807.

21 Secrets, Silence, and Surprise in *Pride and Prejudice*

BRUCE STOVEL

AS LITERARY CONCEPTS, secrecy, silence, and surprise are closely connected: they form a single entity at the very heart of the notion of a plot. A secret consists of information generally unknown, yet understood by a select few—etymologically, something sifted out and set apart. A storyteller's plot is built around a secret, but the storyteller, while continuing to narrate the tale, preserves silence on this secret until the time for divulging it with greatest effect—the time for surprise—has come. Once all the secrets have been divulged, we can no longer be surprised, and the plot is over: the author relapses into literal silence. These ideas underlie the witty title that Henry Fielding gives to book 1 of *Tom Jones*: "Containing as much of the Birth of the Foundling as is necessary or proper to acquaint the Reader with in the Beginning of this History." On the one hand, the author must not give away the nub of the matter: a game of hide-and-seek is no fun if we know the secret hiding places right away. On the other hand, the reader must know a certain amount in order to begin playing the game at all. Narration thus proceeds by indirection—but also moves in a definite, foreknown direction. These ideas are implicit in Aristotle's notion that the best plots are those that build to a simultaneous reversal and recognition (chap. 11).

This set of ideas plays an important part in *Pride and Prejudice*, as we can see in the little comic playlet that is enacted in the opening paragraphs of the novel. Mrs Bennet pesters her husband to visit their new neighbour, Mr Bingley, so that Bingley will be able to marry one of their five daughters; during successive days of badgering, Mr Bennet replies with such masterful indirection that Mrs Bennet finally cries, "I am sick of Mr Bingley," and now the time has come for Mr Bennet, the concealed author of this little drama, to break his silence and reveal his secret: "'I am sorry to hear *that*; but why did not you tell me so before? If I had known as much this morning, I certainly would not have called on him.'...the astonishment of the ladies was just what he wished" (*Pride and Prejudice* [PP] 7).[1]

If Mr Bennet contrives this little comedy, which might be called "The Visit," for his own rather cruel amusement—for an audience of one— Jane Austen has constructed the whole novel on much the same principle, though for a much larger audience and for a much more humane purpose. Secrets, silence, and surprise are of the utmost importance in *Pride and Prejudice*. An attempt to define her handling of them in the novel throws some light on its plot, a construction that George Henry Lewes insisted was more artful, subtle, and economical than the much-praised plot of *Tom Jones* ("Novels" 152; "Word" 175). This approach further emphasizes what many readers and critics have noted: that despite the novel's disposition into three volumes, its plot falls into two halves, separated by the novel's central episode—Darcy's proposal, his letter the next morning, and Elizabeth's ensuing reflections. Before this Aristotelian reversal and recognition, Darcy and Elizabeth are separated by secrets; after this point, secrets unite them. Similarly, the teasing dialogues between Darcy and Elizabeth in the first half of the novel, a form of pseudo-silence similar to Mr Bennet's ironic rejoinders in that speech has served to disguise meaning, are replaced during the second half of the novel, for the most part, by genuine silence: Darcy and Elizabeth are separated, and each now has the material, the opportunity, and the motive for introspection and moral change. Furthermore, the surprises that astonish Elizabeth in the first half of the novel are pseudo-surprises for the reader: beginning with Wickham's non-appearance at the Bingleys' ball and climaxing in Darcy's proposal, each of these developments has been clearly signalled in advance to us. Beginning with Darcy's letter, however, which *is* a major surprise to us as well as to Elizabeth, the last half of the novel contains a series of marvellous comic surprises: events that we could never have anticipated, which suddenly transform pain into pleasure, and which cause the sober truth that Elizabeth has vowed to respect to astonish her.

If we examine the novel's plot, five secrets keep Darcy and Elizabeth apart during the first half of the novel: each secret is known by one of the central pair, but not by the other. Darcy does not know that Jane Bennet, despite her placid demeanour, loves his friend Bingley. Elizabeth is ignorant of four crucial pieces of information: that Darcy had kept from Bingley the knowledge that Jane was in town; that Wickham is a detestable hypocrite; that Darcy is, against his will, increasingly in love with her; and that she herself is, against her will, increasingly in love with Darcy.[2] Elizabeth does know what Darcy does not: that Jane loves Bingley. Darcy clearly knows three of the four things that are hidden from Elizabeth—that he has kept Bingley ignorant of Jane's presence in London, that Wickham is far from being a victim of the Darcy family, and that he himself is in love with Elizabeth (if against his will, his reason, and his character [190])—and he, ironically, is fully convinced of the fourth, of Elizabeth's love for him. He can see in her behaviour to him what she cannot: "I believed you to be wishing, expecting my addresses," he tells her at the novel's end (PP 369).

The proposal scene and its result, Darcy's letter, are thus pivotal. The proposal, itself a secret between them, reveals three of the five secrets: Jane's love for Bingley, Darcy's separation of Bingley from Jane, and Darcy's love for Elizabeth. Darcy's ensuing letter, also a secret between Elizabeth and Darcy, throws further light on all three of the secrets just revealed to Elizabeth. It is especially eloquent on the third secret, Darcy's love, for, despite its haughty opening and its cool tone, it is really a love letter—in its appeal to Elizabeth to share with him in reaching a mutual understanding of their situation, in its painful efforts to be honest and precise, in its trust in her intelligence and ability to keep his confidence. Furthermore, the letter reveals a fourth secret, Wickham's past. By the time Elizabeth has read and absorbed the letter, only one of the five original secrets is unknown to her: her own love for Darcy. That love will slowly become apparent to her as she moves in a series of steps accelerated by her encounter with a transformed Darcy at Pemberley, from credence to respect to approval to esteem to gratitude to affection and, finally, the realization that "he was exactly the man who, in disposition and talents, would most suit her" (312).

From the proposal and letter onwards, then, Darcy and Elizabeth are united by their secret knowledge. This is even more evident when a new secret emerges in the second half of the novel: Wickham and Lydia have eloped and disappeared! The elopement has often been treated with disdain by critics; Tony Tanner, for instance, considers that it presents us with "externalities...mere melodrama" (120). The elopement in itself may have been melodramatic, but Jane Austen carefully limits her presentation of it to its effects upon the other characters, which are not. Elizabeth, moved by impulses that she cannot explain and later regrets, spontaneously tells Darcy about the elopement right after reading Jane's letters announcing it. By entrusting him with this secret, she reciprocates the trust in her revealed by his disclosure to her of Wickham's intended elopement with his sister; perhaps even more important, she conveys to him the message that her love for him has been strengthened, not destroyed, by the battering each gave the other at Hunsford. Mutual confidences and mutual confidence have grown up together. As well, her disclosure allows Darcy to demonstrate exactly the same strengthened love for her: he secretly rescues Lydia and the Bennet family by arranging (and paying for) a marriage that almost guarantees that he will not only be allied to the Bennets, but also have Wickham as a brother-in-law, if he proposes again to Elizabeth and she accepts him. Darcy's secret rescue of the Bennet family has further significance in the plot, since it is only when Elizabeth takes the initiative and thanks him for it that he finds himself able to ask for her hand again. Before that, however, Elizabeth guarantees Darcy's return to

Longbourn by her refusal to divulge a secret—a refusal that, if unsatisfying to Lady Catherine, itself discloses Elizabeth's secret to Darcy.

Two additional points might be made. The first is that the secrets that separate Elizabeth and Darcy in the first half of the novel are really pseudo-secrets: the characters may be ignorant, but we easily see the true state of affairs. Unlike the question of Tom Jones's parentage, which is a secret the author carefully conceals from all but the preternaturally acute reader, Jane Austen has put us in a position to be in on these pseudo-secrets. We know, of course, of Jane's love for Bingley, since Jane confides in Elizabeth and Elizabeth is the point-of-view character. We also know, though less explicitly, that Elizabeth is remarkably obtuse on each of the four remaining questions. She refuses to believe that Bingley has left Longbourn for good because she is convinced that he loves Jane and that "a young man so totally independent of every one" (PP 120) will do just what he wants. She is correct on the first count, Bingley's love for Jane, but wildly mistaken on the second, Bingley's independence: to adapt the words of Colonel Fitzwilliam to Elizabeth just minutes before Darcy's proposal at Hunsford, Elizabeth has lessened the honour of Darcy's triumph very sadly (186). Similarly, Elizabeth can see clearly after reading Darcy's letter just how self-contradictory Wickham's posture of offended virtue has been. As for Darcy's growing love for Elizabeth, Jane Austen leaves Elizabeth's viewpoint several times during volume 1 to give us direct glimpses of both his love and his struggle against it, and during her stay at Hunsford in volume 2, though we remain within Elizabeth's perspective, we can see increasingly clear signs that the struggle is going to be in vain. In fact, Darcy's growing love for her is further evidence to us of the fourth secret, that she is falling in love with him, though without realizing it; E.M. Halliday makes the interesting point that Darcy's secret love for Elizabeth, whom we like immensely, makes him worthy of her love, at least in our eyes (81).

A second important point about these secrets, or more accurately pseudo-secrets, is that Darcy and Elizabeth cannot penetrate them because of their pride and prejudice. Darcy cannot see Jane's love for

Bingley because he is determined not to: he confesses in his letter to the belief that the Bennet family, except for Jane and Elizabeth, have so little propriety that the match would be "a most unhappy connection" (PP 198). He does not admit, in the letter or afterwards, what Caroline Bingley has suggested in her letter to Jane: that Darcy is prejudiced in his assessment of Jane by his desire to arrange a marriage between Bingley and his sister. Similarly, Elizabeth does not want to admit to Darcy's power over Bingley, to Darcy's moral superiority to Wickham, to Darcy's evident admiration for her, and to her own feelings toward him, all for the same reason: to do so would be to lose her independence and her conviction of her own superiority. There is room for growth and change on each side. The final words regarding Bingley and Jane in Darcy's letter contain an unintended precision: "though the motives which governed me may to you very naturally appear insufficient, I have not yet learnt to condemn them" (199). Not yet, perhaps, but he will eventually. It takes more than five months, but, as Darcy explains to Elizabeth, "On the evening before my going to London,...I made a confession to [Bingley], which I believe I ought to have made long ago" (370–71). In the same way, Elizabeth's understanding of her errors and their cause undergoes a long, slow change, culminating, perhaps, in her reaction to the news from Mrs Gardiner that Darcy has secretly arranged the Lydia-Wickham match: "For herself she was humbled; but she was proud of him" (327). Elizabeth, like Darcy, has learned to condemn her earlier certainties.

What I have said about secrets in the novel also applies to the related notion of silence. The relationship between Elizabeth and Darcy during the first half of the novel consists largely of pseudo-silence: Elizabeth may believe that Darcy is a man of silence and twit him repeatedly for being so, but actually their relationship during this section of the novel is a talkative one. All of this is nicely symbolized when Elizabeth finds herself dancing with Darcy at Netherfield: "She began to imagine that their silence was to last through the two dances, and at first was resolved not to break it; till suddenly fancying that it would be the greater punishment to her partner to oblige him to talk, she made some slight observation on the dance" (91). Of course, the key word is "fancying":

Elizabeth grasps neither Darcy's devotion to her nor why she is so determined to punish him. In short, their talk during the first section of the novel is the equivalent of Mr Bennet's evasiveness on the subject of visiting Bingley: it is a confusing disguise, but moves indirectly in a desired direction. The proposal scene and the letter put Elizabeth and Darcy into direct communication, and, as we have seen, this central episode is followed, at least for the most part, by a long period of genuine silence, introspection, and change on the part of each. It is worth pointing out that Elizabeth has had no interest in introspection in the first half of the novel: her attention has been focussed on her attempts to account for the mysterious events that are happening around her. However, we readers are much less uncertain about events than Elizabeth, since what is secret to her is only apparently secret to us, and as a result our attention is drawn to what Elizabeth is determined to ignore: her own motives for her judgements and attitudes. The final sentence in Elizabeth's apostrophe to herself after reading Darcy's letter—the bottom line, as it were—is, "Till this moment, I never knew myself" (208).

To put this another way, Elizabeth begins the novel as someone determined to talk, because she knows exactly what to think. Darcy's proposal, his letter, and their ensuing separation force her to choose to be silent, even to Jane, on some matters, and to understand the value of silence. Her first act in the plot is to entertain everyone with the story of what she has overheard Darcy say to Bingley about her; her decisive act at the end of the novel, when Lady Catherine sweeps up in her chaise and four, shows how much she has learned. Elizabeth has become more like Darcy during the course of their relationship, just as he has gained some of her liveliness and poise.

Secrets and silence lead to surprise. It seems to me that there are five major surprises within the first half of the novel, culminating in Darcy's proposal to Elizabeth, but that these surprises are actually pseudo-surprises—events that catch Elizabeth, but not the novel's readers, unprepared. These surprises are all disturbing shocks to Elizabeth, brought on by her delusions. In the second half of the novel, however, beginning with Darcy's letter and culminating in Lady Catherine's descent upon Longbourn, there are another five surprises, but of a very different kind: each is pleasant, and each is a genuinely astonishing turn of events that no one, neither Elizabeth nor we readers of the novel, could ever have predicted.

Elizabeth's first major unpleasant surprise occurs when Wickham does not attend the Bingleys' ball: "a doubt of his being present had never occurred to her" (89). An even more painful shock occurs when Charlotte Lucas tells Elizabeth that she has agreed to marry Mr Collins:

> that Charlotte could encourage him, seemed almost as far from possibility as that she could encourage him herself, and her astonishment was consequently so great as to overcome at first the bounds of decorum, and she could not help crying out, "Engaged to Mr Collins! my dear Charlotte,—impossible!" (124)

Elizabeth's third surprise comes at about the same time. Bingley has indeed left Netherfield for good, though Elizabeth had been so certain it could not happen: "The idea of his returning no more Elizabeth treated with the utmost contempt" (120). Her fourth unpleasant surprise follows quickly and consists of another defection: Wickham leaves off his attention to Elizabeth and begins determinedly making himself agreeable to a Miss King, whose most remarkable charm is the sudden acquisition of £10,000 (149). Elizabeth is ostensibly cool and unaffected at the loss of her admirer, but her professions of cynical acceptance are so bitter that Mrs Gardiner remarks, "Take care, Lizzy; that speech savours strongly of disappointment" (154). Her fifth and greatest surprise comes when Darcy abruptly enters the drawing-room at Hunsford, where she is sitting alone, and bursts out with the words, "In vain have I struggled" (189). Darcy's proposal is actually, of course, merely the culminating instance in a series of unsettling overtures by Darcy to Elizabeth during the Netherfield and Hunsford scenes.

My point is that all of these surprises are ironic ones: surprises to Elizabeth, but pseudo-surprises to us. For instance, Wickham's tale to Elizabeth is preposterous: he intersperses his maligning of Darcy with claims such as, "Till I can forget his father, I can never defy or expose *him*" (80). Similarly, we have seen Charlotte consistently profess and act upon a credo of cynical opportunism, though Elizabeth has been blind and deaf where Charlotte is concerned. Finally, Darcy's proposal has been looming more and more inevitably: an increasingly obvious flurry of hints while Elizabeth is at Hunsford shows us that his is a kettle about to reach the boiling point. In short, the greatest surprise of all to Elizabeth in the first half of the novel is the event that we most expect.

All of these surprises to Elizabeth are disturbing and even humiliating. They all spring from her prejudices, her determination to think the best of herself and the worst of Darcy, but she chooses to ascribe these surprises to the unsatisfying, undependable nature of reality itself. She tells Jane that Bingley's desertion and Charlotte's marriage are simply "unaccountable" (135).

A great change occurs, however, with Darcy's letter to Elizabeth, the sequel to and even continuation of his proposal. The letter is, in effect, Darcy's proposal, part 2. It is a complete surprise to us as well as to Elizabeth, and such a jolt to the reader's expectations that Mary Lascelles has argued that it shows Jane Austen sacrificing plausibility in order to advance the plot: "The manner is right, but not the matter: so much, and such, information would hardly be volunteered by a proud and reserved man—unless under pressure from his author, anxious to get on with the story" (162).

The letter is the first of five genuinely surprising events in the second half of the novel; each of these surprises (with the partial exception of the central, transitional letter) is pleasant in nature and satisfyingly advances Darcy and Elizabeth's relationship. The second comes when Elizabeth finds herself at Pemberley, finds that the house is gracious, but not ostentatious, and finds, to her special astonishment, that his housekeeper Mrs Reynolds insists that he is a kind master: she has never had a cross word from him in her life, and has known him since he was four years old (PP 218). The crescendo in this series of surprises at Pemberley comes when Darcy himself steps out from behind his house, and the climax is the change in Darcy's manners. The third great surprise is the news of Lydia and Wickham's elopement, though the surprise lies not so much in the elopement itself as in the change it makes in Darcy and Elizabeth's relationship. Five lines after Jane's second letter ends, Elizabeth has run to the door of the room and confronted — Darcy. Then something even more surprising than the elopement happens: Elizabeth finds herself confiding in Darcy. This act is her response to, her reciprocation of, his letter and his reformed behaviour at Pemberley. The fourth great surprise leaps out of a babble of trivia as Lydia describes her wedding day to the assembled Bennets:

> "However, I recollected afterwards, that if he [Mr Gardiner] had been prevented going, the wedding need not be put off, for Mr Darcy might have done as well."
> "Mr Darcy!" repeated Elizabeth, in utter amazement. (319)

Elizabeth now induces her aunt to reveal all Darcy has secretly done to bring about Lydia's marriage, and his actions, of course, have a secret meaning of their own: "Her heart did whisper, that he had done it for her" (326). The fifth and culminating surprise is Lady Catherine's appearance at Pemberley, an appearance that, like all of the other surprising events in this half of the novel, is an extremely happy turn of events: Lady Catherine, who loves to be of use, removes all of Darcy's doubts about Elizabeth's feelings (381). Not only are all of these surprises pleasant, but they are genuine: Elizabeth is no longer self-deceived, and once she begins to see the world as it is, she finds that it far exceeds her expectations. Though, as she tells Wickham, "In essentials...[Mr Darcy] is very much what he ever was" (234), that true identity proves to be far better than she had ever imagined.

AUTHOR'S NOTE

A version of this essay was originally published in *Persuasions: The Jane Austen Journal* 11 (1980): 85–91, and is reprinted by kind permission of the editor.

NOTES

1.   All quotations from Jane Austen's published works are taken from *The Oxford Illustrated Jane Austen*, 3rd ed., ed. R.W. Chapman (Oxford: Oxford UP, 1988), and are documented by short title and page number in the body of the chapter.

2.   The view that Elizabeth unwittingly loves Darcy from the outset is developed by Bruce Stovel in "'A Contrariety of Emotion.'"

WORKS CITED

Aristotle. *Aristotle's Poetics*. Trans. George Whalley. Ed. John Baxter and Patrick Atherton. Montreal: McGill-Queen's UP, 1997.

Halliday, E.M. "Narrative Perspective in *Pride and Prejudice*." *Twentieth-Century Interpretations of* Pride and Prejudice. Ed. E. Rubinstein. Englewood Cliffs, NJ: Prentice Hall, 1969. 77–83.

Lascelles, Mary. *Jane Austen and Her Art*. London: Oxford UP, 1939.

[Lewes, G.H.]. "The Novels of Jane Austen." *Blackwood's Edinburgh Magazine* 86 (July 1859): 99–113. Rpt. as "Lewes: The Great Appraisal" in Southam 148–66.

———. "A Word about *Tom Jones*." *Blackwood's Edinburgh Magazine* 87 (March 1860): 335. Rpt. as "Lewes: A Note on Jane Austen's Artistic Economy" in Southam 175.

Southam, B.C. *Jane Austen: The Critical Heritage*. Vol. 1. London: Routledge and Kegan Paul, 1968.

Stovel, Bruce. "'A Contrariety of Emotion': Jane Austen's Ambivalent Lovers in *Pride and Prejudice*." *International Fiction Review* 14 (1987): 27–33.

Tanner, Tony. *Jane Austen*. Cambridge: Harvard UP, 1986.

22 JA Blues

DOUG BARBOUR

for Bruce Stovel

It's a truth so universal
      that a rich guy needs a wife
a truth universally acknowledged
      that a single man
in possession of a good fortune
must be in want of a wife
so he's got to keep moving
      there's a mother on his trail
      there's a mother wants his life
Let other pens dwell on guilt and misery
      It's the last fair deal goin' down
Let other pens dwell on guilt and misery
      It's the last fair deal goin' down
The death of your daughter would have been a blessing
      rather than she come upon the town
Why the death of your daughter's a blessing
      if she be come upon the town
One half of the world cannot understand
One half of the world cannot understand

the pleasures of the other half
    he's a steady rollin' man
So he gotta keep movin'
    he never read much
    he has something else to do
    he got them old walkin' blues
Three daughters married
Ten thousand a year
Three daughters married
Ten thousand a year
I shall go distracted
in the merriest month of all the year

23 Oh, What a Night

KARI TROGEN

FOR AN AUSTEN DEVOTEE and movie buff like me, Bruce Stovel's Jane Austen in Film class was pure bliss — the dream course I'd been waiting my whole academic life to take.

I think I speak for many of us when I say that on Thursday nights, like Anne Elliot at the end of *Persuasion*, I felt full of *cheerful or forbearing feelings for every creature around* me. That insufferable theorist whose long-winded essay was irking me that morning? I *could pity him*. That annoying loud-mouthed girl in my afternoon lecture? I *had amusement in understanding* her. And with my fellow Austenites, there was *the happy chat of perfect ease*, and *everything of peculiar cordiality and fervent interest* (*Persuasion* 245–46).[1]

It was the poster course for that wonderful liveliness that develops when a group gets talking about literature. Hands shot up in the air as we made our way through the six novels, gleefully savouring the richness of the texts. Sometimes our heated discussions verged on the not-so-deep, such as the "Captain Wentworth is a sexy pirate" theory! Often our talks continued after class, and I mulled them over throughout the week.

Dr Stovel's friendliness, intelligence, and genuine joy in his field were apparent from our very first class. He encouraged us to develop an informal, humorous style of writing in our film reviews as well as a formal one in our essays. He fostered a spirit of collaboration through peer marking and online discussion forums, from which he picked out comments that he particularly liked for us to explore further.

At break, as we bounced through the empty Humanities Building on a tea run, Dr Stovel wrote a list of scenes on the board. Then back we came to fight over who got to act out Mary Bennet's cringeworthy singing—I'm proud to have had that honour!—and who got to do Mr Collins's horrid proposal to Elizabeth. We scattered around the building to rehearse, while Dr Stovel moved from room to room, saying, "Nice accent, Bo!" and "Very Darcy-ish, there, Kari." He was an enthusiastic director who brought out our sense of fun, something I so appreciated as an honours student bogged down with six courses in my final term.

During the film screenings, we revelled in the witty prose, the stunning scenery and costumes of Regency England, the hilarious character actors, and the profound love between the heroes and heroines—or, in the case of some of the lesser adaptations, we fiercely debated the filmmaker's choices. Munching on snacks and scribbling down notes, I felt the energy of a room full of people enjoying a movie together. Dr Stovel was convinced that film should be a communal experience, not merely a solitary activity between an individual and a screen. It was wisdom like this that showed we were being treated to more than just the pleasure of Austen; we were spending time with a gem of a teacher.

Dr Stovel readily shared with us his varied pursuits, telling us about upcoming blues concerts around the city and the radio show he co-hosted with his son. His interests extended beyond Romantic literature and blues music—I remember seeing him at an Alberta Ballet performance of *Alice in Wonderland*, and how warmly he introduced me and another classmate to his son. His passion for art in all its forms was truly infectious, and his love for his family was obvious.

A few months with Dr Stovel taught us, in Mr Bennet fashion, to *make sport for our neighbours, and laugh at them in our turn* (*Pride and Prejudice* 364). The commonplace business of one last semester was made decidedly uncommon, as the experience took us beyond academia and into our wider lives. More than how to critique literature or film, what I will remember from my short time knowing Bruce Stovel is how to live and laugh.

NOTE

1.   All quotations from Jane Austen's published works are taken from *The Oxford Illustrated Jane Austen*, 3rd ed., ed. R.W. Chapman (Oxford: Oxford UP, 1988), and are documented by short title and page number in the body of the chapter.

24 The Bennet Perspective

Narrative Style in Wright's Pride and Prejudice

JESSICA WALLACE

ONE OF THE DIFFICULTIES in adapting novel to film lies in deciding how to compensate for the absent narrator. Jane Austen's *Pride and Prejudice* uses third-person narration to tell the story, although events often unfold from Elizabeth's perspective. In his adaptation, director Joe Wright duplicates Austen's third-person narrative, which Stephen Prince describes as a common filmmaking strategy: "Movies almost always use third-person narration. In most films, the camera assumes a point of view that is detached and separate from the literal viewpoint as seen by each of the characters" (231). However, to remain true to Austen's narrative, Wright must also demonstrate that Elizabeth's point of view connects us to the story. This connection is established with subjective shots, as Prince explains: "There are times when filmmakers wish to suggest a character's literal point of view. To do so, the filmmaker would use a subjective shot or point of view shot in which the camera literally views through the eyes of the character. This kind of shot creates a brief interlude of first-person perspective" (231). During the opening sequence, these subjective shots focus on Elizabeth, indicating to viewers that we will be privy to her personal knowledge and share in her emotional experiences. Though Elizabeth appears on screen more often than not, we can see that the story develops through her point of view. Filmmakers can illustrate first-person perspective implicitly through the actor's performance or camera positioning (231). Wright uses this technique to create subtle connections between the Bennet family members. By providing perspectives from not only Elizabeth, but also other characters, he gives the audience parallel storylines that accentuate the events in Elizabeth's life. During the film's opening scene, Wright sets up the Bennet family dynamic and connects us to important characters through implicit and occasionally explicit first-person perspective.

Wright uses an implicit first-person point of view when introducing us to Elizabeth as she takes pleasure in reading a book. Keira Knightley's performance implies Elizabeth's emotional perspective. The delight she finds in the adventures of the novel's heroine hints at the excitement she will encounter as the story progresses. Wright then switches to a quasi-subjective shot, where we look over Elizabeth's shoulder. This indicates to viewers that, although the movie will use a third-person narrative, the majority of events will be presented through Elizabeth's point of view. The camera continues to follow a thoughtful Elizabeth until she reaches her house and moves off-screen. Wright then consciously breaks away, searching for other characters and hinting at varying narratives. As the camera moves through the Bennet house, third-person perspective foreshadows parallel storylines for the other Bennet sisters. Jane appears first, holding her needlepoint and nearly losing her balance as Lydia and Kitty run past her in a tizzy over the news of Mr Bingley, a bachelor soon to join their community. We see Mary sitting at the piano-forte, providing background music for the scene. This single shot gives us an overview of the Bennet family dynamic: Jane as the sensible oldest sister, Lydia and Kitty as boy crazy, and poor Mary as more of an after-thought. These attributes become more developed as the story moves forward. The camera then takes the audience back to Elizabeth as she pauses to look through a window at her parents. Again Wright uses an over-the-shoulder shot, revealing Elizabeth's perspective while she remains on screen. She smiles to herself while watching her parents, now appearing as an observer within her family.

As the Bennet sisters gather in the hallway to eavesdrop, Wright utilizes an explicit first-person point of view. The camera peers through a crack in the doorway, showing us the perspective of the curious sisters and allowing us to feel their suppressed anticipation. We also witness a connection between Elizabeth and Jane here, as they exchange amused looks over their dramatic younger sisters. Filming returns to the third person as Mr Bennet calmly manages his excited wife and daughters. We follow the family into a sitting room where Wright uses explicit first-person perspective from Mr Bennet's point of view. Mrs Bennet and her daughters stand before him, eagerly waiting to hear about Mr Bingley. We are shown here by the upward camera angle the overwhelming presence of the Bennet women. Mr Bennet's unflustered demeanour demonstrates his strength of character, as he does not succumb to the pressure of marrying his daughters off. The women seem to be positioned in order of prominence within the scene, with Elizabeth closest to the camera until Lydia pushes herself to the forefront. This indicates Lydia's struggle for attention within the family, setting up her disastrous marriage to Wickham. After receiving news of the ball, we find Elizabeth enjoying the excitement of her sisters through an implicit first-person point of view, with help from Knightley's performance. This again positions her as an outsider rather than an active participant in her family, as she finds pleasure in the amusements of others. Elizabeth sets herself apart from her family while remaining loyal to them, thus complicating her upcoming love relationship. Mr Bennet appears behind Elizabeth in the frame, also watching the excitement, though out of focus. This connects Elizabeth and her father for the audience, showing us his quietly supportive role. The camera then backs away from the house in a long shot, creating closure on the first scene. We feel a sense of security for the Bennet family, all tucked away before their adventures begin.

Wright's narrative techniques enable us to connect with the Bennets while understanding their family dynamic. Elizabeth appears at the centre of the plot, and comes across as introspective and concerned for others. We distinguish her from her sisters through implicit first-person narrative, including camera position and Knightley's performance. Subjective shots connect us to members of the Bennet family and allow us to share their perspectives. Although the main plot will revolve around Elizabeth, Wright uses the opening sequence to create impressions of the other Bennet family members that come into play as the story progresses. Elizabeth's perspective is affected by the role she plays within her family, and the roles of her sisters affect the film's outcome.

WORKS CITED

Pride and Prejudice. Dir. Joe Wright. Perf. Keira Knightley, Donald Sutherland, and Matthew Macfadyen. Focus Features, 2005.

Prince, Stephen. *Movies and Meaning: An Introduction to Film*. New York: Pearson Education, 2004.

25 Making Implicit Themes Explicit

Cinematic Intervention in Sense and Sensibility, Persuasion, and Mansfield Park

KERRY TAILLEFER

IN THE DVD COMMENTARY on her 1995 adaptation of Jane Austen's *Mansfield Park*, director Patricia Rozema suggests that the radical nature of the shift from literary to cinematic text precludes the creation of an exact or pure film adaptation of a novel. Indeed, one can argue that the process of adaptation is inherently a process of reinvention, and that each film adaptation is the product of a radical reshaping of the original text. Because each medium is limited by the form and unique expressive vocabulary that define it, distinctively literary techniques must be translated into cinematic ones, and the novel's substance is at once temporally compressed and visually inflated. The centrality of such change to the adaptive process is clearly reflected by the points of similarity that link three scenes from Roger Michell's *Persuasion*, Ang Lee's *Sense and Sensibility*, and Patricia Rozema's *Mansfield Park*. While these films reflect three very different approaches to filming Jane Austen's novels — ranging from British low-key telefilm, to star-studded Hollywood feature, to stylized interpretation — each film relies on cinematic equivalents (and not just the original text) to convey the irony, social observation, and wit that infuse Jane Austen's novels with such richness. In this paper, I will compare the different ways in which Marianne's stormy walk at Cleveland Park in *Sense and Sensibility*, the opening sequence of *Persuasion*, and the epilogue of *Mansfield Park* (three scenes specifically fabricated by, and consistent with the approaches of, the filmmaker) make use of cinematic techniques to approximate the novel's depth by visually expressing its implicit themes.

Cinematography is one of the most fundamental means of infusing the superficial elements of plot with the larger themes and concerns of the original text. Indeed, it is the manipulation of camera position that situates the dramatic, and completely fabricated, scene wherein Marianne walks to the edge of Cleveland Park to see Willoughby's estate within the thematic framework of Austen's *Sense and Sensibility*. The series of close and medium shots that begin the scene establish a sense of foreboding: the camera slowly tracks past a twisted hedge, and the sound of Marianne's footsteps precedes her entrance into the frame. Lee's camera closely follows Marianne as she stares fixedly ahead at something the viewer cannot see, and the wind, as it rustles through the hedge and tears at her clothes, dominates the soundscape. After cutting to an anxiously watchful Elinor, Lee suddenly enlarges the viewer's field of view with an extremely long shot of the edge of the park and the black clouds of the gathering storm, and, by using a short vertical tilt—a camera movement that suggests a connection between images— (Prince 28), he links this shot with the subsequent one of Marianne. The connection between Marianne and the natural world that is suggested by the camera movement builds on a relationship that is introduced earlier in the film. Indeed, during a similar stormy walk at Barton Cottage, wherein Marianne drags a reluctant and rather miserable-looking Margaret through the rain, Lee's use of long shots serves to integrate Marianne into her environment and visualize that romantic perception of nature that has Marianne eagerly chasing blue skies.

Through his use of the long shot, then, Lee conflates Marianne's inner feeling with the natural world, and this relationship reaches its visual climax near the end of her walk at Cleveland. While Marianne's final sighting of Willoughby's estate provides the narrative climax of the scene, it is the aerial shot immediately preceding it that provides the thematic one. By turning her back on Cleveland, Marianne turns her back on Elinor and the sensible moderation of feeling she represents, and this wilful submission to unchecked grief (one that anticipates the subsequent submission of health and hope to illness and despair) is powerfully conveyed by the aerial shot that reduces her to a small white figure in a boundless sea of green; in a final visual expression of the excessive sensibility that shapes Marianne's world view, a sensibility that demands the complete abandonment of self and intellect to imagination and feeling, the camera abandons Marianne to the raw elements of weather and landscape. Exploiting the way in which camera-to-subject distance manipulates viewer's response (Prince 12), Lee's cinematography not only evokes the creed of sensibility that leads Marianne to Willoughby's estate and a "grief...voluntarily renewed" (*Sense and Sensibility* [*ss*] 7),[1] but its inherent danger—a thematic statement central to Austen's novel.

While the fabricated opening sequence of Roger Michell's 1995 film *Persuasion* is comparatively unobtrusive on the level of narrative, it is one that profoundly shapes the viewer's understanding of the proceeding narrative action. Indeed, with a subtlety characteristic of his low-key and more literal adaptive approach, Michell creates a visual equivalent of the novel's thematic framework. While the images of this opening sequence are themselves infused with meaning, as are the images in Marianne's stormy walk, it is the *arrangement* of these images that succeeds in fully expressing the scene's underlying concerns. By intercutting images of a horse-drawn gig and man-powered boat, as they make their way to landed estate and naval ship, respectively, Michell establishes the central thematic tension between the landed gentry and the rising professional class of the navy. Indeed, the clash of lifestyles and of the values that underlie them is implicit in the contrasting images on which the scene is built. The first set of contrasting details in the opening sequence introduces a quick sensual opposition between sea and land. The sounds of the initial underwater shot and rhythmic splashing of oars, and the viewer's underwater and eye-level point of view, give way to the sounds of horses' hooves hitting the pavement and an eye-level blur of carriage wheels in motion. In the next series of shots, however, this contrast of land and sea is extended into that of landowner and sailor. Images of the gig making its easy way past the labourers to Kellynch Hall are intercut with images of rough hands working oars, and the lined and weary faces of the sailors—images that visually evoke Anne's claim that "sailors work hard enough for their comforts" (*Persuasion* [P] 19).

Indeed, while the montage invites the viewer to draw graphic comparisons across cuts, it also suggests intellectual and thematic ideas (Prince 164–68), and thus the visual tension between land and sea also suggests an ideological tension. The criticism of the landed gentry implicit in Anne's claim is a criticism also implicit in Michell's montage. The clamour of men demanding overdue payments herald Sir Walter Elliot's financial troubles and (by extension) the decline of the landed gentry, and the cinematography itself highlights the sterile emptiness of Kellynch Hall and the lifestyle it represents. During Lady Russell's arrival at Kellynch, camera movement is minimal. Situated within the hall's entrance and perfectly centred so as to create a symmetrical *mise-en-scène*, the camera remains static as Lady Russell's carriage appears within the door frame, and then gracefully tracks forward to meet her with the same deliberate calculation as the six waiting servants who file out to attend her. The camera's static impersonal distance, the cool whites and blues of the interior, and the symmetrical harmony of the *mise-en-scène* suggest an emphasis on contrived display over real substance, and this overall visual design—one also used for the shots of the Elliots' new lodgings at Camden Place, with its echoing floors and white-washed interior—visually expresses Anne's, and Austen's, criticism of the shallowness of the gentry's "usual style of give-and-take invitations, and dinners of formality and display" (P 98).

Standing in direct contrast with Lady Russell's arrival at Kellynch is the subsequent shot wherein Admiral Croft meets with his fellow sailors on board ship. Consistent with the previous montage shots of the sailors, the camera is extremely mobile. Circling the room freely, and rather roughly, its field of vision is more egalitarian than that at Kellynch and Bath; privileging no one in particular, not even the central speaker of the scene, the camera roams with an intimate freedom among the sailors as they share a circle around a rectangular table. As in an earlier shot wherein the camera positions itself right in the row-boat amongst the sailors, the camera's mobility and intimacy express the virtues of this rising professional class—one that is based on achievement and camaraderie, rather than birth and inheritance. Indeed, in the same way in which the camera's distant formality during Lady Russell's arrival at Kellynch "correlat[es] as a visual design, with important issues in the narrative," the camera's free movement during the admiral's meeting is "metaphoric and symbolic" (Prince 33). The freedom of the camera suggests the freedom and possibility represented by the sea (and later captured in the dazzling seascapes of Lyme), and the self-determination of those who sail it; the camera's spontaneous intimacy embodies those qualities that Anne so admires in Captain Wentworth and that set the navy apart from the cool formalities of the card parties of Camden Place.

In the same way in which my chosen scenes from *Sense and Sensibility* and *Persuasion* reflect each film's overall adaptive approach, the epilogue from the 1999 film *Mansfield Park* is characteristic of the film's stylized interpretation. In marked contrast to the strict adherence to continuity that characterizes both Ang Lee's mainstream Hollywood movie and Roger Michell's low-key telefilm, *Mansfield Park* often relies on spatial and temporal distortion to convey the novel's underlying themes. Indeed, in the final scene of the epilogue of *Mansfield Park*, director Patricia Rozema deliberately breaks the illusion of temporal continuity so as to visually evoke the novel's concern with art and fiction. Like the preceding snapshots into the lives of Mrs Norris and Maria, and Mary and Henry Crawford, the final scene of the Bertrams assembled on the lawn is characterized by its theatrical quality. Using a long take—a shot of long duration that relies on elaborate composition and character movement rather than editing to maintain the viewer's interest (Prince 168–69)—Rozema constructs a visual experience akin to watching theatre. After following Julia to her chair, the camera remains centred and fixed, leaving the viewer's eye to range freely over the frame, as it does when viewing a stage. Each character takes a position that corresponds with his or her role in the narrative itself: Sir Thomas leans over Tom, who sits near Julia in the foreground, Lady Bertram sits aloofly to one side of the middle ground, and Suzie stands distant, but central, in the background. The frame appears to freeze, as the actors pause in mid-action, and this showy theatricality not only recalls the earlier theatricals at Mansfield Park but also the nature of the novel as a whole; while the novel's theatricals represent a means of transgression—a way for Henry and Maria to pursue an increasingly dangerous intimacy—they also point to art's power of conferring agency. In the same way in which acting allows Henry to change roles fluidly—from lover of Maria to rescuer of poor Fanny Price—writing allows Austen to intervene in, and shape the lives of, her characters for her own purposes.

Indeed, the novel's ending is infused with "an awareness of the fictionality of fiction" (Rozema, DVD commentary), as Austen directly addresses the reader, stating that she is "impatient to restore every body, not greatly in fault themselves, to tolerable comfort, and to have done with all the rest" (*Mansfield Park* [MP] 461). In a visual expression of Austen's metafictional narrative voice, then, Rozema uses Fanny's voice-over narration, the theatrical composition of the scene, and the deliberate pauses heralded by a recurrent musical cue to "break the illusion that the spectator is watching a real, authentic world on screen rather than a movie" (Prince 293).

Rozema further suggests the writer's agency by the way in which Fanny's own character is exempt from the epilogue snapshots. Because Rozema's Fanny is given Austen's pen, writing and then reading (directly to the camera) lines from Austen's earlier fiction, it is she who presents these scenes through voice-over, and in doing so points to their contrived nature by suggesting that "it could have all turned out differently." Rozema's epilogue, then, attempts to visually convey the role of art and fiction, and thus, a film that begins with the act of writing ends (in a "By the way..." closing scene distinct from the epilogue) with the act of publishing.

While Ang Lee's *Sense and Sensibility*, Roger Michell's *Persuasion*, and Patricia Rozema's *Mansfield Park* represent three very different approaches to adaptation, and make use of widely differing cinematic techniques, each film depends on cinematic intervention to approximate the depth of the original text. Each film is linked to its book by a fabricated and uniquely cinematic scene that situates the narrative action within the novel's thematic framework, and it is this intervention that characterizes the adaptive process, emphasizing the fact that the shift from literary to cinematic text is fundamentally one of reinvention.

NOTE

1.   All quotations from Jane Austen's published works are taken from *The Oxford Illustrated Jane Austen*, 3rd ed., ed. R.W. Chapman (Oxford: Oxford UP, 1988), and are documented by short title and page number in the body of the chapter.

WORKS CITED

Mansfield Park. Dir. Patricia Rozema. Miramax, 1999.

Persuasion. Dir. Roger Michell. BBC Films, 1995.

Prince, Stephen. *Movies and Meaning: An Introduction to Film*. 3rd ed. Boston: Pearson, 2004.

Sense and Sensibility. Dir. Ang Lee. Columbia Pictures, 1995.

26 Dancing

A Visual Equivalent of Austen's Language

KELSEY EVERTON

ADAPTING A NOVEL AS A FILM is a great challenge. Novels employ words, which sweep across the page and give the reader often limitless possibilities for imagination. Films, in contrast, use images to create a visual, and therefore allegedly definitive, interpretation. This presents both problems and opportunities. On the one hand, to admirers of a beloved novel, a film adaptation that presents a different visual representation than the one they had envisioned may be judged unfaithful to the original and limiting to their own imagination. On the other hand, film adaptations have the advantage of using visuals to depict intricate situations that are assumed to be background information and prior knowledge in the novel. In all Jane Austen's novels, "[s]cenes set at balls and assemblies are an important structural feature....In such scenes, [Austen] subtly explores the pressures and pains of dancing, and of the matchmaking and social mixing ritualized in its elaborate rules of polite behavior" (Jones 389). Very few references are made to the details of the dance: for instance, only brief allusions are made to Elizabeth and Mr Darcy having "gone down the dance" (*Pride and Prejudice* [PP] 92) or Emma "not yet dancing; she was working her way up from the bottom" (*Emma* [E] 327).[1] Certainly, Austen's contemporary readers would understand the logistics of social dancing; besides, the dance itself is secondary, providing a setting that enables interactions and offers layers of social commentary. In the film adaptation, though, the dance setting becomes an enticing visual equivalent that filmmakers are unlikely to do without.

In *Emma*, Jane Austen writes, "It may be possible to do without dancing entirely. Instances have been known of young people passing many, many months successively, without being at any ball of any description, and no material injury accrue either to body or mind;—but when a beginning is made—when the felicities of rapid motion have once been, though slightly, felt—it must be a very heavy set that does not ask for more" (247).

It seems as though that might also be the philosophy of those adapting Austen's novels as films, particularly in period pieces that set the action of the story in the late eighteenth or early nineteenth century. Obviously, the dance scenes enhance the validity of the time frame of the film. Dancing is displayed in a way that modern audiences find extremely formal and even foreign. This fulfills Prince's requirements for good production design: "Viewers look to the cinema to provide images, narrative, and spectacles that transform their sense of life and the world, but they also demand reference to life and correspondence with experience" (101). In an Austen film adaptation, the medium of dance, in its unfamiliar form, provides an attractive visual image for moviegoers, but also parallels the action of the plot and comments on what is taking place.

Simon Langton's miniseries *Pride and Prejudice*, regarded by many as the quintessential Austen adaptation, employs dance scenes extensively. Much longer than a feature film, the miniseries takes advantage of the extra time that it has to work with by featuring longer dance sequences than other Austen adaptations. Most particularly, the scene where Elizabeth and Mr Darcy dance at the Netherfield Ball is given special attention. It is their first dance together, and, accordingly, one of the first times that they have really had exclusive contact with one another. The camera highlights this by focussing on their hands as they join together at the beginning of the dance; the two are interacting in the public sphere for the first time. However, Elizabeth and Darcy are silent for an extended period, which remains faithful to Austen's narrative: "They stood for some time without speaking a word" (PP 91). Instead, they stare intensely at each other, almost a wordless battle of wills. Elizabeth eventually initiates conversation out of necessity for propriety and perhaps her own discomfort, and, despite Darcy's apparent unwillingness to speak, the tension between the two is heightened. Elizabeth subtly mocks Darcy's unsociable disposition, and Darcy's sarcastic "This is no very striking resemblance of your own character, I am sure" is delivered perfectly. Their conversation progresses to Elizabeth attacking Darcy's treatment of Mr Wickham, to which Darcy has little to say in reply except to advise Elizabeth tersely not to "sketch [his] character at the present moment." They part, as Austen writes, "on each side dissatisfied" (94). The undeniable chemistry between the two leaves the characters each wishing the dance had not ended quite so soon, although Elizabeth herself would certainly not admit it.

If the same dialogue between Elizabeth and Darcy had taken place in an alternative setting, such as over dinner, it would not carry the same emotional force. The scene gains energy by placing the civil and restrained argument into the fluidity and motion of the dance. However, the dance is by no means quick and energetic. Just prior to Elizabeth's dance with Mr Darcy is Elizabeth's dance with Mr Collins. That dance is light and quick, suitable to Mr Collins's comedic inability to dance. In Elizabeth and Darcy's dance, however, there is no longer any lighthearted skipping; the situation here is of much greater gravitas. The editing attempts to convey this. According to Prince, the audience sees "a rapid succession of individual shots on screen accompanied by an ever-changing series of camera positions and angles...what viewers *experience*, however, is the impression of a smoothly flowing, unbroken stream of imagery in which the story and the characters come convincingly to life" (147). The dance scene uses a sequence of different camera angles: from the front, from an angle, but most often from a position to the side, as if one were watching the dance from the sidelines. Indeed, the editing seems to emphasize the private conversation between Elizabeth and Darcy taking place in a very public setting. The layered shots often show the audience in the background observing the dance, including Mr Collins and Mary. As if to reinforce the concept of being on display, Sir William Lucas even stops them to compliment them on their "superior dancing." Elizabeth and Darcy weave around the other couples on the dance floor in an intricate design; they are navigating through the world of societal requirements as well as their own entangled feelings; yet even though there are so many people present, Elizabeth and Darcy seem to have their own space as well. They are often apart from everyone else physically; no one gives any indication of overhearing their private conversation. This dance scene, then, serves as a setting for a powerful verbal duel and visually reinforces what is taking place.

The music that Elizabeth and Darcy dance to in Langton's *Pride and Prejudice* is identical to the music that Emma and Mr Knightley dance to in Douglas McGrath's *Emma*. In *Emma*, as well, the dance setting is used widely. Before Emma and Mr Knightley dance together at the Crown Inn, Emma dances with Frank Churchill to a lively and energetic piece of music. She is alarmed as she observes Mr Elton deliberately snub Harriet, but Emma's distress turns to joy as Mr Knightley graciously saves Harriet from embarrassment by asking her to dance. For a brief moment, Emma and Mr Knightley are partnered during this dance, and Emma's wordless thankfulness and delight are evident. Afterwards, Emma and Mr Knightley step outside for a more private conversation, with the dance still visible as a backdrop through large open windows. In contrast to the novel, in which a meal separates the dance and the conversation, the film adaptation places their conversation immediately after Mr Knightley dances with Harriet, which gives the events connectedness and continuity. Afterwards, the two dancers return inside to dance together. As in *Pride and Prejudice*, this seems to be the first time that the future lovers have ever danced together, judging from Emma's comment, "You have shown that you can dance, and you know we are not really so much brother and sister as to make it at all improper" (331). Unlike *Pride and Prejudice*, though, the two have no need to converse during the dance itself. Their conversation takes place prior to the dance, which is fitting, since Emma and Mr Knightley are already close friends and trust each other implicitly. Mr Knightley's affectionate urging of Emma to "confess, now, old friend" captures the warmth of their relationship, and the choice to stage the scene with the dance in the background emphasizes the interaction and interplay between public and private social realities.

The actual dance scene is extremely graceful and fluid—one can truly appreciate that dancing is an art form. The dance emphasizes the suitability of Emma and Mr Knightley for one another. They move elegantly and in perfect synchronization. The entire scene is filmed in one long shot: "If a filmmaker chooses to construct a scene using the long take, this decision will substitute for the normative practice of building a scene by cutting among different camera set-ups. In other words, the long take becomes the foundation of the scene, not editing" (Prince 168). This practice is typical for much of *Emma*, as is the choice to film scenes from the front, as if the audience were watching a piece of theatre. The camera is stationary throughout, and, though there are other couples dancing, our focus is centred firmly on Emma and Mr Knightley. They are leading the dance, and, accordingly, are in view much more than any of the other couples. The dancing in this film adaptation gives colour and spectacle, with beautiful, lavish costumes and refined, graceful motion, but it provides commentary as well. Once again, the audience standing around the dance is present, albeit in a slightly diminished role, but this still strengthens the sense of dancing as an important social interaction. Emma and Mr Knightley's compatibility on the dance floor visually echoes their suitability for each other, as shown in their lively disagreements and intimate conversations.

While undoubtedly these dance scenes involve emotion and intensity, it is of a subtle and constrained nature that is fitting with the elaborate social rules of the dance. In Joe Wright's adaptation of *Pride and Prejudice*, the dance at Netherfield between Elizabeth and Darcy is preserved, but is infused with much more obvious passion. This *Pride and Prejudice* is much more dramatic than the subtle miniseries or the light, comedic *Emma*. The dance scene between our heroine and (unbeknownst to Elizabeth) her future husband is charged with emotion and heightened intensity. The tone of the dance here is sharply contrasted with the boisterous and raucous country ball where Mr Darcy is introduced for the first time. Everyone at Netherfield is very elegant and refined, and the music in Elizabeth and Darcy's dance is a powerful force in conveying this message: "Movie music emphasizes emotional effects most often by direct symbolization: the music embodies and symbolizes an emotion appropriate to the screen action" (Prince 188). The emotional magnitude of the music, a baroque piece by English composer Henry Purcell, alerts the audience that this is an important scene indeed. There is a definite layered sense to the image: visually, there is the pretense that Elizabeth and Darcy are dancing, when there is actually also a mental battle ensuing between the two.

Like the miniseries, this sequence starts with a shot of Mr Darcy standing on the right of the screen followed by a shot of Elizabeth standing on the left; as in *Emma*, much of the rest of the scene is constructed through a single shot. The filmmakers use a medium shot, and the camera follows Elizabeth and Darcy alternately as they slowly and deliberately weave in a complex pattern around the others participating in the dance. Indeed, the visual presence of others in the scene is striking and almost overwhelming. The shot is crowded with those observing the dance from the sidelines and with couples crossing closely in front of and behind Elizabeth and Darcy; the room is crowded nearly to the point of claustrophobia. Again, the dance seems to be a formal façade for what is really going on between the two. Their conversation lacks the wit of the equivalent scene in the miniseries and warmth of the scene in *Emma*, but substitutes instead deep emotion. The dialogue becomes a heated mental battle, with each seemingly playing mind games and saying less than he or she means. This culminates as Darcy challenges, "Why do you ask such a question?" At this point, the two seem to forget that they are dancing; they freeze in position in the middle of the room, staring at each other with anger and intensity, while the dance continues around them. As they rejoin the dance, the camera swirls around the couple in a sweeping fashion, and it now appears as though they are the only two people in the room. This seems somewhat of a clichéd device—after all, according to popular tradition, this happens frequently to those who are truly head-over-heels in love. It is used rather cleverly here, though; Elizabeth would certainly not yet admit to being in love with Mr Darcy, and the tone suggests that each is trying to solve the enigma of the other. It also nicely visualizes the distinction between the worlds of public and private life. Elizabeth seems almost shocked when the dance has ended and everyone begins to clap, as if for a moment she had been lost in a private world. The dance, then, acts to channel emotion and present an image of the competing, and yet interacting, public and private domains.

Novels such as Jane Austen's are very dependent on the subtleties and intricacies of language, and, accordingly, film adaptations must find some way to parallel this through visual nuances. Langton's *Pride and Prejudice*, McGrath's *Emma*, and Wright's *Pride and Prejudice* find success in their varying treatments of the dance setting. In all three, even though the camera angles and techniques vary, the impression of being on display is apparent. Additionally, there is the sense that dancing is a sort of trial for marriage. Austen's Henry Tilney would likely agree with this, for he considers a dance to be "an emblem of marriage" that, "once entered into, [the man and the woman] belong exclusively to each other till the moment of its dissolution" (*Northanger Abbey* 76–77). In Austen's time, dancing was an acceptable form of social interaction between young men and women, and, appropriately, the three dance scenes convey physical and intellectual attraction. Dance is a private interaction between characters, in these films between our heroine and hero, but it is carried out in a public social environment. It provides a visual representation of tension, suitability, grace, and emotion.

NOTE

1. All quotations from Jane Austen's published works are taken from *The Oxford Illustrated Jane Austen*, 3rd ed., ed. R.W. Chapman (Oxford: Oxford UP, 1988), and are documented by short title and page number in the body of the chapter.

WORKS CITED

Emma. Dir. Douglas McGrath. Perf. Gwyneth Paltrow and Jeremy Northam. Miramax,
1996.

Jones, Vivien. Appendix B. *Emma.* By Jane Austen. Ed. James Kinsley. New York:
Oxford UP, 2003.

Pride and Prejudice. Dir. Simon Langton. Perf. Colin Firth and Jennifer Ehle. A&E, 1995.

Pride and Prejudice. Dir. Joe Wright. Perf. Keira Knightley and Matthew Macfadyen.
Universal, 2005.

Prince, Stephen. *Movies and Meaning: An Introduction to Film.* 3rd ed. Boston: Pearson,
2004.

27 Emma's Search for a True Friend

BRUCE STOVEL

THE CAREFULLY WORKED, understated artistry of *Emma* has perhaps
never been better defined than in a single sentence written by Reginald
Farrer some 75 years ago: "Only when the story has been thoroughly
assimilated, can the infinite delights and subtleties of its workman-
ship begin to be appreciated, as you realize the manifold complexity of
the book's web, and find that every sentence, almost every epithet, has
its definite reference to equally unemphasized points before and after
in the development of the plot" (65). The miraculous thing, Farrer suggests, is that the references that together weave the novel's web are
both "definite" and yet "unemphasized": because they are definite the
reader builds up a store of imaginative and emotional connections, but
because they are unemphasized these connections may remain unrec-
ognized. Only after reflection, assimilation of the novel's subtleties, do
such connections become conscious. In this essay, I would like to give
full emphasis to the strand in the web constituted by the word "friend,"
which occurs prominently in the novel's opening pages and many times
thereafter, most notably in its two pivotal moments, Mr Knightley's
rebuke of Emma after Box Hill and the scene in which he proposes to
her. This particular set of connections has not been remarked on by
critics of the novel, though I am sure its resonances are felt by attentive
readers; furthermore, this strand is a prime instance of the way in

which the novel raises great issues on its constricted stage, since by the novel's end Emma has not only discovered that Mr Knightley is the friend who will fill the gap in her life created by the marriage of Miss Taylor at its outset, but she has also changed her conceptions of friendship, love, and marriage. The anonymous French translator of the novel in 1816 had good reason to entitle it *La Nouvelle Emma*.

The novel's opening suggests that it will present the story of Emma's search for a true friend. The discovery of true friendship had been a central subject of eighteenth-century fiction, at least since the time of Sarah Fielding's popular novel of 1744, *The Adventures of David Simple: Containing an Account of His Travels Through the Cities of London and Westminster, in the Search of a Real Friend*. Nothing was more admired in Richardson's *Clarissa* (1747–1748) than its depiction of the tested and true friendship of Clarissa and Anna Howe—a friendship without which the novel would, quite literally, not exist. The idea of friendship became so interconnected with the novel form that when Jane Austen, aged 14, brought together in one 30-page mélange all the clichés of sentimental fiction, she entitled it *Love and Freindship: A Novel in a Series of Letters* and gave it a resounding epigraph: "Deceived in Freindship & Betrayed in Love." *Emma*, however, reveals Jane Austen giving this conventional subject a dramatic, carefully formulated, and most unconventional treatment.

Friendship is, in fact, the central concern of the novel's first chapter. It presents Emma's dilemma for the rest of the novel: who can take Miss Taylor's place as Emma's special friend? The chapter also suggests that Emma's relationship with Miss Taylor has not really been friendship; shows that Emma does have a good friend, though she hardly realizes it, in Mr Knightley; and uses friendship as a way of defining the split in Emma between her egocentric Woodhouse side and her more kind, rational, and good-hearted Knightley side. By the time the chapter is over, both the course of future events and a conception of friendship that underlies those events are clear.

Let me take up each of these claims in turn. Emma's past relationship with Miss Taylor is summed up in the novel's third paragraph:

Sixteen years had Miss Taylor been in Mr Woodhouse's family, less as a governess than as a friend, very fond of both daughters, but particularly of Emma. Between them it was more the intimacy of sisters. Even before Miss Taylor had ceased to hold the nominal office of governess, the mildness of her temper had hardly allowed her to impose any restraint; and the shadow of authority being now long passed away, they had been living together as friend and friend very mutually attached, and Emma doing just what she liked; highly esteeming Miss Taylor's judgment, but directed chiefly by her own. (*Emma [E]* 5)[1]

I take these sentences to be our introduction to the novel's distinctive narrative method, free indirect speech: the narrator shifts slowly and almost imperceptibly from objective narration to an ironic depiction of facts as Emma sees them. The reader of *Emma* soon learns that hidden quotation marks exist within the most straightforward relation of fact; for instance, "The lovers were standing together at one of the windows" (90), in chapter 10, really tells us, "The lovers [*as Emma persisted in thinking of Harriet and Mr Elton*] were standing together at one of the windows." In the same way, the words "highly esteeming Miss Taylor's judgement, but directed chiefly by her own" (5) are Emma's summary of a very satisfactory situation: she has been free to say and do what she likes. Miss Taylor, as a dependent, has had to acquiesce. The passage asserts that the two lived together, not as teacher and student, but as independent equals, "friend and friend very mutually attached"; at the same time it suggests that, although the two may have seemed to be and thought of themselves as friend and friend, they were actually independent employer and dependent employee. Mr Knightley offers the same ironic picture of the relationship in his discussion with Mrs Weston[2] in chapter 5: "You might not give Emma such a complete education as your powers would seem to promise; but you were receiving a very good education from *her*, on the very material matrimonial point of submitting your own will" (38).

Of course, Emma has seen things very differently. On the novel's second page, she thinks tenderly of "the equal footing and perfect unreserve" in which she lived with Miss Taylor:

> It had been a friend and companion such as few possessed, intelligent, well-informed, useful, gentle, knowing all the ways of the family, interested in all its concerns, and peculiarly interested in herself, in every pleasure, every scheme of her's;—one to whom she could speak every thought as it arose, and one who had such an affection for her as could never find fault. (6)

If this is what Emma considers an equal footing, no wonder that she will find a replacement for Miss Taylor in the lowly Harriet Smith, who repeatedly addresses Emma as one would a divinity: "Whatever you say is always right....You understand every thing....Nobody is equal to you!—I care for nobody as I do for you!...You...who can see into everybody's heart" (74, 76, 268, 404). In fact, the strange locution "It had been a friend and companion..." is echoed when Emma meets Harriet and we hear, "Altogether she was quite convinced of Harriet Smith's being exactly the young friend she wanted—exactly the something her home required" (26). (As one critic, Darrel Mansell, remarks, this puts Harriet in the same category as Regency mirrors [152]). Just as Emma claims in chapter 1 to have "made" the marriage between Mr and Mrs Weston, so she will choose as her friend someone who will allow her to fulfill the managerial task she sets herself at the end of the chapter: finding a wife for Mr Elton. Emma has something very specific in mind when, immediately after meeting Harriet in the novel's third chapter, she resolves to "detach her from her bad acquaintance, and introduce her into good society" (E 23).

Even more ironically, this opening chapter shows that Emma does have a good friend, Mr Knightley. Ostensibly, he calls on Emma and her father because he has just returned from London "and now walked up to Hartfield to say that all were well in Brunswick-square" (9), but it is clear that he sympathizes with Emma's feelings of loss and comes to restore her spirits. Late in the novel, when it seems that Mr Knightley is about to marry Harriet and will make such visits to Hartfield no more, Emma recalls how he came that particular evening and "dissipated every melancholy fancy" (422). Furthermore, Emma and Mr Knightley really do display an "equal footing and perfect unreserve" in their lively debate here. "We always say what we like to one another" (10), Emma explains to her father. If Mr Knightley's rebukes are stringent—"Your time has been properly and delicately spent, if you have been endeavouring for the last four years to bring about this marriage. A worthy employment for a young lady's mind!" (12)—Emma's reply is equally unrestrained, "I pity you.—I thought you cleverer" (13). At this point, Emma takes this serious yet bantering relationship for granted; only when she is threatened with its loss will she realize how important Mr Knightley's friendship is to her.

Chapter 1 of the novel also uses the idea of friendship to dramatize the split within Emma herself. Falling into self-pitying loneliness, Emma reflects, "there was some satisfaction in considering with what self-denying, generous friendship she had always wished and promoted the match; but it was a black morning's work for her" (6). Emma rallies herself to combat the unmitigated sorrow of her father, who, "from his habits of gentle selfishness and of being never able to suppose that other people could feel differently from himself,...was very much disposed to think that Miss Taylor had done as sad a thing for herself as for them, and would have been a great deal happier if she had spent all the rest of her life at Hartfield" (8). When Mr Knightley calls, however, Emma takes the plaintive pose again, but now her own generous and rational position is uncompromisingly urged upon her by Mr Knightley: "Emma...cannot allow herself to feel so much pain as pleasure. Every friend of Miss Taylor must be glad to have her so happily married" (11). The notion of friendship has served to crystallize the moral issues: Emma has a Woodhouse self and a Knightley self, a self capable only of "gentle selfishness" and another capable of self-denying generosity. In fact, as the novel will demonstrate, Mr Knightley embodies Emma's deepest and best self. The phrasing suggests this at several points—for instance, when we are told, "[Emma] had had many a hint from Mr Knightley and some from her own heart, as to her deficiency" (i.e., in not calling upon Miss Bates and her mother [155]). The patterning of events often makes it even clearer: for instance, Emma in chapter 14 roundly condemns Frank Churchill's failure to visit his father and his new stepmother, but in her heated argument on the subject with Mr Knightley four chapters later, she "perceive[s] that she [is] taking the other side of the question from her real opinion, and making use of Mrs Weston's arguments against herself" (145). When Emma marries Mr Knightley at the novel's end, then, the union is also a psychic one: when Emma ceases being Miss Woodhouse and becomes Mrs Knightley, she has become reunited with a part of herself that she had neglected. Neglected, perhaps, but hardly banished: against all of her intentions, the Knightley side of Emma has been responding to him all along—in fact, leading him on. During their arguments, her propositions are often provocations: "Were you, yourself, ever to marry, [Harriet] is the very woman for you" (64). She later adds, "There will be but one subject throughout the parishes of Donwell and Highbury; but one interest—one object of curiosity; it will be all Mr Frank Churchill; we shall think and speak of nobody else" (149–50). This split within Emma is, I think, what makes the novel so profoundly comic.

The first chapter of *Emma* has thus presented a rich and humane conception of friendship. Friendship is a mutual exchange of sympathy, emotional sustenance, and esteem; it can only exist between independent equals, since each person must have freedom of speech and action; it entails some degree of sacrifice, of placing the other person's immediate happiness before one's own; friendship exists when the two friends are essentially alike—each other's alter ego. Samuel Johnson's definition of the word "friendship" in his *Dictionary of the English Language* (1755) is helpful at this point. Johnson, so much admired by Jane Austen and so well known for his own friendships, distinguishes five shades of meaning in the word "friendship": "1. The state of minds united by mutual benevolence. 2. Highest degree of intimacy. 3. Favour; personal kindness. 4. Assistance; help. 5. Conformity; affinity; correspondence; aptness to unite." Johnson gives instances of usage with each sense, and the first instance cited under the first meaning is particularly illuminating; Johnson cites Francis Bacon's *Essays*: "There is little *friendship* in the world, and least of all between equals, which was wont to be magnified: that that is, is between superior and inferior, whose fortunes may comprehend the one the other." Bacon intends to shock his reader into thought, as does Johnson in citing him; Bacon asserts that, despite the common idealized view that friendship exists between equals, the friendships that we actually find in the world are compacts for mutual advantage between superior and inferior.

Chapter 1 of the novel has also suggested, even more interestingly, that Emma will find her true friend, not in another woman, but in the man who becomes her husband. This, too, was a common enough idea. The marriage ceremony in the *Book of Common Prayer*—that ceremony, as Emma says late in the novel, "in which N. takes M. for better, for worse" (E 463)—states that the third of the three "causes for which Matrimony was ordained" is "for the mutual society, help, and comfort, that the one ought to have of the other, in both prosperity and adversity." In 1750, Johnson, in the first of several *Rambler* essays devoted to the topic of marriage, wrote, "Marriage is the strictest tie of perpetual friendship;...there can be no friendship without confidence, and no confidence without integrity" ("Unhappiness of Marriage" 103). Samuel Richardson's *Sir Charles Grandison* (1753–1754), Jane Austen's favourite work of fiction and one that she adapted into a drama for family performance, has at its centre the proposition that, in the heroine Harriet Byron's words, "marriage is the highest state of friendship that mortals can know" (1:184).

These ideas about friendship are borne out in all that follows the novel's opening. Emma's relationship with Harriet Smith is summed up in one sentence by Mr Knightley: "You have been no friend to Harriet Smith, Emma" (E 63). These words echo in Emma's mind at two key moments: after her first fiasco, ashamed of the blunders that have led Mr Elton to propose to her and not Harriet, but unwilling to inquire into their cause, she reflects, "I have been but half a friend to her" (137); in the novel's climactic pages, when the worm has turned and Harriet has not only chosen for herself, but chosen Mr Knightley, Emma thinks,

"Mr Knightley had spoken prophetically, when he had once said, 'Emma, you have been no friend to Harriet Smith'" (402). Genuine friendship would, Emma feels, undermine her supremacy: this is why she shuns Jane Fairfax, who is her equal in so many ways, and not only entertains, but spreads, her spiteful suspicion that "This amiable, upright, perfect Jane Fairfax was apparently cherishing very reprehensible feelings" for Mr Dixon (243). When Emma comes to self-knowledge,

> She bitterly regretted not having sought a closer acquaintance
> with [Jane], and blushed for the envious feelings which had cer-
> tainly been, in some measure, the cause....had she endeavoured
> to find a friend there instead of in Harriet Smith, she must, in
> all probability, have been spared from every pain which pressed
> on her now. Birth, abilities, and education, had been equally
> marking the one as an associate for her, to be received with
> gratitude; and the other—what was she? (421)

Significantly, Jane and Emma are exactly the same age, about to turn 21, while Harriet is only 17.

Emma's great discovery, however, is not that she has been no friend to Harriet, nor that she should have befriended Jane, but that Mr Knightley is, and has always been, the friend she has been seeking. His most "knightly" act in the novel, his rescue of Harriet Smith from humilia-tion by the Eltons at the Crown Inn, is plainly aimed at rescuing Emma as much as Harriet, as Emma immediately recognizes: "She was all pleas-ure and gratitude, both for Harriet and herself" (328). Paradoxically, the stronger their differences of opinion, the stronger their friendship becomes. When they disagree heatedly over Harriet's rejection of Robert Martin, Emma feels that she "[can] not quarrel with herself" (69), since she considers herself in the right, but she is very unhappy until she and he agree amicably to disagree: they shake hands cordially and she can feel, with relief, that "they [are] friends again" (98). Mr Knightley's unwelcome pronouncements, warnings, and predictions are all offered as acts of friendship. When in the extraordinary chapter—volume 3, chapter 5—in which we enter his mind and share his discovery that there seems to be a secret relationship between Jane Fairfax and Frank Churchill, he decides, "he must—yes, he certainly must, as a friend—an anxious friend—give Emma some hint, ask her some question. He could not see her in a situation of such danger, without trying to preserve her" (349). Emma, however, laughs off his suspicions, saying that she can answer for Frank Churchill's feelings (351), and the way is thus prepared for the novel's central scene, the expedition to Box Hill, one chapter later.

Emma is at her worst at Box Hill; Mrs Elton subsides into a muttering nonentity for once. As everyone prepares to leave, Mr Knightley finds Emma alone and addresses her with the words, "Emma, I must once more speak to you as I have been used to do"; his ensuing rebuke ends, "This is not pleasant to you, Emma,—and it is very far from pleasant to me; but I must, I will,—I will tell you truths while I can, satisfied with proving myself your friend by very faithful counsel, and trusting that you will some time or other do me greater justice than you can do now" (374–75). His words "Once more," "while I can," "some time or other," and "now" all show that he believes Emma's head has been turned by Frank and that she is about to become engaged to him. Emma is shattered by his speech, and the tears that follow are caused, I suspect, less by simple remorse at having humiliated Miss Bates than by the pain she feels at the prospect of having lost his good opinion and at having responded to his words "in apparent sullenness" (376). Of course, given Mr Knightley's identity and the author's comic vision, these two feelings ultimately are one, but Emma's immediate response suggests where the emphasis falls: "The truth of his representation there was no denying. She felt it at her heart. How could she have been so brutal, so cruel to Miss Bates!—How could she have exposed herself to such ill opinion in any one she valued! And how suffer him to leave her without saying one word of gratitude, of concurrence, of common kindness!" (376). Cruelty to Miss Bates is dispatched in the first of the three parallel exclamations; the second and third are reserved for the breach with Mr Knightley. Emma is so anxious to regain Mr Knightley's regard that she without delay makes a penitential visit to Miss Bates; her act succeeds in making them "thorough friends" (386) again. There is no handshake this time, and Emma is unaccountably disappointed at Mr Knightley's "little movement of more than common friendliness," when he seizes her hand — "she might, perhaps, have rather offered it" — only to hesitate and then suddenly let it go. Even so, "She could not but recall the attempt with great satisfaction. It spoke such perfect amity" (386).

Emma's divided feelings here point to the book's culminating irony: the clearer it becomes to Emma that Mr Knightley is truly her friend, the less conceivable it is to her that he can be her lover. Emma has believed from the start that she is an expert on matters of the heart: Mr Knightley has not assessed Mr Elton's intentions, she tells herself, "with the skill of such an observer on such a question as herself" (67); others may have seen nothing, but *she* would have made discoveries, she tells Frank Churchill, if she had been on the sailboat when Mr Dixon rescued Jane Fairfax (218). Love, Emma believes, is a romantic obsession that overrides all other considerations. Once the lover is imprinted, nothing else matters to him or her: Mr Dixon, or Jane, or probably both of them, will never be the same after that stormy day at sea; once Frank Churchill saves Harriet from the gypsies, the emotions of each will naturally be fixed on the other (335). That is why, Emma tells Harriet, her attachments will be limited to her nephews and nieces: "it suits my ideas of comfort better than what is warmer and blinder" (86). This is why Frank Churchill quickly decides that it is safe to flirt with Emma: "Amiable and delightful as Miss Woodhouse is, she never gave me the idea of a young woman likely to be attached" (438), he says in his final letter. He is right; Emma, on her side, repeatedly thinks that she and Frank are no more than friends: "The conclusion of every imaginary declaration on his side was that she *refused him*. Their affection was always to subside into friendship" (264). At the Crown Inn, when she notices Mr Knightley "often observing her" while she dances with Frank, she is unworried: "There was nothing like flirtation between her and her partner. They seemed more like cheerful, easy friends, than lovers" (326).

All of Emma's assumptions about love and friendship come into play at the plot climax. After Harriet confesses her love for Mr Knightley and her belief that it is returned, Emma makes a whole series of realizations: that she has always stood first with Mr Knightley; that this relationship is "inexpressibly important" to her; that "he had loved her, and watched over her from a girl, with an endeavour to improve her, and an anxiety for her doing right, which no other creature had at all shared" (415). All the same, she considers, she can have no hope:

> Harriet Smith might think herself not unworthy of being pecu-
> liarly, exclusively, passionately loved by Mr Knightley. She could
> not. She could not flatter herself with any idea of blindness in
> his attachment to her. She had received a very recent proof of its
> impartiality.—How shocked had he been by her behaviour to
> Miss Bates! How directly, how strongly, had he expressed him-
> self on the subject!—Not too strongly for the offence—but far,
> far too strongly to issue from any feeling softer than upright
> justice and clear-sighted good will.—She had no hope, nothing
> to deserve the name of hope, that he could have that sort of
> affection for herself which was now in question. (415–16)

She can hope, however, that Mr Knightley will at least not marry Harriet: "Let him but continue the same Mr Knightley to her and her father,...let Donwell and Hartfield lose none of their precious intercourse of friendship and confidence, and her peace would be fully secured" (416). The new, humble Emma, who for the first time underestimates her own claims, still assumes that friendship and love are entirely different: Mr Knightley's upright justice and clear-sighted good will demonstrate his friendship, but also prove that he cannot feel "that sort of affection for herself which was now in question."

These reflections occur in chapter 12 of volume 3; in the very next chapter Emma's sentimental education is to be completed. Mr Knightley and Emma meet in the garden; he proposes marriage, and in so doing gives the word "friend" a dramatic new meaning, but only after the two have performed a dance of comic misunderstanding. Mr Knightley has come once again "to soothe or to counsel her" (432), believing that she is crushed by the news of Frank Churchill's secret engagement to Jane Fairfax; Emma, thinking he has come to consult her about his love for Harriet, is also anxious to play a friend's part: to listen, sympathize, advise. Emma manages to convey the fact that she has been blinded by Frank Churchill and yet "it was my good fortune—that, in short, I was somehow or other safe from him" (427). At this point, Mr Knightley is eager to raise a new topic; Emma, however, believes him to be within half a sentence of Harriet, and when he says, "Emma, I must tell you what you will not ask, though I may wish it unsaid the next moment," she abruptly cuts him off with the words, "Oh! then, don't speak it, don't speak it....Take a little time, consider, do not commit yourself." After he thanks her and falls silent, she changes her mind:

> Emma could not bear to give him pain. He was wishing to con-
> fide in her—perhaps to consult her;—cost her what it would,
> she would listen. She might assist his resolution, or reconcile
> him to it; she might give just praise to Harriet, or, by repre-
> senting to him his own independence, relieve him from that
> state of indecision, which must be more intolerable than any
> alternative to such a mind as his. (429)

Emma has finally achieved the "self-denying, generous friendship" she ascribed to herself in the novel's opening pages, and, as with her remorse over another all-too-natural speech at Box Hill, she immediately acts upon it.

At this point in the scene, Emma takes the initiative. Just as she had invited Mr Knightley to ask her to dance, just as she had perhaps rather offered her hand to him during their reconciliation, her initiative brings on Mr Knightley's proposal. She suggests that they take another turn through the garden and makes a carefully worded speech to him: "I stopped you ungraciously, just now, Mr Knightley, and, I am afraid, gave you pain.—But if you have any wish to speak openly to me as a friend, or to ask my opinion of any thing you may have in contemplation—as a friend, indeed, you may command me. I will hear whatever you like. I will tell you exactly what I think" (429). Emma's repeated use of the word "friend," which signifies her new determination to be selfless, her awakened gratitude for his friendship, is at first, but only for a moment, misunderstood: "As a friend!...Emma, that I fear is a word—No, I have no wish—Stay, yes, why should I hesitate—I have gone too far already for concealment.—Emma, I accept your offer—Extraordinary as it may seem, I accept it and refer myself to you as a friend.—Tell me, then, have I no chance of ever succeeding?" (430). It seems that in the course of the speech Mr Knightley realizes that in proposing marriage what he wants Emma to become is, simply, his friend—and that realization is only possible because she has, for the first time, acted as his friend. He has often been her friend; she is now his. The notion that Mr Knightley's wife will be his friend had been suggested just pages earlier in the novel, when Emma imagines how wretched she will be "if Harriet were to be the chosen, the first, the dearest, the friend, the wife to whom he looked for all the best blessings of existence" (423). Now it turns out that it is to Emma that he looks, and that she is as much the chooser as the chosen. The way is clear, if not quite smooth, to the novel's final sentence, in which we leave the just-married hero and heroine at the centre of a "small band of true friends" (484).

There are many more striking references to friendship in *Emma*. There is Mrs Elton's "friendship" with Jane Fairfax, which parodies Emma's relationship with Harriet and is only possible because Emma has neglected Jane; there is Emma's reflection, overtly about Mr Weston but covertly about Mr Knightley, that "General benevolence, but not general friendship, made a man what he ought to be.—She could fancy such a man" (320). Enough has been said, however, to establish my point: that Emma's search for and discovery of a friend constitutes one of those definite but unemphasized networks pointed to by Reginald Farrer.

Emma is such a rich and various novel that Jane Austen's use of this particular pattern has been largely ignored by her critics. J.F. Burrows, in his monograph on *Emma*, notes Mr Knightley's recurring use of the word "friend," but considers it to be a mounting irony at Mr Knightley's expense: *he* thinks he is acting simply as Emma's friend, but we know differently (107). The advent of feminist criticism has led to new interest in the idea of friendship in Jane Austen's novels; but, as the title of Janet Todd's 1980 book, *Women's Friendship in Literature*, suggests, the assumption has been that friendship in the novels is a matter of friendship between two women. Janet Todd's book contains a long and thoughtful analysis of Emma's friendship with Harriet and of "what could have been the most fulfilling female friendship in all her novels," Emma's relationship with Jane Fairfax, but notes, regretfully, "Austen chops off the relationship at its inception...we have the introduction of two friends but not the friendship" (301). The same view is advanced in a provocative essay by Ruth Perry, "Interrupted Friendships in Jane Austen's *Emma*" (1986). Perry argues that Jane Austen was forced by the fictional conventions of her day to write narratives of love and marriage—"trapped as an author as her characters were trapped as women" (200)—and that the subtext of *Emma* consists of a counter-narrative, the story of Emma's and Jane's mutual need for friendship. She concludes, "The repeated frustration of women's friendship in a novel that emphasizes the importance of friendship, and the book's emotional unsatisfactoriness on this central crux (for Emma never does find a proper friend to 'replace' Mrs Weston)—these ellipses must alert us to suggestions about the limitations of the form itself" (192). This sentence serves to highlight all that I have been arguing: that *Emma* is "a novel that emphasizes the importance of friendship" and that Emma's search for a proper friend is the novel's "central crux." My view, of course, is that Emma does find a true friend in Mr Knightley, and this is what makes the novel emotionally satisfactory.

In fact, I would go one step further. The novel depicts Emma as an everyman figure in her movement from narcissism to community; I think it also presents her as most women, if not everywoman, in her movement from having a best friend in another young woman to finding that friend in her husband. "An old story, probably—a common case—and no more than has happened to hundreds of my sex before" (E 427), is Emma's rueful summary of her career during the proposal scene; her words apply to far more than her flirtation with Frank Churchill. Near the end of the novel, she considers "her wilful intimacy with Harriet Smith" has been "the worst of all her womanly follies" (463); by contrast, her chosen intimacy with Mr Knightley is her greatest piece of womanly wisdom.

AUTHOR'S NOTE

A version of this essay was originally published in *Persuasions: The Jane Austen Journal* 13 (1991), 58–68, and is reprinted by kind permission of the editor.

NOTES

1. All quotations from Jane Austen's published works are taken from *The Oxford Illustrated Jane Austen*, 3rd ed., ed. R.W. Chapman (Oxford: Oxford UP, 1988), and are documented by short title and page number in the body of the chapter.
2. Mrs Weston is Miss Taylor's married name.

WORKS CITED

The Book of Common Prayer. London: 1662.

Burrows, J.F. *Jane Austen's "Emma."* Sydney: Sydney UP, 1968.

Fielding, Sarah. *The Adventures of David Simple: Containing an Account of His Travels Through the Cities of London and Westminster, in the Search of a Real Friend*. London: A. Millar, 1744.

Farrer, Reginald. "Jane Austen, ob. July 18, 1817." *Quarterly Review* 228 (July 1917) 1–30. Rpt. in *Emma: A Casebook*. Ed. David Lodge. London: Macmillan, 1968. 64–69.

Johnson, Samuel. *A Dictionary of the English Language*. London: Printed by W. Strahan, 1755.

———. "The Unhappiness of Marriage." *Rambler* 18 (1750). Rpt. in *The Rambler*. Ed. W.J. Bate and Albrecht B. Strauss. New Haven: Yale UP, 1969. 97–103. Vol. 3 of *The Works of Samuel Johnson*. 14 vols. 1958–1978.

Mansell, Darrel. *The Novels of Jane Austen: An Interpretation*. Macmillan: London, 1973.

Perry, Ruth. "Interrupted Friendships in Jane Austen's *Emma*." *Tulsa Studies in Women's Literature* 5 (Fall 1986): 185–202.

Richardson, Samuel. *Clarissa*. London: Printed for S. Richardson, 1747–1748.

———. *Sir Charles Grandison*. 1753–1754. Ed. Jocelyn Harris. Oxford: Oxford UP, 1986.

Todd, Janet. *Women's Friendship in Literature*. New York: Columbia UP, 1980.

28 The Complexity of Marriage in Jane Austen's Novels

AMY STAFFORD

IN *JANE AUSTEN'S NOVELS: SOCIAL CHANGE AND LITERARY FORM* (1979), Julia Prewitt Brown argues that Jane Austen "gave meaning to domesticity for the first time in English fiction. Her novels are the first to fully assert the cultural significance of marriage and family" (1). The centrality of marriage in Jane Austen's novels is obvious; the majority of her characters, whether major or minor, female or male, are actively engaged in the business of matrimony. The perfect marriages achieved by her heroines demonstrate Austen's grasp of the economic and social realities for women in her society, while the wide-ranging differences she depicts among already-married couples are an indication of her thorough understanding of human nature. *Sense and Sensibility*, *Pride and Prejudice*, *Mansfield Park*, and *Emma* most effectively illustrate her commentary on the institution of marriage and its significance in her society.

While the marriages of Austen's heroines and heroes combine true affection with practical or monetary considerations, her minor characters demonstrate interesting deviations from this standard. A brief survey of the heroes and heroines will help to establish Austen's tenets on marriage, which will provide a basis for exploring the relationships of the minor characters. Minor characters fall into one of three marriage categories: married characters of the older generation make a statement on the varying results of marriage; many younger peripheral characters endeavour to enter the happy state for a variety of reasons; some characters, both old and young, are excluded from marriage altogether for reasons that comment on social realities for women in Austen's society.

Put simply, Jane Austen's work always acknowledges the social truth that, although marriages can be functional without love, they cannot be successful without money. The most heart-warming marriages—the ones worthy of Austen heroines—are those based on mutual esteem and affection, as well as material comfort. Emma is the only female character that has the luxury of declaring that she does not need to marry to secure her own comfort and economic security: "I have none of the usual inducements of women to marry...without love, I am sure I should be a fool to change such a situation as mine. Fortune I do not want; employment I do not want; consequence I do not want" (*Emma* [E] 84).[1] Emma's is a rare situation for women in eighteenth- or nineteenth-century society. All other Austen heroines, and some heroes, too, have to take their financial situations into account when considering potential mates. We are reminded repeatedly that affection is not enough to make a couple happy in marriage.

Even Elinor and Edward, "one of the happiest couples in the world" (*Sense and Sensibility* [SS] 374), are not "quite enough in love to think that three hundred and fifty pounds a-year would supply them with the comforts of life" (369). The threat of poverty hangs over the heads of all the heroines except Emma. The Dashwood girls are forced out of their homes and given only £500 per year to live on; Mrs Bennet's eagerness to marry her daughters off stems from the entailment of Mr Bennet's estate away from the female line; Fanny Price is threatened with the poverty of her former home at Portsmouth if she does not marry Mr Crawford. The economic and social reality for women in Jane Austen's society often made them dependent on making good marriages to secure a comfortable income. All Austen heroines are motivated to marry by affection, but economic security is the underlying assumption of their marriages.

In the case of Bingley and Jane Bennet, Darcy and Elizabeth, and Colonel Brandon and Marianne, wealth on the gentleman's side ensures that, once the heroine's affections are gained, their marriages are considered perfect models of conjugal felicity. For Edward and Elinor and Edmund and Fanny, however, marriage is not the complete picture of bliss, despite their mutual affection, until sufficient income is attained. Edmund and Fanny, for example, establish a marriage that "must appear as secure as earthly happiness can be," but their "picture of good" is still not complete until they acquire the Mansfield living, which occurs "just after they had been married long enough to begin to want an increase in income" (*Mansfield Park* [MP] 473).

Although they primarily marry for love, economic stability is a crucial ingredient of every major character's marriage. The minor characters exhibit a wider range of motivations and strategies for marrying and varying degrees of contentment with their choices, but their actions reinforce the economic realities of eighteenth- and early nineteenth-century society and effectively illustrate that mutual affection was not necessary for comfort in matrimony. Some level of domestic contentment was always attainable, provided the couple was not impoverished and neither spouse was in love with someone else.

The older generation of minor characters in the novels provides an interesting evaluation of different motives for marriage. Sir John and Lady Middleton in *Sense and Sensibility*, for example, have united for the purpose of domestic comfort rather than mutual affection. As Juliet McMaster points out in *Jane Austen on Love* (1978), "The Middletons seem to suit each other in their very distance, as his incorrigible sociability and her invariable insipidity drive them both to seek any company but each other's" (76). Although they are not in love, the Middletons find sufficient satisfaction and contentment in a marriage based on their shared desire for domestic security and comfort.

The Bennets in *Pride and Prejudice*, unfortunately, do not fare so well. Mr Bennet "married a woman whose weak understanding and illiberal mind, had very early in their marriage put an end to all real affection for her. Respect, esteem, and confidence, had vanished for ever; and all his views of domestic happiness were overthrown" (*Pride and Prejudice* [PP] 236). Between a disappointed father who derives no pleasure from his wife's company, except "as her ignorance and folly" contribute to his "amusement" (236), and an obnoxious mother who demonstrates impropriety at every turn, it is easy to see why Elizabeth Bennet's home sorely lacks domestic comfort. The Bennets' less-than-perfect situation demonstrates an important lesson: Mr Bennet's unhappy fate may be imputed to the mistake of marrying only for "youth and beauty," without consideration of his long-term needs in a domestic companion (236).

Mr Bennet's brother-in-law, Mr Gardiner, is an example of a man who married for better reasons, and therefore fared better in married life. Mr and Mrs Gardiner share mutual affection and intellectual equality; they are well-suited companions. Along with the Westons in *Emma* and the Crofts in *Persuasion*, the Gardiners are one of only a few couples in Jane Austen's work that provide an active example of matrimonial felicity for the younger characters.

Mansfield Park provides further commentary on the married state, beginning with the three Ward sisters, whose narratives open the novel. These three sisters, who become Lady Bertram, Mrs Norris, and Mrs Price by marriage, offer an informative contrast of different motivations for marriage and the corresponding consequences. Lady Bertram, like Mrs Bennet, seems to have her looks to thank for her "good luck" in captivating Sir Thomas, and in being "thereby raised to the rank of a baronet's lady, with all the comforts and consequences of an handsome house and large income" (MP 3). This marriage, especially on Sir Thomas's side, cannot be highly rewarding or fulfilling. The Bertrams share none of the mutual affection, attraction, or intellectual stimulation enjoyed by the Gardiners, but each partner seems content enough. The eldest Ward sister, Mrs Norris, only "found herself obliged to be attached to the Rev. Mr Norris" due to a lack of other options, but her marriage "was not contemptible" (3).

Mrs Price, in contrast, suffers greatly from her choice. After marrying a man "without education, fortune, or connections," simply because she loves him, Mrs Price finds herself struggling to support her numerous children on an insufficient income (3). When Fanny goes back to Portsmouth to stay with her family, she witnesses a scene of poverty, drunkenness, and domestic discord, "the very reverse of what she could have wished. It was the abode of noise, disorder, and impropriety" (388).

In her 1999 film adaptation of *Mansfield Park*, writer-director Patricia Rozema articulated the implications of Mrs Price's situation directly by adding a new scene in which Mrs Price urges Fanny to consider marrying Crawford. She tells Fanny, "There is no shame in wealth, my dear....Just remember, Fanny, I married for love." Rozema emphasizes an important precept from the novels with this statement. Mrs Price, the only Ward sister to marry for love without consideration of wealth, is also the only sister to be completely unhappy, the only sister who lacks all domestic comfort. The example of the Ward sisters reinforces the idea that adequate contentment can be achieved regardless of affection, provided there are sufficient means, but affection is necessary to greater happiness.

The younger set of minor characters includes those in the process of securing their mates in the novels. Jane Austen implies that, based on their strategies for getting what they want, the motivations of this group of characters fall into varying positions along a spectrum of acceptability. In other words, we must assume, as Margaret Doody does in her introduction to Austen's *Catharine and Other Writings* (1998), that Jane Austen believed in "fiction's truisms, its pattern of exemplary rewards and punishments." This means that "the world is orderly, that Virtue is Rewarded," and that the consequences of each character's marriage reflects the social acceptability of his or her actions leading up to that marriage (Doody xxxviii).

For example, Mr Collins and Mr Elton (from *Pride and Prejudice* and *Emma*, respectively) share the remarkable ability to shift their violent passions speedily from one woman to the next as convenience dictates. Neither practises too serious a deception. They merely produce insincere, conventional expressions of love and admiration, whenever called for, in the name of wooing a potential wife. Accordingly, neither clergyman faces terribly grave consequences: they have to endure only brief moments of humiliating rejection at the hands of their first choices. In the end, however, Mr Collins secures a sensible and respectable wife to bring home to Lady Catherine de Bourgh in Charlotte Lucas, and Mr Elton finds his "Miss Somebody else" with £10,000 in Augusta Hawkins (E 135).

Both men seem perfectly content in their domestic situations, although the reader may discern some deficiencies in these marriages when compared with those of the major characters. After observing their situation for two weeks, Elizabeth is forced to acknowledge to Mr Darcy that the Collinses are happier than she expected them to be (PP 178). Mr Elton has also managed a match that contents him. Shortly after Mrs Elton is introduced in all her vulgarity, we are told that "there was no reason to suppose Mr Elton thought at all differently from his wife. He seemed not merely happy with her, but proud. He had the air of congratulating himself on having brought such a woman to Highbury" (E 281). The reader realizes, with Emma and Mr Knightley, that the Eltons share a pettiness that allows them to be happily spiteful (or spitefully happy) together, although we also recognize that they will never be as truly happy as the Knightleys.

Charlotte Lucas is probably the most infamous Austen character, in terms of marriage, because she so bluntly states her pragmatic motivations for marrying the loathsome Mr Collins; she is practically the poster child for the marriage of convenience. We know her to be an exceptionally sensible person until she suddenly accepts his proposal, but cannot deny that she defends herself in a characteristically sensible manner: "I ask only a comfortable home; and considering Mr Collins's character, connections, and situation in life, I am convinced that my chance of happiness with him is as fair, as most people can boast on entering the marriage state" (PP 125). Charlotte recognizes Mr Collins as her last chance to avoid spinsterhood and perpetual dependence and therefore willingly enters into a connection with a man whom she can never truly esteem. In this desire for comfort she resembles many other Austen characters who marry strictly for material considerations, but the frankness with which she pursues her goal ensures that we feel no resentment against her, although we also feel no pity for her when reminded, by her "expectation of a young olive-branch" (PP 364), of the somewhat sickening implications of living with Mr Collins.

Lucy Steele, Mr Willoughby, and Mr Wickham, in contrast, all practise wilful and cunning deceit in the pursuit of their agendas. Lucy, two-faced and false with everyone, is especially cruel and taunting to Elinor. The reader feels it is only Lucy's just desserts to end up married to the foppish Robert Ferrars, looking forward to a long life of obsequious grovelling at the feet of his egocentric mother. Willoughby, too, is detestable when, despite all his attentions and expressions of devotion, he instantly gives Marianne up in favour of Miss Grey and her inheritance. Wickham is also extremely changeable: his attentions swing quickly from Elizabeth to Miss King (and her inheritance) and then, eventually, to Lydia. Furthermore, his conduct toward Georgiana Darcy is as unscrupulous as Willoughby's to Marianne. Both men are guilty of the careless seduction of helpless women (Colonel Brandon's young ward Eliza Williams by Willoughby, and Lydia Bennet by Wickham). Thus, both men are abhorrent to the reader and seem to escape too easily by feeling only somewhat unsatisfied in their married lives; neither Wickham nor Willoughby suffers as much as they ought to for their crimes. Although they are not blissfully happy, they are content enough. As illustrated by the case of Maria Bertram, however, women do not fare so well when they commit similar transgressions.

Maria Bertram commits the only error, besides marrying for love without money, that can cause absolute misery in a marriage—namely, marrying one man whom she dislikes while she is in love with another. Despite her preference for Henry Crawford, she marries Mr Rushworth; her marriage inevitably ends in disaster and divorce when she can bear her husband no longer and runs away with Crawford. Austen tells us that, although Rushworth is also to blame for the failed marriage, as he "had been very much aware" (MP 464) that Maria loved another, Maria's punishment will be far more severe than her husband's: "*He* was released from the engagement to be mortified and unhappy…while *she* must withdraw with infinitely stronger feelings to a retirement and reproach, which could allow no second spring of hope or character" (MP 464). Maria's fate brings to mind the advice that Austen offered her niece Fanny Knight in a letter of 1814, when Fanny was struggling with a decision about a marriage proposal. Austen's own words leave little doubt about her feelings on the matter: "Nothing can be compared to the misery of being bound *without* Love, bound to one, & preferring another" (*Letters* 286).

Maria also illustrates the catastrophic consequences faced by women who fell prey to seduction in Austen's world. Sex outside marriage, as evident in the cases of Maria, Lydia Bennet, and Colonel Brandon's Eliza, leads to the ostracism and downfall of female offenders, although male offenders do not suffer such harsh penalties, as proven by Willoughby, Wickham, and Crawford. Lydia is fortunate enough to be rescued by Mr Darcy, but Maria and Eliza are beyond all help after they "fall." Even Maria's own father rejects her: Sir Thomas disowns and banishes her to live alone except for the company of Mrs Norris, which is, of course, punishment in itself. Eliza is fatally lost: she literally dies after falling into vice, while Maria suffers only a figurative, social death. Eliza, too, married a man she did not care for while in love with another, but her situation is altogether more pitiable than Maria's because she was forced into her unhappy marriage, whereas Maria chooses her fate with open eyes.

Seduction was not the only danger women could avoid by marrying. Spinsterhood, embodied in the person of Miss Bates, threatened women with economic dependence. Miss Bates, though boring, is a harmless old lady, not an unpleasant character. She serves as a reminder of the precarious position of single women in Austen's society because, having no male relatives to provide for her, she is sunk into poverty. This is a harsh economic reality that nearly all the female characters—the heroines as well as the minor characters like Jane Fairfax, who would be forced to work as a governess if she did not marry Frank Churchill—hold in common.

If we look beyond her characters to Austen's own life, we find further evidence of her feelings about matrimony. The events of 2 December 1802 immediately spring to mind. Harris Bigg-Wither, a friend of the family, asked Jane to marry him, and she accepted, only to change her mind by the following morning and withdraw her acceptance. Many years later, her niece Caroline speculated that "the advantages he could offer, & her gratitude for his love, & her long friendship with his family, induced my Aunt to decide that she would marry him *when* he should ask her—but that having accepted him she found she was miserable & that the place & fortune which would certainly be *his*, could not alter the *man*" (qtd. in Le Faye, Austen-Leigh, and Austen-Leigh 121–22). Combined with her advice to Fanny Knight, this refusal seems to clearly indicate that Jane Austen disdained to marry where she did not love.

Those of us who love Jane Austen prefer to interpret this incident as an indication of the moral integrity she shared with her heroines, which prevented her from marrying solely for the purpose of material security. We believe that she modelled her protagonists after herself and her own opinion that true happiness in marriage can only be obtained if there is love, or, in the case of Marianne Dashwood, at least "strong esteem and lively friendship," between spouses (ss 378). However, even if Austen chose not to marry for security, she never forgot about those who did when realistically representing human nature in her writing.

Thus, the couples that are lucky enough to find exquisite happiness in marriage, such as Elinor and Edward, Marianne and Colonel Brandon, the Gardiners, Jane and Bingley, Elizabeth and Darcy, Fanny and Edmund, and Emma and Knightley, are only the fortunate few in terms of Jane Austen's total inventory of characters. Whether because she modelled her protagonists on her own beliefs about marriage, or because she understood her audience's desire for happily-ever-after endings, Austen decided to focus her novels on these few. However, she knew from her own experience that, in the real world, perfect marriages such as these are not possible for everyone, and so her minor characters illustrate a range of other marriage types and possibilities. Austen's novels illustrate that marriage is as complex and varied a topic as human nature itself.

NOTE

1. All quotations from Jane Austen's published works are taken from *The Oxford Illustrated Jane Austen*, 3rd ed., ed. R.W. Chapman (Oxford: Oxford UP, 1988) and from *Jane Austen's Letters*, 3rd ed., ed. Deirdre Le Faye (Oxford: Oxford UP, 1995), and are documented by short title and page number in the body of the chapter.

WORKS CITED

Brown, Julia Prewitt. *Jane Austen's Novels: Social Change and Literary Form*. Cambridge: Harvard UP, 1979.

Doody, Margaret Anne. Introduction. *Catharine and Other Writings*. By Jane Austen. Oxford: Oxford UP, 1998. ix–xxxviii.

Le Faye, Deirdre, William Austen-Leigh, and Richard Austen-Leigh. *Jane Austen: A Family Record*. New York: Simon / British Library, 1989.

Mansfield Park. Dir. Patricia Rozema. Miramax. 1999.

McMaster, Juliet. *Jane Austen on Love*. Victoria, BC: U of Victoria P, 1978.

29 Classifying the Husbands

JULIET MCMASTER

Dear Bruce — wherever you are, since you left us so suddenly —

Remember the radio interview we did with CBC?

"So what's so great about Jane Austen?" asked the announcer, in his "answer-in-five-words-or-less" voice.

"She wrote intelligent love stories," you answered promptly.

My answer was longer and much less pointed. We were glad of the interview, because we needed the publicity: we were launching the Edmonton Chapter of the Jane Austen Society of North America, preparatory to hosting JASNA's annual conference at Lake Louise: and the chapter happened, and swung into action alongside us in co-convening that grand occasion, which brought some 600 Janeites to Alberta.

So it was appropriate that the Edmonton group we founded, which still flourishes (though we lost you as our Mr Knightley), chose "Marriages and Weddings" as the theme for its 2007 gala. We wanted to explore those intelligent love stories.

This is the paper I gave there, and I scripted it for a present and sympathetic audience of friends. Wish you'd been there. Wish I could have heard you speak as the expert. At least you'd have been pleased that your student Amy Stafford delivered a paper there that you had given her an A for in your class on Jane Austen. It gave us a sad but satisfactory sense of your hovering around as a tutelary spirit.

Yours — missing you — Juliet

JANE AUSTEN CLEARLY THOUGHT long and hard about marriage, and not only during that sleepless night between accepting Harris Bigg-Wither's proposal in the evening and rejecting him the next morning. Single all her life, she looked at those doubles around her, both in her life and her fiction, and wondered at the strange composite being that results from the surprising conjunction of individuals. Plato humorously proposed that male and female were originally one body, a creature with two heads, two trunks, four arms, and four legs—fairly bristling with supernumerary limbs! Austen's wonder at the astonishing nature of some of the couples she saw—and invented—was hardly less: "Mrs Hall of Sherbourne [she famously wrote to Cassandra] was brought to bed yesterday of a dead child...oweing to a fright. I suppose she happened unawares to look at her husband" (*Letters* 17).[1] How could those two have gotten together? Or, to turn to her fiction: "Mrs Allen was one of that numerous class of females, whose society can raise no other emotion than surprise at there being any men in the world who could like them well enough to marry them" (*Northanger Abbey* [NA] 20). With the sexes reversed, one might say the same of, say, John Thorpe or Robert Ferrars.

However, given the fact that society—and novels—are so arranged that most men and women must and do marry, what are the rules by which they come together? The rules include the matter of suitability of fortune, class, and family, of course. Shared principles and shared interests are important too: but what about *personality*?

I'll pause over that term: what does it mean? Johnson defines it, not very helpfully, as "the existence or individuality of anyone"; but I'm using it in the modern sense, the *Shorter Oxford Dictionary*'s third definition, "Distinctive individual character, especially when of a marked kind," current from 1795. Austen herself doesn't use the term, but her use of "disposition" and "temper" come close to our understanding of personality. The Middletons of *Sense and Sensibility*, we hear, are "dissimilar in temper and outward behaviour" (32). The matter of "outward behaviour" is relevant, because "personality," however created in an individual psyche, has much to do with the way the individual is perceived by

surrounding people—as genial or surly, outspoken or reticent, asser-
tive or "creepmouse" (*Mansfield Park* [MP] 145).

In the matter of personality so understood, then, should you, in
choosing a spouse, be looking for your soulmate and double, the *matching*
personality—someone of the opposite sex who is as like yourself as
possible? Or should you look for your contrast and complement, someone
who will make up for your deficiencies and benefit from your strengths,
so that that new composite creature, the Couple, will be well balanced
and happy? Should like marry like, to create a doubling effect, or should
contrast prevail? This was a question that clearly fascinated Austen,
especially in *Sense and Sensibility*, and she answers it in various ways.

In *Sense and Sensibility*, the antithesis of the title carries on into the
relation between many pairs of characters. As Elinor and Marianne are
contrasting sisters, so are Anne and Lucy Steele—one all babbling impru-
dence, one sharply calculating; and so are Lady Middleton and her sister
Mrs Palmer: "Mrs Palmer was several years younger than Lady Middleton,
and totally unlike her in every respect" (*Sense and Sensibility* [SS] 106).
One is all elegant reserve, one all gushing smiles. The same goes for the
married couples. The Middletons are completely "dissimilar in temper
and outward behaviour": Sir John is gregarious, and never happy but
with a houseful of neighbours and young people; Lady Middleton is
elegant, taciturn, and tolerant only of those who will dote as she does
on her awful children. Their choice of activities likewise contrasts: "He
hunted and shot, and she humoured her children" (32).

What of the matches that are made in the course of the novel, the
ones that are not already *faits accomplis*? Marianne and Willoughby are
soulmates, almost twins: "They speedily discovered that their enjoyment of dancing and music was mutual, and that it arose from a general
conformity of judgement in all that related to either....Their taste was
strikingly alike. The same books, the same passages were idolized by
each" (SS 47).

They share not only interests but also their eager and outgoing personalities. This is not, however, a marriage made in heaven. Marianne
has to learn that a soulmate doesn't always make the right marriage

partner. She settles for a contrast, not a double: not Willoughby, the eager extrovert like herself, but Colonel Brandon: older, dourer, reticent—and trustworthy.

Are there spouses in *Sense and Sensibility* who are doubles rather than contrasts? Yes: for instance, the Dashwoods. We are told that John Dashwood, who could have been improved by a contrasting wife, is actually confirmed in his worst habits of mind by the woman he does marry, because she is just like him, only worse: "He was not an ill-disposed young man, unless to be rather cold hearted, and rather selfish, is to be ill-disposed....Had he married a more amiable woman, he might... even have been made amiable himself....But Mrs John Dashwood was a strong caricature of himself:—more narrow-minded and selfish" (*ss* 5). If you weren't very nice to begin with, the doubling effect of like marrying like makes you doubly unpleasant.

The only successful matching of like to like in *Sense and Sensibility* is that of Elinor to Edward. Both are sensible, reticent, self-controlled—perhaps *too* self-controlled! We are permitted to believe that their niceness will be doubled, just as the Dashwoods' nastiness is.

The consideration of contrast and mirror image is followed through in the later novels, too, though the patterns are less clear and schematic than in *Sense and Sensibility*. The marriage of the pretty, gabby, thoughtless Mrs Bennet to the withdrawn and cerebral Mr Bennet is hardly a success. However, the marriage of the vivacious Elizabeth to the serious and taciturn Darcy seems to be a match designed to "teach the admiring multitude what connubial felicity really was" (as Elizabeth reflects wryly), for each is to be the other's appropriate complement:

[Elizabeth] began now to comprehend that he was exactly the man, who, in disposition and talents, would most suit her. His understanding and temper, though unlike her own, would have answered all her wishes. It was an union that must have been to the advantage of both; by her ease and liveliness, his mind might have been softened, his manners improved, and from his judgement, information, and knowledge of the world, she must have received benefit of greater importance. (*Pride and Prejudice* [*PP*] 312)

The other courtship and marriage, of Bingley and Jane, is an example of the best kind of matching of like to like, though Mr Bennet perhaps overstates the case a little: "Your tempers are by no means unlike. You are each of you so complying, that nothing will ever be resolved on; so easy, that every servant will cheat you; and so generous, that you will always exceed your income" (348). There we have it again: niceness doubled.

In the later novels, Edmund and Fanny are like Jane and Bingley, a marriage of like to like. Both are quiet, serious, moral in their actions and judgements. Edmund was initially attracted to his opposite, however, the vivacious and lax-moralled Mary Crawford. His moral journey is the opposite of Marianne's: she had to learn to renounce the dangerous affinity of Willoughby and embrace the sterling moral qualities of Colonel Brandon; Edmund has to learn to resist the dangerous difference of Mary Crawford and to recognize Fanny, his eager disciple, as his true and appropriate partner.

Emma and Mr Knightley are contrasts: she hot-headed, scheming, loquacious; he circumspect, highly principled, observant. She needs his moral probity; he is attracted to her vivacity and eagerness. Like Marianne, Emma is for a while attracted to her male twin, Frank Churchill. In *Emma*, a different possible coupling is briefly suggested, of two matching pairs: the quiet ones, Mr Knightley and Jane, both thoughtful and intelligent; and the lively, scheming, talkative ones, Emma and Frank. However, Mr Knightley, pressed on whether he might marry her, responds thoughtfully, "Not even Jane Fairfax is perfect. She has a fault. She has not the open temper which a man would wish for in a wife" (*Emma* [*E*] 288). (For "a man" read "*this* man.") Frank, too, subscribes to the principle of contrast, and loves his other, Jane Fairfax, for all her reserve; and she — surprisingly, perhaps — loves *her* other too, the ebullient and not-altogether-trustworthy Frank.

The marriage of like to like in this novel is the Eltons,' and they are like the John Dashwoods, each doubling the other's worst qualities. At Mr Elton's meanest moment, when he is pointedly snubbing Harriet on the dance floor, Mrs Elton is "even encouraging him by significant glances" (E 327) — like Mrs Dashwood helping to reduce her husband's donation to his needy sisters from £3,000 to zero.

Anne Elliot and Wentworth, again, are contrasts in personality, rather than soulmates: she thoughtful, patient, constant, long-suffering; he eager, impulsive, resentful. In a reaction from her early rejection, he courts her contrast, the strong-willed, unthinking Louisa Musgrove. Anne has other potential love interests as well, in the bereaved and grieving Captain Benwick and the quietly calculating William Elliot. Rather than matching with their doubles, however, Anne and Wentworth gravitate back to each other, responding to the stronger attraction of opposites.

Why this contrast? There are aesthetic reasons, of course. Henry Fielding laid it down in *Tom Jones* that the "principle of contrast" pertains in all great works of art. There's the attraction of the unexpected: we delight that Beatrice should marry Benedick, whom she has singled out for mockery, and that Elizabeth should marry Darcy, the man she loves to hate. A thousand Harlequin romances follow the formula of the dark-browed, steamy, surly hunk who at last reveals that he has been head-over-heels in love with the blond and vivacious heroine from square one. There is increased potential for drama, as dark and fair, light and heavy, vivacious and saturnine, move through conflict to reconciliation.

Lest the unexpected should occur so regularly as to become expected after all, however, Austen does vary the pattern. Of the marriages among the principals, the quiet ones, Elinor and Edward, and Fanny and Edmund, are the only couples to exemplify the fortunate marriage of like to like. Perhaps it's not surprising that for these same two couples there is no dramatized proposal scene. All the other principals, with the possible exception of Catherine Morland and Tilney (and the issue doesn't seem important in *Northanger Abbey*), present the marriage of contrasting personalities—where, of course, there is more potential for conflict and drama.

While I am dealing with recurring patterns in the courtship and marriage plots, I'll mention a couple of others. Of the dramatized scenes—that is, where we have dialogue, and specified time and place—all the unsuccessful proposals take place indoors. Think about it: John Thorpe, Mr Collins, Darcy the first time, and Henry Crawford all propose indoors, and in vain. Mr Elton and Emma are out on a snowy night—you might call it outdoors—but they're packed together claustrophobically in a carriage, with no chance of getting away from each other: "In this state of swelling resentment, and mutually deep mortification, they had to continue together a few minutes longer" (E 132). It's about as close as Austen ever comes to a depiction of hell! Even Frank Churchill's almost-confession, which Emma believes is an almost-proposal and is resolved to refuse, happens indoors. We can be sure that Mr Rushworth proposed to Maria Bertram indoors; and she made the mistake of accepting him. "I cannot get out," she quotes Sterne's caged starling, as she frets before the locked gate at Sotherton (MP 99).

All the *successful* proposals happen outdoors, in the fresh air and amidst natural scenery. Henry Tilney and Darcy (the second time) propose on a walk; Mr Knightley and Emma are strolling in the shrubbery at Hartfield, where she has been appreciating "the exquisite sight, smell, sensation of nature, tranquil, warm, and brilliant after a storm" (E 424). Anne and Wentworth, when they finally pledge their love, are walking—appropriately enough—in Union Street in Bath.

Why should Austen be so consistent to this pattern? It is part of her unobtrusive use of symbolism. The confinement of the carriage when Mr Elton proposes suggests a constriction that is all too like a bad and inescapable marriage. When Mr Collins formally requests a private interview with her, Elizabeth tries to leave the room: "Upon Elizabeth's seeming really, with vexed and embarrassed looks, about to escape, [her mother] added, 'Lizzy, I *insist* upon your staying and hearing Mr Collins'" (PP 104). Her attempt to "escape" suggests a kind of imprisonment. Similarly, Fanny is almost frantic to escape Henry Crawford's importunate advances in the breakfast room, twice drawing back her hand from his grasp, and "twice attempt[ing] in vain to turn away from him" (*MP* 301). Hearing Sir Thomas approaching, "she rushed out at an opposite door" (302). Again, escape is necessary. The proposal, in fact, is a kind of rehearsal for the marriage itself; and the heroine's sense of entrapment, especially since these sanguine suitors won't take *No* for an answer, suggests something like a rape.

The outdoor proposals, in contrast, with their fresh and spacious settings, present an unconstrained and mutual coming together that is likely to be propitious for both partners. In the cases of both Elizabeth and Emma, the woman has as much to do with initiating the actual proposal as the man. Mistaking his feelings, Emma has silenced Mr Knightley at a crucial moment:

> They had reached the house. *[Don't go inside, Emma, whatever you do!]*
>
> "You are going in, I suppose," said he. *[That would put an end to his hopes, of course.]*
>
> "No"—replied Emma—quite confirmed by the depressed manner in which he still spoke. "I should like to take another turn....I stopped you ungraciously just now, Mr Knightley."
> (*E* 429)

"Another turn" round the shrubbery does the business, just as "going in" would have put an end to it. Similarly, on that walk from Longbourn, Elizabeth gives Darcy the crucial prompting that precipitates his renewed proposal; after which "they walked on, without knowing in which direction" (*PP* 366). No mothers or uncles breathing down their necks, no drawing-room decorum to worry about, no trap, no need to escape: "They wandered about, till she was beyond her own knowledge" (372).

Having explored the rule by which most heroines (but not all) marry a contrasting personality, and the rule about necessarily outdoor proposals, I offer a further consistent rule in Austen's fiction: among her potential suitors, the heroine marries the first that she meets. For all

Austen's mockery of "first impressions" and the convention of love at first sight, that chap the heroine has encountered *first* is the one who eventually gets her. Catherine meets Tilney before Thorpe; Elizabeth is attracted to Wickham, but she met Darcy first. Fanny is courted by Henry Crawford, but she met Edmund first. Emma is attracted by Frank Churchill, but Mr Knightley was there all along. Anne is courted by William Elliot (never outdoors, mind you!), but she is constant to Wentworth, her first love. Even Marianne, who falls for Willoughby more or less at first sight, actually marries Brandon, who came first into her life.

There's one more way of categorizing the husbands. For all the minute differentiations of their individual characteristics, the men the heroines marry, I have noticed, fall into one of three categories: the brother-husband, the father-husband, and the lover-husband.

"Brother-husband?" He is the friendly, supportive man that the heroine has come to know over time, and in a domestic context. He's helpful rather than daunting. In the other pattern of marriage of like to like or of contrasting personalities, he is apt to be *like* the heroine rather than her contrast and complement. She sees him in his literal brotherly relation to his siblings — as Catherine sees Henry Tilney at Northanger Abbey, in his intimate joking with Eleanor, and sympathizes with them in their visible nervousness before their father. So Elinor Dashwood comes to know Edward Ferrars as the brother of her sister-in-law, and Fanny Price is brought up as a cousin-cum-sister alongside Edmund. Moreover, the names we know them by signal this intimate and friendly relation. We know them by first-and-last name, as *Henry* Tilney, *Edward* Ferrars, *Edmund* Bertram.

The father-husband comes with title-and-last-name: *Colonel* Brandon, *Mr* Darcy, *Mr* Knightley. Emma is offended when Mrs Elton refers to "Knightley," *tout court*, and herself declares, "I never can call you any thing but 'Mr Knightley'" (E 463). The father-husband has a certain somewhat daunting authority. (Even Bingley says of his intimate friend, "I declare I do not know a more aweful object than Darcy, on particular occasions" [PP 50].) The heroine looks up to him: he is her superior in age and experience, like Colonel Brandon, or in class and influence, like Mr Darcy, or in moral probity, like Mr Knightley.

What of the lover-husband? One would expect him to be the most romantic prospect for the heroine and for the reader; but in fact his appeal, which is physical and initially strong, is usually revealed to be spurious. Only one of the heroines, Anne Elliot (who is likewise the most romantic in spite of being the oldest) is allowed to marry the lover-husband and be happy with him. What is he called? He usually comes as "last-name-only"; and it helps—as it happens—if that last name begins with a W. He is Willoughby, Wickham, Wentworth. (William Walter Elliot has some of the characteristics of this category too, but the nomenclature doesn't mark him out.)

Mrs Dashwood and her daughters regularly call Marianne's love interest "Willoughby," though they employ the full formal title for all the other males they meet in Devon. ("Edward" is a different matter—he is seen as a family member, of the younger generation, and so gets called by his first name.) Usually last-name-only is the way men refer to and address each other: Edmund talks of "Crawford," Mr Knightley of "Elton"; and "Wickham" is so referred to by his brother officers in the militia. Mrs Bennet (who calls her own husband "Mr Bennet") also addresses him as "Wickham," and so does Lydia. The last-name-only, when used by women, signals a particular kind of intimacy, but one that is different from the more familial application of the first name.

In talking of brother-husbands and father-husbands, I am invoking an analogy only and not suggesting any incestuous implication. Austen uses these names and associations only as rough characterizations of a *kind* of relation. Catherine and Henry, Elinor and Edward, and Fanny and Edmund are to love each other as husband and wife, but their relation partakes in the familial. It is less characterized by awe and surprise than the matches of other principals. The man who is your friend's brother is demystified, congenial, equal. Henry teases Catherine; Edmund makes sure Fanny has a horse to ride.

The man the heroine thinks of as "Mr," though, is more authoritative, someone to be looked up to. Darcy's "judgement, information, and knowledge of the world," which Elizabeth recognizes as what she needs

(PP 312), are the qualities one hopes to find in a father. Emma once thinks of marrying a lover-husband, the stranger who erupts into the familial community of Highbury from the outside; but "Frank Churchill" is really the potential brother-husband, the stepson of her surrogate mother; and besides the fact that his affections are otherwise engaged, Emma is the kind of heroine who needs a father-husband. Frank Churchill can eventually become indeed something like a real brother to her.

Brothers and fathers are known quantities, and have been subject to that wearing down of rough edges that happens in the give-and-take of family life. The brother is "one of us"; and so is the father. The lover, though, is the outsider, the mystery man, who brings with him unknown connections and antecedents. He is a risk, and perhaps the more attractive for being so. Austen doesn't go for Casanovas, however, and the trouble with lover-husbands is that making love tends to be habit-forming. No heroine wants to think of herself as part of a series; nor do we readers care to see her that way. Two loves are permissible to some men: Colonel Brandon is allowed his first passionate love without being considered burnt out (unless by the young and unreformed Marianne); and Edward Ferrars is lured into an imprudent early engagement, and is allowed to learn the error of his ways, as is Edmund. *Three* loves exceed the mark, however. Willoughby has been a lover to Eliza (and who knows how many others?) before Marianne, and then moves on to Miss Grey. Wickham dangles after Georgiana Darcy, then Elizabeth, then Miss King, and finally Lydia. William Walter Elliot flirts with his cousin Elizabeth, marries a rich wife and buries her, courts Anne, and shacks up with Mrs Clay. These are not the material for heroes. Captain Wentworth (and I have to admit that "Captain" does often come before his name) is also a man with a past: and the redeeming feature that makes him a viable husband, as Willoughby and Wickham are not, is the fact that his "past" is also his future: Anne Elliot.

Austen chooses to differentiate the *kinds* of marital relation that her heroines enter into, and also to signal the differences by the labels she attaches to the suitor. It is one more element in the rich artistic patterning that makes her six novels with their seven marriage plots endlessly comparable and endlessly different.

Now that the recurring patterns in Austen's marriage plots are established, perhaps those of us with husbands or wives should analyze our *own* marriages. Did you marry your double, or your contrast and complement? Was the proposal delivered outdoors or in? Is your spouse a brother-husband, a father-husband, or a lover-husband? Does his or her name perchance begin with a W? Better still, now you have my useful analysis of the courtship patterns in Austen's novels, you are equipped to write an Austen novel of your own!

AUTHOR'S NOTE

A short version of the last part of this paper appeared in *Re-Drawing Austen: Picturesque Travels in Austenland*, edited by Beatrice Battaglia and Diego Saglia (Napoli: Liguore Editore, 2004), 437–40.

NOTE

1. All quotations from Jane Austen's published works are taken from *The Oxford Illustrated Jane Austen*, 3rd ed., ed. R.W. Chapman (Oxford: Oxford UP, 1988) and from *Jane Austen's Letters*, 3rd ed., ed. Deirdre Le Faye (Oxford: Oxford UP, 1995), and are documented by short title and page number in the body of the chapter.

WORK CITED

Shorter Oxford English Dictionary. 2 vols. Reprinted with corrections. Oxford: Clarendon Press, 1959.

30 "Our Miss Austen"

Women Writers Reading Jane Austen through Two Centuries

ISOBEL GRUNDY

THE TITLE IS A KIND OF PUN OR JOKE. Reading through two centuries, *for* two centuries? Imagine a writer who just pulled a book off the shelf because she wanted to reread some scene—perhaps Elizabeth Bennet standing up to Lady Catherine de Bourgh, or Anne Elliot confiding in Captain Harville—and once she'd started reading she couldn't stop...!

The reading here is not a marathon, but a relay race. Ever since she got into print, Jane Austen has *deeply* interested her fellow writers, and especially women writers. The material for this essay comes out of *Orlando: Women's Writing in the British Isles from the Beginnings to the Present*, published by Cambridge University Press Online in 2006. This is fitting because I was working with many others on this project for almost the entire period of my friendship with Bruce Stovel. The subject is fitting in another way, too. Before the Orlando Project began, Bruce and I team-taught a graduate course on women novelists of the eighteenth century: pre-Austen novelists. In a way, this essay continues a story begun in that course.

In fact, however, the essay will begin with more recent years and move backwards in time to treat Austen's early reception in rather more detail. We have, most recently, entered a period not only of Austen canonized, but of Austen almost beatified. Novels in dialogue with her go back at least as far as E.M. Delafield's *The Optimist* (1922), which reworks *Mansfield Park*, and reach forward to the likes of *Bridget Jones's Diary*. Today we are almost drowning in sequels to her works, by Joan Aiken and Emma Tennant and myriad others, and in spinoffs like *The Jane Austen Book Club*, not to mention TV and movie versions, including the wonderfully cross-cultural *Clueless* and *Bride and Prejudice*. (The gap between refilmings of each novel is steadily decreasing.) As we look back, we see the period of canonization, the period preceding canonization, and the period during which Austen was little known.

Scholarly work on her by creative writers is now in full flower, but it began almost as soon as the little-known period was over. Sarah Tytler published a biography in 1880 and Anne Thackeray Ritchie put Austen in *A Book of Sybils* three years later. Sarah Woolsey, author of *What Katy Did*, edited a selection of her letters in 1892. Any number of novelists have written introductions to her books, both during and before the recent boom: Rebecca West, Margaret Drabble, Penelope Fitzgerald, and many more. Sylvia Townsend Warner published a book about her. G.B. Stern and Sheila Kaye-Smith published two collaborative books about her in the form of critical dialogues, bouncing ideas off each other. The Irish writer Mary Lavin did an MA thesis on her, and later said that Austen's principles had shaped her own writing. The detective novelist P.D. James has lectured about *Emma*—*Emma* as a detective story! Carol Shields published a life of Austen. Fay Weldon and Deborah Moggach have each written a film script for *Pride and Prejudice*.[1]

Austen's admirers are free to love her without feeling in awe of her: they cheerfully take liberties with her, just as she took liberties with her own predecessors. She is now the common on which they graze. Margaret Drabble, tongue-in-cheek, calls the denouement of her own *The Realms of Gold* a "Jane Austen ending" because her archaeologist heroine decides to go back to her long-term lover (Stovel 74).

Comments about Austen in our own and the recent century occasionally sound like the comments that Henry Crawford and Edmund Bertram make in *Mansfield Park* about Shakespeare. Henry says he's part of every Englishman's birthright, like a kind of family heirloom— for someone belonging to the right nation, gender, and class, it isn't necessary actually to *read* him because he's in the cultural air and can be absorbed through the pores. Admiration for Austen has reached a stage not unlike that, and undoubtedly she has been praised by some who have not read her, if only by, for instance, dignitaries opening conferences.

One writer who thinks it "probable that [Austen] is the greatest of all novelists," Brigid Brophy, nevertheless despises Austen's common admirers or cult followers, whose worship she sees as both condescending and demeaning (107). This modern novelist seems to feel that Austen's ordinary readers are not good enough for her, as if Austen could be appreciated exclusively by the writers among her posterity. Though I don't agree with Brophy, I do feel that writers' comments on Austen have a special value for us, the ordinary readers. The writers making those comments include some men, including such disparate figures as Rudyard Kipling and W.H. Auden, but very many more women. During the last several generations, women writers have presented a pretty much united front on this topic, and retaliation has lain in wait for anyone stepping out of line. The Victorian poet Alice Meynell, in her weekly column "The Wares of Autolycus" (specifically directed at women) concurred with Charlotte Brontë's disparaging opinion of Austen, and added that Austen was a "frump" (qtd. in Tuell 192). A generation later, Virginia Woolf, in an article on Meynell, reported her "frump" comment and added that Meynell herself was a MULE (which she spelled in capital letters for emphasis) to say such a thing (Woolf, *Letters* 2:503). It's a safe bet that more people have read Meynell's comment as quoted in Woolf's article than in its original place, and that most of those will have sided with Woolf, and thought better of her for springing to the defence of Austen.

What would critics do without Austen? I've lost track of the novelists whose critics or reviewers, casting around for a supreme compliment, liken their subject's works to those of Jane Austen. It perhaps began with James Edward Austen-Leigh naming Charlotte Yonge as his aunt's successor. More recently named have been Mary Lavin, Ivy Compton-Burnett (who both certainly admired her), and Barbara Pym (surprising perhaps, when readers have objected to Pym's non-romantic endings—apparently not everyone feels with Margaret Drabble that a happy ending is such a defining feature of Austen!). A very recent recipient of the heir-of-Austen award was Penelope Fitzgerald in her obituaries.[2] I love Fitzgerald's novels, but I don't think they quite deserve that accolade.

Presumably, those who make the comparison intend to do honour to Austen as well as to her successor. Presumably sequels also set out to pay tribute; but the reviewer and the sequel writer, too, are also trying for a tiny share in Austen's cultural capital, hitching their wagons to her star. For a novelist to catch any reflected light from Austen is not easy, but Margaret Drabble did it when she spoke at the annual Jane Austen Society of North America conference at Lake Louise, Alberta, in 1993. She wrote, not a sequel, but a kind of daughter of *Persuasion*. In her story, "The Dower House at Kellynch: A Somerset Romance," we are in the twentieth century, and Austen's characters are long forgotten, but Austen's places are still there. The dower house once occupied by Anne Elliot's friend Lady Russell is now an immensely covetable architectural gem from the eighteenth century. This particular Drabble heroine does not fall in love with a man: she falls in love with the house. Since it is hanging in the balance between different owners, different occupants, she makes up her mind to marry whichever man gets the house! Drabble has both enriched her story with memories of Austen and offered a potential enrichment, not a distraction, to readers of *Persuasion*.[3] This kind of improvising on Austen has surely something in common with the art of the blues.

Other successful tributes of an improvised, blues-like kind consist of a single detail in a novelistic panorama. Some of the most pleasing are offered with a pinch of Austen's own irony: celebrating her subtlety by creating characters who don't get her, in fact, by creating unworthy fans—only, unlike the fans whom Brigid Brophy finds unworthy, these characters are generally full of intellectual pretension. In Virginia Woolf's very first novel, *The Voyage Out*, a character called Clarissa Dalloway (who has not yet grown into the character of that name in Woolf's later *Mrs Dalloway*) gushes about how she adores Austen and never travels without her. This Clarissa is a snob and a social butterfly; she has no real interest in books, and not an ounce of irony in her. Having expatiated on her adoration, she says she's brought *Persuasion* to read on this voyage because it's "perhaps less threadbare" than the other novels! In other words, her religion of adoring Austen is an affectation, a fake (Woolf, *Voyage* 62–67).

Molly Keane pays similarly ironical tribute to Austen in *Time after Time*. This is a novel about aged siblings who share, perforce, since they cannot afford to live elsewhere, a crumbling great house in Ireland: each one is greedy, selfish, and at daggers drawn with the others. April, the only one ever to have been married (not happily), reads *Mansfield Park* in bed, but her Austen habit is "less for pleasure than as a counteraction to those French books...which Barry liked her to study before he tried to follow out their instructions and illustrations in bed" (Keane 47). April evidently doesn't like sex, but she does like (or wish for) material comforts. She thinks Fanny Price was an idiot to refuse Henry Crawford, whom she apparently finds pleasingly unlike her own late unlamented husband. April condemns herself out of her own mouth, and she does so with comic incongruity.

Fay Weldon's *Letters to Alice: On First Reading Jane Austen* (published the next year, 1984) make another complex and ironical response. They purport to be written by a novelist, Aunt Fay, to her niece at college, who has met Austen on the syllabus and doesn't like her. Weldon issued this book four years after doing her Austen TV screenplay, and as an alternative to writing the critical book on Austen that she planned but never published. In a way, this book does offer comment: on Austen's writings, on the Romantic-era context, and on the art of novel writing. Its irony lies in the fact that at the end the niece — not the aunt — achieves success as a popular, romantic novelist. It's as if Weldon is confessing that she herself is *not* Austen's heir — and suggesting that the true heir is not the literary critic but the popular romance writer.[4]

One more recent, apparent Austen allusion is baffling. If it's a tribute it's a very odd one. A.S. Byatt's novel *The Biographer's Tale* has been called "an addict's book about the dangers of literary addiction" (Lee 18). In it we meet a Victorian explorer gone native, "who lived amongst a crew of drug-dealers and slave-traders, dressed in a leopardskin, with a shaven head and Moslem tuft"—and he is called "the wild Mansfield Parkyns" (Byatt 61). Mansfield Parkyns is his *name*. Of course, the actual explorer named Mungo Park must have something to do with this, but Jane Austen is surely present, too. Are we to imagine a Victorian Janeite who married a man named Parkyns and christened her son Mansfield in tribute? Or are we to imagine Austen's *Mansfield Park* as the ordered, restrictive environment whose grandsons, perhaps, reacted by going native? Or is this a riposte to Byatt's sister's "Dower House at Kellynch"—a kind of defiant refusal on Byatt's part to pay tribute? It is in any case one of the most puzzling literary allusions I have encountered.

Things were a little different before the days of St Jane, but it's not easy for us to judge just how different. When Elizabeth Bowen voiced her opinion that Austen was infinitely preferable to the over-intellectual George Eliot, she surely felt she was challenging the received view in a way that she would not have felt later. When Kathleen Innes, a suffragist and the prime mover of the Women's International League for Peace and Freedom, expressed her pride at counting herself a Hampshire woman like Austen, did she take pleasure in belonging to a small, select band of Austen appreciators—and how did that feel?[5]

It's even harder to assess the climate of literary opinion two centuries back, in the days of Austen's contemporaries or near-contemporaries. (I would say that Austen was little known during her lifetime—despite the generous praise of Sir Walter Scott—and remained so until well after Maria Jane Jewsbury's appreciation in 1831.) I daresay we all know already the regrettable case of Charlotte Brontë. Brontë wrote, "She does her business of delineating the surface of the lives of genteel English people curiously well....but what throbs fast and full, though hidden, what the blood rushes through, what is the unseen seat of Life and the sentient target of Death—; *this* Miss Austen ignores" (128). This is perhaps the Romantic viewpoint, because Mary Shelley is somewhat similar. She voiced discriminating admiration for Austen's "humour... vividness and correctness," but still could not forget that Harriet Martineau had "higher philosophical views" (qtd. in Crook 424n29).

Others were more perceptive. I've found no comments on Austen from Frances Burney, the most admired of her immediate predecessors (who of course outlived her younger admirer by several decades); but Frances's younger sister, Sarah Harriet Burney (also a novelist, and a good one), admired the "careless originality" of *Pride and Prejudice* ("my prime favorite of all modern Novels") and then went on to feel "glee" in reading *Emma* (201). (I'd love to be able to ask Sarah Harriet after she finished *Emma*: "Is *Pride and Prejudice* still your favourite?") Imagine living early enough to be making up your mind about Jane Austen, with no teachers, no critics, no movies—only your own unaided powers of perception and responsiveness! It's remarkable to me that so many women cottoned on so quickly to her exceptional quality.

Sarah Harriet's language about Austen is generous as well as warm, with no hint of envying the other author's originality or wishing she could give that "glee" to her own readers; yet Sarah Harriet was always inclined to feel envious of the very great literary success of her own elder sister. Born a little more than 20 years before Jane Austen, she had a hard life. She never married; she spent her life caring for her somewhat unappreciative aged father. After his death, she supported herself by governessing and writing novels; but she was an omnivorous and highly discriminating reader, personal in her tastes and without intellectual pretensions.

Some of Austen's earliest admirers, however, were fully paid up (though not professional) intellectuals, successors to the original bluestockings, less outsiders than Burney, who read a lot of non-fiction (history, biography, travel, politics, philosophy) and rather looked down on novels. (Though some moderns condescend to women of an earlier period for lacking formal education, many of them were self-educated to an impressive degree long before English literature was a subject of academic study, and their critical standards, like Austen's own, were very high.) At least two of the earliest to mention Austen in their letters are quite surprised to find a novelist whose work they can really respect.

Both Catherine Hutton (whose name is identified with Birmingham) and Anne Grant (whose name is identified with Laggan in the Highlands of Scotland, though she lived latterly in Edinburgh) first mention Austen's works as an easy read, as diversions from serious study, as trifles, though enjoyable trifles. It's fascinating to watch them gradually revising their opinion as they register her seriousness, even her importance. Catherine Hutton was a friend of Sarah Harriet Burney—I wish I knew which one put the other one on to Jane Austen! She wrote novels herself, in which she incorporated non-fictional material—like the unconnected essay or critique or history that Austen believed, or professed to believe, she needed in *Pride and Prejudice* (though she emphatically did not write the "solemn specious nonsense" that Austen joked about) (Austen, *Letters* 203).[6] Hutton had some reputation. She was one of those invited in 1816 to contribute to an abortive plan for a magazine by and for women, bearing the distinguished names of Anna Letitia Barbauld, Elizabeth Inchbald, Maria Edgeworth, and Elizabeth Hamilton. Catherine Hutton admired the novels of Inchbald, Edgeworth, and Hamilton (and of Henry Fielding and Tobias Smollett), but reckoned Walter Scott the best going. She herself published in various periodicals, but considered the "greatest of her works" her collection of almost 1,500 fashion prints, in eight large folio volumes, with commentary and indexes (Hutton 215). This history of costume, the first in the world, remained unpublished because publishers judged it too expensive to produce, and after her death the collection was dispersed.

Hutton, a socially conscious intellectual, was a gradual Austen convert. She first encountered Austen's writing in summer 1821 and thought of it as frivolous though enjoyable. About a year later, she had read all the novels and developed a serious admiration for the wise personality expressed in them. She went so far as to write, "her character is either something like mine, or what I would wish mine to be" (Hutton 183).

Anne Grant, a Scotswoman of the same age as Burney and Hutton, had a very different life. She spent her childhood in upstate New York, and later wrote a wonderful book about colonial and Mohawk culture called *Memoirs of an American Lady*. Back in Scotland, she married a minister with a parish in the deep Gaelic-speaking Highlands. Her children grew up bilingual—those who grew up at all, because, alas, many of her family succumbed to tuberculosis. By the time her husband died, after 22 years of marriage, four of their twelve children were already dead, and by the time she died herself, at around 80, there was only one son left alive. Meanwhile, as a widow with eight children and no income, Grant had very reluctantly embarked on a career as a professional (and non-fictional) author.

Grant was reading *Mansfield Park* within seven months of its appearance (not bad, considering she was in Edinburgh) and recommending it to Catherine Fanshawe (another underestimated woman writer of the time)—warmly, but strictly as light reading. Austen's impression stayed with her, however. After another five months, she was using *Mansfield Park* as a touchstone to explain what she thought was wrong with other recent novels by Laetitia Matilda Hawkins and Mary Brunton (even though Brunton was a close personal friend). The Austen novel was by then "a great favourite with me, on account of its just delineation of manners and excellent moral, which is rather insinuated than obtruded throughout—the safest and best way, I think" (Grant 2:84).

Mary Russell Mitford, too, who supplies the title for this paper, was a gradual convert. Probably most of us know her sharp comments on Austen's appearance and alleged disposition: about her being a husband-hunting butterfly when she was young, and a stiff, starched old maid later on. Mitford's information came partly from her mother, but mostly from a neighbour who had a lawsuit against some of the Austen family. Mitford admitted this gossip was probably prejudiced; but it's been much repeated without her own warning about its unreliability, and without her later, gradually increasing, praise of Austen's works.

When Mitford first read *Pride and Prejudice*, her comment might recall Keane's character, who wanted Fanny Price to marry Henry Crawford. She pronounced Austen *almost* the perfect novelist—except for a certain deficiency in taste or elegance. Elizabeth Bennet, she said, is pert and worldly, lacking in the dignity that a heroine needs. She joked that

Elizabeth would have been well matched with Wickham: "I can not forgive that delightful Darcy for parting them" (*Life* 1:231). (Could she have been writing this before she got to the end of the novel? Was she serious, or is this an example of the irony that so many readers caught from Jane Austen?) She does say in the same place that she prefers Austen to Maria Edgeworth, partly because Austen "preaches no sermons" (*Letter* 54), but this passage—the only one of Mitford's many musings on Jane Austen that is included in Brian Southam's *Critical Heritage* volume on Austen—is predominantly dismissive.

It was not the only comment that Mitford made. She kept reading. In due time she decided her favourite Austen novel was *Emma*. When Austen died, she responded not only with grief but with shock: "our Miss Austen" was a terrible loss (*Life* 1:272). Still, that's not all. By 1821, Mitford was planning to write and publish a critical essay on Austen, whose works, she said, "are by no means valued as they deserve" (1:357). I wish she had acted on this plan—but it was just then that she got involved in writing and publishing the sketches that brought her fame when they were collected as *Our Village*. In 1824, with the first volume of *Our Village* in print and wildly successful, she was trying to get up her courage to move on to a novel; she wrote, "Of course I shall copy as closely as I can Nature and Miss Austen" (2:39). Being something of a learned lady, she probably remembered here Pope's line in *An Essay on Criticism*: "*Nature* and *Homer* were, he found, the *same*" (Pope 135).[7] A very cool way of adding value to her compliment—yet she paid a more Austen kind of compliment when she gave Austen's fictional characters a place in her own life, as if they were real people—her own letters, she casually remarked, were getting too much like Mr Collins's!

These women—Sarah Harriet Burney, Catherine Hutton, Anne Grant, and Mary Russell Mitford—read Austen's novels when they were new. They surely came close to whatever ideal reader Austen herself might have had in mind. Mitford was already looking to the future, concerned to ensure her favourite a place in the developing, or perhaps the narrowing, canon—as was Lady Louisa Stuart (whom I love *partly* because she was the granddaughter of Lady Mary Wortley Montagu). Stuart was a close friend of Sir Walter Scott, the friend he trusted most for pre-publication criticisms of his own novels. When Scott was over-seeing his big, canonical collected edition of novels, Lady Louisa urged him to include various women writers. She wanted him not to omit Charlotte Lennox, Charlotte Smith, Frances Burney, Elizabeth Hamilton, Maria Edgeworth, or Jane Austen. To us today this might sound pre-dictable, canonical. At the time, however, Lady Louisa was fighting a rearguard action. This was 1826 (about ten years after Scott's favourable review of *Emma*), and several of the women novelists whom she men-tions were just about to lose what *had* been canonical status.

While Lennox and Hamilton slipped from view, Austen was be-coming a touchstone for others besides Sarah Harriet Burney and Mary Russell Mitford. Lord Dudley, for instance, a long-time admirer of Maria Edgeworth, decided that he liked Austen better (Butler 271–72). A journal called *Atlas* praised Anne Brontë's *Agnes Grey*, but compared it to its disadvantage with Austen (a coarse and less memorable imita-tion of Austen, it said—does that help to explain the motivation of Charlotte Brontë's disparagement?) ("From an unsigned review" 232–33).

Since Mitford never wrote her projected critical evaluation, the first formal, printed comment by a woman on Austen the novelist was Maria Jane Jewsbury's in the *Athenaeum* in 1831. Unfortunately it has been hidden from history not only by its original anonymity (which was common to all contributions to this and other magazines) but also by the fact that it was reprinted as a single unit with Richard Whately's essay of 1821, and most readers forgot or never knew that it had begun as something separate, by a different critic.

Early response to Austen by other authors came not only in the form of comment but in the form of echoing and borrowing. They couldn't keep their hands off her novels—and especially the openings. It's no surprise that the Scottish novelist Susan Ferrier could not resist Austen, since she was an almost obsessive user of literary allusions. We don't have to look at this as actual plagiarism: Ferrier expected her readers to notice and appreciate her allusions, just as readers of eighteenth-cen-tury poetry, or eighteenth-century parliamentarians listening to speeches, had enjoyed literary quotation. Ferrier, another Edinburgh lady of let-ters, was also a friend of Anne Grant and Walter Scott. Her novel *The*

Inheritance (1824) opens, "It is a truth, universally acknowledged, that there is no passion so deeply rooted in human nature as that of pride" (qtd. in Cullinan 75). At least one of her readers reacted with something other than straight appreciation. Sarah Harriet Burney, reading or rereading *The Inheritance* 20 years after it appeared, remarked that it was "excellent, & perhaps Miss Ferrier's best"; but, she went on, "I quite, & always did, prefer Miss Austen" (Burney, *Letters* 469). Perhaps Ferrier made an error of judgement in inviting the comparison!

A rather stranger case of allusion is presented by Mary Ann Kelty, a less-remembered novelist than Ferrier. Kelty's highly derivative first novel, *The Favourite of Nature* (1821), draws on Austen, Frances Burney, and the novel of sentiment. It introduces its heroine, Eliza Rivers, as "Young, beautiful, and highly accomplished" (Kelty 1), which sounds like an echo of Austen's introduction of Emma as "handsome, clever, and rich" (*Emma* [E] 5). Eliza, indeed, has a good deal in common with Emma. She too lives in a quiet village, and is talented, impetuous, and thoughtless. She too has a friend and neighbour whom she feels, unhappily, to be in some ways superior to herself. She too scribbles to-do lists (with scraps of poetry mixed in): buy things for poor children, get hold of *Pride and Prejudice* and *Sense and Sensibility*. Here it seems that Kelty, with a sense of humour lacking in Ferrier, is acknowledging her own indebtedness with appropriate, improvised irony: her Austen-influenced heroine wants to read Austen. More than Ferrier, however, she runs up debts because she lacks a clear literary direction of her own. This same novel includes an underbred Mrs Bartley with four daughters to marry off (Mrs Bennet in *Pride and Prejudice*) and a character called Lady Delville (Frances Burney's *Cecilia*), who writes in an ample epistolary style (Lady Bertram in *Mansfield Park*). The book ends with Eliza's godly, penitent death, which is far removed from anything that Austen might ever have written. Perhaps Eliza's reminders to herself to get *Pride and Prejudice*, get *Sense and Sensibility*, are really memos from Mary Ann Kelty to herself saying, "Try to write more like Jane Austen!"

If so, it was a resolution that Kelty was not designed to keep. If only she had wished, like Catherine Hutton, to *be* more like Jane Austen, or if only she could have chosen sense over sensibility! She did write another novel, *Trials; A Tale* (1824), which opens in an Austen manner, with 15-year-old Catherine Dorrington being rebuked by her aunt for running in the shrubbery with no gloves on. Like almost all Kelty's novels, it ends with the heroine's pious death. Kelty was plagued all her life by religious doubts and scruples: she was a natural magnet for dubious gurus and self-styled evangelists; she once gave up her music in case it was not pleasing to God; she very nearly burned her piano; she was often on the point of giving up writing; and as time went on, almost everything she wrote became overtly religious. She relates all this in her *Reminiscences of Thought and Feeling* (1852) — a very endearing book, but totally unlike Jane Austen.

Emma was not really Mary Ann Kelty's kind of heroine, for Kelty belonged in spirit to the more earnest age that was dawning. There are Victorian heroines whom we might never have had without Emma, like those of *Miss Marjoribanks*, by Margaret Oliphant, and *The Clever Woman of the Family*, by Charlotte M. Yonge. Oddly enough, however, the former's first name comes from a novelist almost the polar opposite of Austen, namely Hannah More. Oliphant's protagonist is Lucilla Marjoribanks, and Lucilla Stanley is the impossibly perfect heroine of More's *Coelebs in Search of a Wife* — the very character who made Austen herself say, "pictures of perfection...make me sick [and] wicked" (*Letters* 335). Lucilla Marjoribanks and Rachel Curtis (Charlotte Yonge's clever woman of the family) are perhaps the closest thing possible to being Victorian Emmas — but that is not really close, because their authors cannot resist the temptation to harp on their heroines' flaws and to highlight their reformation. Rachel must be saved from her organizing schemes (though they are more socially benevolent than Emma's) by the love of a good, dominant man. Lucilla must repent the political ambition that makes her choose a husband willing to be bossed around and to let her live vicariously through his public career. Thank heavens, we cry, for Austen's delicacy in *not* connecting Emma's happy ending to her moment of truth at Box Hill!

I feel (and as a non-Victorianist I may be mistaken) that the Victorians saw Austen as a relic of an earlier age, out of style, though offering some good ideas. Their immediate predecessors, however, the women writers of *almost* Austen's own generation who knew her before she was famous, related to her almost as to a private possession of their own. She was the original tune around which they could weave their own performance—and this was appropriate, for it is how Jane Austen herself related to the women writers who went before her.

Let's think for a moment about her relations with those predecessors. She laughed at them wickedly in her juvenilia. As an adult she did the same, with more ambivalence and more regular touches of affection, in her letters. She famously wrote beyond the ending of Frances Burney's *Camilla*. In that novel, the heroine is persecuted nearly to death by the mentor-hero and particularly by the hero's misogynist tutor, Dr Marchmont. Jane Austen wrote a stop-press note inside the cover of her copy about "a circumstance of some assistance to the happiness of Camilla...namely that Dr. Marchmont has at last died" (qtd. in Doody 272). In *Northanger Abbey*, she honoured just a few novels as the highest productions of human genius, and those were exclusively novels by women: Frances Burney and Maria Edgeworth. She demanded high standards from her peers. Of *Clarentine*, the first novel by her later fan Sarah Harriet Burney, Austen said that it was good on the first reading, not quite so good on the second reading, and unnatural and forced on the *third* reading (*Letters* 120). She evidently required that Sarah Harriet should stand up to innumerable readings—two centuries' worth, perhaps!

Austen also felt free to browse on the common of her female predecessors. Loraine Fletcher, biographer of Charlotte Smith, has a lot of fun presenting her readers with a schoolgirl called Jenny avidly devouring each new Smith novel as it appeared. It took a while, when I myself read Fletcher, for the penny to drop: Jenny is Jane is Austen. From every Smith novel, the child Jenny was processing details that she would use, some straight and some parodically, in her own mature novels. Or take Sophia Lee's *The Life of a Lover*, a novel published in 1804 though written years earlier, a sentimental, epistolary work six volumes long, unlike the politically conscious Charlotte Smith and very, very unlike Jane Austen. Lee writes in her preface something that might sound familiar: "every tender and silent suffering," she says, "is the sad distinction of my sex," and therefore women are the best qualified to write about such feelings (qtd. in Alliston xxxvi). Lee's plot here has to do with a woman harbouring her love for years before her feelings are finally rewarded. It is possible, then, that a memory of Sophia Lee lay in Austen's mind as she planned and wrote *Persuasion*, with the conversation between Anne Elliot and Captain Harville about women's sad superiority in loyalty and suffering. The differences between the two novels are obvious, yet it seems Austen found Lee helpful, and used her.

It seems to me that Austen related to her predecessors in much the same way that her immediate successors—leisured letter writers and hard-pressed novelists alike—related in their turn to her. These women wrote, whether privately or for publication, to pinpoint and express the meaning of their lives, and their reading was an important constituent of that meaning. Women writers of the 1820s hurried to share with each other the discovery of a little-known novelist who spoke to them as women and as writers; women writers today, when Austen is a majority taste, even a mass taste, feel that they have some special claim on her. Though almost no comments by the women discussed here are included in the *Critical Heritage* volumes on Austen (Southam), they add something important to our understanding of the way her reputation grew. She was always a word-of-mouth discovery, and so we owe those women, poised between the Romantic and the Victorian ages, a debt of gratitude for their perception as readers.

NOTES

1. Susan Brown, Patricia Clements, and Isobel Grundy, eds. *Orlando: Women's Writing in the British Isles from the Beginnings to the Present*. Cambridge: Cambridge University Press Online, 2006. <http://orlando.cambridge.org/>. Results of Tag Search query on tag <name> containing "Jane Austen" within lives and writings of all writers in textbase, 25 September 2007.

2. Susan Brown, Patricia Clements, and Isobel Grundy, eds. *Orlando*. Results of Tag Search query on tag <name> containing "Jane Austen" within lives and writings of all writers in textbase, 25 September 2007.

3.	Susan Brown, Patricia Clements, and Isobel Grundy, eds. *Orlando*. Margaret Drabble entry. Writing screen. 25 September 2007.

4.	Susan Brown, Patricia Clements, and Isobel Grundy, eds. *Orlando*. Fay Weldon entry. Writing screen. 25 September 2007.

5.	Bowen writes of Austen in *English Novelists* (1942), and Innes in *Hampshire Pilgrimages* (1948). Susan Brown, Patricia Clements, and Isobel Grundy, eds. *Orlando*. Austen entry. 25 September 2007.

6.	All quotations from Jane Austen's published works are taken from *The Oxford Illustrated Jane Austen*, 3rd ed., ed. R.W. Chapman (Oxford: Oxford UP, 1988) and from *Jane Austen's Letters*, 3rd ed., ed. Deirdre Le Faye (Oxford: Oxford UP, 1995), and are documented by short title and page number in the body of the chapter.

7.	The "he" who discovered this was Virgil. Mitford thus ingeniously places a mere novelist in dizzyingly exalted company, in the sequence Homer, Virgil, Pope, Austen.

WORKS CITED

Alliston, April. Introduction. *The Recess*. By Sophia Lee. Lexington, KY: UP of Kentucky, 2000. ix–lii.

Brontë, Charlotte. Letter to W.S. Williams. 12 April 1850. Excerpted as "Charlotte Brontë on Jane Austen" in Southam 127–28.

Brophy, Brigid. *Reads*. London: Penguin Sphere, 1989.

Brown, Susan, Patricia Clements, and Isobel Grundy, eds. *Orlando: Women's Writing in the British Isles from the Beginnings to the Present*. Cambridge: Cambridge UP Online, 2006. <http://Orlando.cambridge.org/>

Burney, Sarah Harriet. *The Letters of Sarah Harriet Burney*. Ed. Lorna J. Clark. Athens: Georgia UP, 1997.

Butler, Marilyn. *Maria Edgeworth: A Literary Biography*. Oxford: Clarendon, 1972.

Byatt, A.S. *The Biographer's Tale*. London: Chatto and Windus, 2000.

Clark, Lorna J., ed. Editor's Introduction. *The Letters of Sarah Harriet Burney*. Athens: Georgia UP, 1997.

Crook, Nora. "Sleuthing towards a Mary Shelley Canon." *Women's Writing* 6.3 (1999): 413–24.

Cullinam, Mary. *Susan Ferrier*. Boston: Twayne, 1984.

Doody, Margaret Anne. *Frances Burney: The Life in the Works*. New York: Cambridge UP, 1988.

Drabble, Margaret. "The Dower House at Kellynch: A Somerset Romance." *Jane Austen's Business: Her World and her Profession*. Ed. Juliet McMaster and Bruce Stovel. London: Macmillan, 1996. 206–22.

Fletcher, Loraine. *Charlotte Smith: A Critical Biography*. Basingstoke: Macmillan, 1998.

"From an unsigned review, *Atlas*." *The Brontës: The Critical Heritage*. Ed. Miriam Allott. London: Routledge and Kegan Paul, 1974. 230–33.

Grant, Anne. *Memoir and Correspondence of Mrs Grant of Laggan*. 3 vols. Ed. J.P. Grant. London: Longman, 1844.

Hutton, Catherine. *Reminiscences of a Gentlewoman of the Last Century: Letters of Catherine Hutton*. Ed. Catherine Hutton Beale. Birmingham: Cornish Brothers, 1891.

Jewsbury, Maria Jane. "Literary women. No. II. Jane Austen." *Athenaeum* 27 August 1831: 553–54.

Keane, Molly. *Time after Time*. London: A. Deutch, 1983.

Kelty, Mary Ann. *The Favourite of Nature*. London: Whittaker, 1821.

———. *Reminiscences of Thought and Feeling*. London: W. Pickering, 1852.

———. *Trials; A Tale*. London: Whittaker, 1824.

Lee, Hermione. "Losing the Thread in the Labyrinth of Life." *Guardian Weekly* 8–14, June 2000.

Mitford, Mary Russell. Letter to Sir William Elford. Excerpted as "Miss Mitford on Jane Austen" in Southam 54.

———. *The Life of Mary Russell Mitford: Told by Herself in Letters to her Friends*. Ed. Alfred Guy Kingham L'Estrange. New York: Harper and Brothers, 1870.

Pope, Alexander. *An Essay on Criticism*. 1711. *Critical Theory since Plato*. Ed. Hazard Adams. San Diego: Harcourt Brace Jovanovich, 1971. 278–86.

Southam, B.C., ed. *Jane Austen: The Critical Heritage*. London: Routledge and Kegan Paul, 1968.

Stovel, Nora Foster. "Introduction to Margaret Drabble." *Persuasions* 15 (1993): 74.

Tuell, Anne Kimball. *Mrs. Meynell and her Literary Generation*. 1925. New York: Dutton, 1970.

Woolf, Virginia. *The Letters of Virginia Woolf*. Ed. Nigel Nicolson and Joanne Trautmann. 6 vols. London: Hogarth, 1975–80.

———. *The Voyage Out*. London: Hogarth, 1975.

The Blues

OVERLEAF: *Bruce Stovel and Lazy Lester at* CKUA *Radio, March 4, 2000.*
Photo: Holger Petersen.

31 Anne Elliot's Blues

ELAINE BANDER

For Bruce, who so generously shared his love of Jane Austen

That man o' mine, he sailed away from me.
That man o' mine, he sailed away from me.
An' a woman alone is all I'm gonna be.
Been sittin' here, seven long years alone.
Been sittin' here, seven long years alone.
Since I lost my baby, Lor,' I even lost my home.
I'm blue today, gonna be blue tomorrow.
I'm blue today, gonna be blue tomorrow.
Lord, a woman's life ain't nothin' but strain an' sorrow.
Gotta help my sisters, help my poppa too.
Gotta help my sisters, help my poppa too.
Oh lord, lord, what's a woman alone to do?
My baby come back, but he didn't come back to me.
My baby come back, but he didn't come back to me.
He's brought his rod, but he's fishin' in other seas.
Until I die, he's still gonna be my man.
Until I die, he's still gonna be my man.

I'll love my baby any ol' way I can.
That man o' mine, he sailed away from me.
That man o' mine, he sailed away from me.
An' a woman alone is all I'm ever gonna be.

32 A Galvanizing Force

Sneeky Pete's was a dingy, dark, and not particularly inviting joint that served as one of the many short-lived blues music venues in Edmonton during the nineties. The nondescript room was also the place where I was first introduced to Bruce Stovel, at a gig that wasn't nearly as memorable as that initial contact with someone for whom I would come to have a deep respect and fond affection.

I can still see Bruce leaning up against the bar in the funky night-spot, appreciating all that was going on around him, from the sounds from the stage, which were being dispensed by the legendary Billy Boy Arnold, to the camaraderie that makes our local blues scene hum.

A bit of light spilled out of the beer coolers behind the bar and backlit Bruce and friends on that night. Over the course of an hour or so, it was apparent that there was no shortage of individuals who wanted a bit of his time and, with that, his insight and opinion on what was happening on the stage, with various characters on the local blues front, or with any of our festivals.

A warm smile, an easy laugh, and a man who looks you in the eye when conversing are good calling cards. Just as much as his opinion was solicited, he wanted to know what those around him thought and felt.

As the years went by the opportunity to watch Bruce interact with his students and associates in the Humanities Centre on the University of Alberta campus was presented, and it wasn't any different—a nice balance of respect and affection, giving and receiving.

He seemed to be a completely unselfish individual, one who only wanted us to better ourselves and appreciate what we were accomplishing as we walked through this life.

Galvanizing forces don't come along very often, but Bruce was exactly that, and a member of a club that in this city included another champion of the blues, the late, great Big Miller. Like Big, Bruce arrived in this city after spending his formative years a long way from Edmonton. He comfortably slipped into the community, and so many of us were the better for it.

Bruce encouraged and supported young blues musicians and, most importantly, our local and regional players. He understood what sits at the core of a scene and what makes a scene strong. His championing of players like Jim Guiboche, Chris Brzezicki, members of the Rockin' Highliners, Graham Guest, Kat Danser, Dave Cantera, and others, including his son Grant, is part of the brick and mortar of this city's roots music scene.

His work with CJSR Radio, his vision in programming blues at the Yardbird Suite, and his work at the university, where he developed a course that was built around the written content and structure of "the blues," were all part of that same foundation.

Bruce Stovel did everything for the right reasons, whether it concerned his family or his academic associates or his friends in the blues community. He was a brilliant man, his academic achievements nothing short of amazing, and when those kinds of gifts are rolled together with humility, grace, and a genuine love of life, we end up in the company of an unforgettable and beautiful human being.

33 Blues in the Academy

INING TRACY CHAO, BRUCE STOVEL,
& NORA FOSTER STOVEL

Introduction

TOO OFTEN, computers become the focus of a technological integration endeavour in education. Instructors may be excited about the potential uses of computer-assisted education, but at the same time feel lost in a high-tech jungle. However, computer technology is just a means to an end. The real question for instructors and course designers is how to understand a course holistically, including its goals, content, structure, teaching methods, and even the underlying theories of learning. This holistic analysis helps determine the best way to incorporate technology, or a variety of technologies, to deliver a course effectively. This essay describes, through a case study, this holistic approach toward course design and presents the implications for using educational technologies in a conventional classroom setting.

This case study focusses on an undergraduate course at the University of Alberta. English 483, Studies in the Literature of Popular Culture: Blues Lyrics as Lyric Poetry, was a one-term course offered by Bruce Stovel for advanced undergraduates. Given the subject matter, the advanced level of the students, and the instructional goals for this course, a traditional, lecture-centred teaching method was considered inappropriate. The instructor believed that students must experience the music and the lyrics for themselves, and form their own interpretations from that experience. Thus, the design of the course and the use of technology were based upon two considerations: (1) how to expose students to an authentic learning environment where they could experience blues music as an artistic form, and (2) how to guide students to interpretations of blues songs that take account of their contexts in social history and blues traditions as well as their intrinsic literary value. The two considerations called for constructivist philosophy and principles. This course serves as an excellent example of the marriage between constructivist design principles and the actual practices in a classroom.

A variety of activities and technologies were implemented to materialize the design principles and to accomplish the aforementioned goals. As in traditional English courses, the students were asked to buy textbooks, to complete readings from them, to submit—on paper—a long essay, and to write a final examination. However, the instructor played selected blues recordings in each class and then invited analysis of them, assigned CDs of blues music, and invited the students to explore other blues recordings. He then asked the students to submit assignments to a course website and to critique other students' work on the website. In addition, the instructor conducted both face-to-face and online asynchronous discussion, arranged an interview with a blues musician (at first via a web-based chatroom and later by telephone), held live concerts in class, encouraged the students to consult a set of videos that were placed on reserve, and required an oral presentation from each student at the end of the term—and many of these presentations involved the student presenter showing a video or playing a recording to the class. This multi-faceted instruction allowed the students to understand the subject of the course and to interact with the instructor, musicians, and each other through face-to-face contact and computer-mediated communication.

This essay will discuss in detail the constructivist principles applied to the design of English 483, the way this course was conducted, and the outcomes as a result of the technology integration. The story and the reflection are meant to provide instructors in higher education with

insights into designing courses that incorporate technology into classroom teaching.

Constructivist Design Principles

Constructivism is central to the design of English 483. Students were
not expected to memorize the lyrics to blues songs nor to learn to interpret them objectively. On the contrary, students were to experience the
performed art in order to understand the poetic nature of the songs.
Personal experience and immersion in an authentic environment were
required to meet the instructional goals. Constructivism offers a strong
theoretical foundation for this course.

Constructivist philosophy is founded on the premise that we each
construct our own understanding and that learning occurs through the
association of previous experience with newly acquired knowledge. It
is up to the learners to make sense of a concept and to express their
own perspectives. There is no one correct meaning, since individuals
differ in their sense-making and viewpoints, as T.M. Duffy and D.H.
Jonassen observe in *Constructivism and the Technology of Instruction*.

Many theorists have articulated this philosophy in terms of its
application in education. John Dewey and L.S. Vygotsky are two of the
theorists who offer insights on this matter. For Dewey, education
depends on action. Knowledge and ideas emerge only from a situation
in which learners are induced to draw them out of experiences that have
meaning and importance to them. These situations have to occur in a
social context, such as a classroom where students join in manipulating
materials and thus create a community of learners who build knowledge individually and collectively. In *Mind in Society*, Vygotsky further
states that learning is a social process. Learners acquire knowledge by
interacting with peers and with a subject expert. The zone of proximal
development provides a clear application of Vygotsky's principle. Learners
can learn from others who possess the desired knowledge, thereby
acquiring and constructing their own knowledge.

Dewey's and Vygotsky's views can be expanded into an argument for
an authentic learning environment. It is believed that learning im-

proves when it occurs in a meaningful and authentic context. In other words, the context must be an integral part of the content to be learned (Spiro, Feltovish, Jacobson, and Coulson 57–75). Constructivism promotes the idea that a learning activity must be situated and authentic (Brown, Collins, and Duguid 32–42). The authenticity contextualizes learning; authenticity therefore helps learners see the usefulness of the knowledge and helps them transfer what they have learned to a real-world situation.

Another principle that is at the heart of constructivism is active learning. Ernst Von Glaserfeld argues that constructivism requires self-regulation and the building of conceptual structures through reflection and abstraction. The emphasis is on an individual's autonomy in the learning process, as well as on knowledge construction instead of reproduction. It is more effective for learners to build their own knowledge from their experiences than to receive it passively (Perkins 45–55). By constructing knowledge, learners are actively trying to create meaning. They are more likely to retain it because they have interpreted and assimilated it into their previous knowledge. D.J. Cunningham suggests that a constructivist learning environment should promote active learning and facilitate the knowledge construction process; in other words, a constructivist approach to teaching should help learners construct their own plausible interpretations.

In short, from a constructivist standpoint, learning is viewed as a social function, and the focus is on knowledge construction. An individual must be an active agent in the learning process, and learning should occur in an authentic context. Later in this section of the essay, we will describe the ways in which these constructivist principles have been applied to the design of the course.

The Course

English 483 was taught over a 13-week term; the class contained 22 students, most of them third- or fourth-year honours English students or English majors. The course is one of some 20 variable-content 400-level English courses offered each year that are meant to provide sophisticated and specialized instruction to advanced students. The class met once a week, at night, for three hours.

The course explored the poetic art in the lyrics of selected blues songs, taking as its point of departure the claim made by Brooks, Lewis, and Warren that "The blues was one of the few unique contributions— perhaps the only unique contribution—that America has made to the world of art" (2753). They argue that, even "Waiving their value as musical art, blues songs represent a body of poetic art unique and powerful" (2759). The course aimed at allowing students to experience and understand blues lyrics, not as poems in the usual sense (words on a page), but as performed poetry—in other words, as elements in the songs in which they appear. Another goal was to help students understand the social context in which the blues developed: the life of the black population of the United States in the twentieth century, a life that changed dramatically during the century as the majority of blacks moved from the country to the city and from the Deep South to the North. The course surveyed the development of blues music by studying a different period or style each week, beginning with women blues singers of the 1920s and continuing to the present. At the end of eight weeks of such a chronological survey, one week was devoted to studying the work of each of two immensely influential blues artists, Muddy Waters and B.B. King. The second-to-last meeting of the class consisted of student presentations, and the last week's class, according to university practice for night classes, was the final exam.

The students were asked to buy three textbooks and two anthologies of recordings of a wide variety of blues songs. Some 30 additional books and articles bearing on the course were placed on reserve in the university library, and an additional CD anthology was an optional purchase available in the campus bookstore. The students also proved able to make excellent use of the thousands of blues LPs and CDs in the university's Music Library and in the city's library system. In addition, students were invited to consult ten videos of blues performances placed on reserve in the Audio Visual Centre.

In-Class Activities

Each three-hour class fell into three parts. The first hour was presided over by the instructor, who gave a lecture accompanied by question-and-answer discussion on the phase of blues studied that week. The second hour of each class focussed on four blues songs in the style of music under study that week: the students were divided at the start of the term into four groups, each containing five or six students; each group would listen to its assigned song, consult about its striking features and its significance, and then report back to the class, playing the song on the CD player and presenting their conclusions. The final hour of each class was allotted to "fun." Eight of these one-hour sessions were devoted to live performances by blues artists living in Alberta; a video on blues music was shown in one final-hour segment; a panel discussion by local figures in the blues business (such as DJs, booking agents, and, in one case, the head of a recording label) was held one week, and once a prominent blues artist (Ann Rabson, founder of the acoustic trio Saffire) was to be interviewed through a web-based chatroom facility in WebCT.

The eight concerts were especially important. Each lasted for one hour and coincided in style with the kind of music under study that week; they were held in a separate classroom that is an amphitheatre, and members of the public were invited to attend. The series was advertised as "Blues in the Academy," and since the performers were all well known, the audiences at several of these concerts contained many people who were not students in the class. The performers spoke between songs about the music they were performing, and many of these comments made a deep impression on the students. The blues artists all performed for free out of love for their music; this donation by the musicians was itself something that the students appreciated.

At the end of the term, each student submitted a term paper of 2,500 words (eight to ten typed pages) on a topic of his or her choice: the only requirements were that the essay had to deal with the issues of the course and to discuss in some detail at least one blues song. Each student had a scheduled interview with the instructor about one month before the due date; this allowed students a chance to air their ideas and receive suggestions. Then, in the second-to-last class meeting, each student gave a brief oral presentation (ten minutes maximum) outlining his or her essay, and invited responses from the class and the instructor. Finally, the essay was submitted two weeks later, one week after the final exam was written. The term papers were arresting and original in conception and execution. Most of the students used recordings on CDs or segments from videos in making their presentations.

The final exam was an important part of the learning experience. It covered the course as a whole and asked the students to synthesize the knowledge and insights that they had been accumulating all term; whereas the focus all term had been on the study of individual artists and songs, now the students were asked to step back and try to fit things together and see what it all meant. The exam was 2.5 hours long, and the most important question—to be completed in 1.5 hours and so worth 60 per cent of the exam mark—was one in which the students were asked to choose one of six large topics and write an essay on it, referring to a variety of artists, styles, and periods. The exam also asked the students to apply their knowledge to new material that had not been studied in class: two shorter exam questions were given to them in advance, to be done in 30 minutes each, dealing with contemporary blues music. The questions asked each student to define the qualities that a blues song must have to become a blues standard and to identify the qualities that distinguish songs by the best blues songwriters from the majority of blues songs.

Course Website

The course website was designed as an integral part of the course. WebCT was the delivery platform. Many of the students were already veteran Internet users, but some were novices who did not have access to a computer. The first hour of the second class meeting was devoted to an orientation session, conducted in a university computer lab, showing students how to access and use the course website and also how to make use of the university's computer labs. This session was to help students understand the role of the course website and provide them with necessary instruction so they would not feel too frustrated when they encountered problems. The web components, including the course outline and syllabus, which contained a weekly schedule, were handed out in class and posted on the course website. They provided overall guidance to the students and spelled out the course requirements.

Weekly assignments formed the core elements in the course. Every week for nine weeks, each student was asked to choose a blues song, transcribe it, and write a brief commentary. Students had to report on songs they had actually heard; the songs had to be chosen from given chronological periods (for instance, for the first four weeks, the songs chosen had to have been recorded before 1945). Students found these songs on the assigned CDS or on CDS and LPS they discovered on their own. Each assignment was to consist of two pages, one page of transcription and one page of commentary. Each commentary had to have at least one factual paragraph, identifying the performer, the songwriter, the accompaniment, the place and date of the original recording, and the like, and at least one paragraph of interpretation. A sample weekly assignment, by Josh Nodelman, is given in the next chapter of this volume.

These assignments were posted to the course website and gradually formed an anthology called "Nothing but the Blues." In fact, the students were allowed to hand in these assignments on paper and by email to the course website; students were urged to post their work to the website, so that their ideas could be shared, but there was no penalty for those who handed in the assignment on paper only. The students quickly found it fascinating to read each other's work on the website, so that by the end of the course more than 90 per cent of the assignments had been placed on the website.

The vehicle by which the students submitted their assignments was the email function in WebCT. Email allowed students to send their assignments as private submissions to the instructor. The instructor could then provide feedback to the students, mark the assignments, and post them in "Nothing but the Blues." This process allowed the instructor to make minor editing changes to ensure that the assignments were all in the same format and to index each assignment. The students were to indicate each week whether or not they wanted their submission to the website to be identified as theirs; as a result, about 80 per cent of the assignments found in "Nothing but the Blues" identify the student authors; the remainder are anonymous. The great advantage of the web anthology is that the students could read each other's work, week by week, and the assignments thus not only built up a store of songs known to all, but also established a body of thought that could be built upon. Often, students in their weekly assignments alluded in their commentary to points made in previous assignments by other students. The students also made frequent use of the ideas advanced by other students in "Nothing but the Blues" when they produced their presentations, term papers, and final exams.

Nothing but the Blues

Every week, the instructor collected the students' emailed assignments, added the song titles to an index, and posted the assignments in "Nothing but the Blues" on the course website. The anthology thus became a core repository of the course materials. This anthology served a variety of purposes. The primary benefit was the intellectual one noted above: a body of songs and a body of thought were defined as the course's primary concern. Another benefit was that students were actively engaged in publishing their work. This allowed the students to regard their work as a public contribution to an ongoing project and encouraged professionalism.

Students were also forced to consult "Nothing but the Blues" before completing each assignment, if for no other reason than to be sure of not writing on a song already in the collection. In fact, it occasionally happened that two or three students would write on the same song in the same week; it then became very interesting to compare the differences in the transcriptions and the different perspectives taken in the commentaries. In general, students not only learned by completing their own assignments, but also benefitted from the multiple perspectives reflected in the anthology.

The instructor used a web-authoring tool—Dreamweaver (1999)—to edit the web pages for "Nothing but the Blues." Because submissions were done through email, the instructor was able to index the song titles and then cut and paste the submissions onto the course website. The instructor thus served as the editor of the emerging anthology, guaranteeing that it had consistency and clarity and also allowing the submissions to be identified by author or to remain anonymous, depending on each author's preference.

Constructivism in Action

So how were the constructivist principles applied to the design of English 483? The method employed can be described as an approach to building a rich, authentic environment for active learning (Grabinger and Dunlap 5–34).

The live concerts were probably the most authentic experiences students had in this class. The instructor also made an effort to invite a well-known musician to meet the class online; although the plan for the online interview fell through, the interview was conducted by telephone, and the students were still able to ask Ann Rabson questions. The emphasis was authentic interaction between the students and blues music and musicians. In addition to first-hand encounters with musicians in the live concerts, listening to music recordings was an activity for every class. Discussions were all based on these experiences. The instructor also provided information about blues performances around the city and on the radio. It is important to note that the authenticity varies in degree in different situations. Listening to music recordings in class may be less authentic than attending a live concert. Given the constraints and the resources available for classroom teaching, music recordings seemed to be a reasonable solution for exposing students to many blues songs from the past to the present. J. Cronin argues that authenticity exists on a continuum. Authenticity was accomplished in this course through the arrangement of various events in class and encouragement for students to explore blues music outside class.

Throughout the course, students were engaged in the listening and interpreting process. Weekly assignments were the outcome of this active learning process. Later in the course, the students worked on an essay and the accompanying oral presentation to externalize their learning. This promoted ownership of learning and turned students from passive recipients of instruction into active agents of learning. In addition to each individual's knowledge construction through writing weekly assignments and preparing his or her presentation and essay, the students were led by the instructor to explore course issues in in-class discussion. The topics in the online forums broadened the range of discussion and helped students learn from one another. With all of these elements working together, students were exposed to multiple perspectives on the subject of the course. Alternative perspectives are viewed by most constructivists as an effective approach to knowledge construction and as a way to deepen one's understanding of a subject (Spiro et al. 57–75).

Instructor's Perspective

The instructor believes the students advanced further in both knowledge and in sophistication than they would have, had the course been taught in a more conventional manner. It seemed that the students came to know each other unusually well and to rely on each other's insights to an unusual degree as a result of reading each other's work on the website as well as from face-to-face interaction in class. The atmosphere in class was relaxed, friendly, and mutually supportive. The students also became very adroit at using Internet research (in addition to the course textbooks and other reference books) to support their ideas in the weekly assignments and in the end-of-term presentations and term papers. One bonus of having so much of the coursework completed on the website was that the hour of class time devoted to lectures each week could be used to tackle interesting issues that emerged from the weekly assignments—subtleties, qualifications, complications, implications, historical explanations, and the like—since the students had already displayed a grasp of the elementary issues at stake.

Lessons Learned

The case study and the description of the outcomes provide a clear picture of what was planned: the holistic design approach and the integration of technology into the course on constructivist principles. To offer instructors and course designers in higher education insights into the integration process, this section gives practical suggestions for those who are in a position to apply and are interested in applying constructivism in university courses.

First, it is very important to consider pedagogical issues as primary, even though an instructor's immediate goal is to integrate technology into teaching. Without clear instructional goals, technology may not help at all. Tony Bates observes, "Good teaching may overcome a poor choice in the use of technology, but technology will never save bad teaching; usually it makes it worse" (12). Some key questions about the instructional goals must be considered: What do we expect students to learn from this course? What learning activities will help students acquire the essential skills? How can technology help to achieve the instructional goals? These questions established the foundation for the course design and provided directions for decisions on the selection of course materials, learning activities, and the use of web components.

Constructivism is the underlying philosophy for English 483. However, it is worth mentioning that constructivism was integrated into a conventional classroom teaching model. This partial implementation might be optimal for the majority of students (Bostock 225–40). As the students' evaluations revealed, a small number of students resented the open-ended, student-directed kind of learning they were asked to do and wanted to have more lectures, more guidance from above as to what they should think and do. Also, those who responded negatively to the web components of the course may have seen technology as restricting and daunting because they were not used to learning in this fashion. It is, though, quite encouraging to find that most students embraced the opportunity to explore and appreciated the chance to pursue active learning in an authentic environment. It seemed that an effective strategy is to apply constructivist principles to a course while maintaining a certain degree of instructor presence and guidance.

Student resistance may be an issue in a course like this. The instructor was very adaptive and allowed flexibility. For instance, the students could opt out of the online submission of weekly assignments. However, students realized that their own contributions were valued and that they could all benefit from sharing their work. By the end of the course, almost all of the students' assignments had been submitted online. It is true that individuals have different learning styles, and some simply will not like the openness in a constructivist environment. However, this course suggests that, once students come to understand the benefits of such an environment, they will seize the opportunity, and resistance will dwindle to a relatively insignificant level.

Providing a rich and constructivist learning environment is also intended to increase the equality of learning opportunities among students. Since students respond differently to different types of media, a mix of in-class and online activities simply gives students more options. The issue of access must be addressed, however. In the student evaluations, it was apparent that the lack of easy access to a computer and the Internet imposed a great constraint on a very few students' ability to adapt to this new course format. The instructor tried to address the access issue by booking several hours each week in university computer labs for use by his students. This solution may not be completely satisfactory, though it did guarantee that students without their own computers had access to computers on campus.

Providing support to students is another critical issue, and one related to the issue of access. This support encompasses the orientation students received in the beginning of the course and the ongoing troubleshooting for both technical and pedagogical issues. This burden of support can be quite challenging for an instructor, especially one who was, in this case, learning how to use the technology just a step ahead of the students. In the case of English 483, the support unit—the University of Alberta Faculty of Arts Technologies for Learning Centre—was aware of the issue. Thus, the instructional designer and the technical support staff supported the course throughout the implementation phase by being available for consultation by both the instructor and students.

Conclusion

More and more instructors in higher education are beginning to see the potential of using technology in their courses. The mixed-modes model in which technology and classroom teaching are integrated will become an increasingly common practice in higher education. Through

English 483, we learned that the key to successful integration lies in solid design principles and adequate support for instructors and for students. What technology to use and how to use it are, at the same time, only a part of the whole picture for the instructor. The most challenging task is to be creative and imaginative when applying constructivism to classroom teaching and to find a balance between an open learning situation and instructor's guidance. The mindset and attitudes students have toward the new paradigm of learning can be another challenge. An instructor must communicate clearly — and then demonstrate — the purposes that the technology serves. The more students understand this, the more likely they are to flourish in the new environment and the less likely they are to resist and resent the innovations.

WORKS CITED

Bates, T. *Technology, Open Learning and Distance Education*. London: Routledge, 1995.

Blues Classics [3 CDs]. Los Angeles: MCA, 1996.

Bostock, S. "Constructivism in Mass Higher Education: A Case Study." *British Journal of Educational Technology* 29.3 (1998): 225–40.

Brooks, C., R.W.B. Lewis, and R.P. Warren, eds. *American Literature: The Makers and the Making*. New York: St. Martin's, 1973.

Brown, J. S., A. Collins, and P. Duguid. "Situated Cognition and the Culture of Learning." *Educational Researcher* 18 (1989): 32–42.

Cronin, J. "Four Misconceptions about Authentic Learning." *Educational Leadership* 50.7 (1993): 78–80.

Cunningham, D.J. "Assessing Constructivism and Constructing Assessment: A Dialogue." Duffy and Jonassen 35–44.

Dewey, John. *Democracy and Education*. New York: Free Press, 1994.

Dreamweaver [Computer software]. Vers. 3. Macromedia, 1999.

Duffy, T.M., and D.H. Jonassen. *Constructivism and the Technology of Instruction: A Conversation*. Mahwah, NJ: Lawrence Erlbaum, 1992.

Grabinger, R.S., and J.C. Dunlap. "Rich Environments for Active Learning." *ALT-Journal* 3.2 (1995): 5–34.

Perkins, D.N. "Technology Meets Constructivism: Do They Make a Marriage?" Duffy and Jonassen 45–55.

Spiro, R.J., P.J. Feltovish, M.J. Jacobson, and R.L. Coulson. "Cognitive Flexibility, Constructivism and Hypertext: Random Access Instruction for Advanced Knowledge Acquisition in Ill-Structured Domains." Duffy and Jonassen 57–75.

Von Glaserfeld, E. *Radical Constructivism: A Way of Knowing and Learning.* London: Falmer, 1995.

Vygotsky, L.S. *Mind in Society.* Cambridge, MA: MIT Press, 1978.

WebCT [Computer software]. Vancouver, BC: University of British Columbia, 1998.

34 "Evil," by Willie Dixon, Performed by Howlin' Wolf

J.N. NODELMAN

If you're a long way from home, can't sleep at night,
Grab your telephone, something just ain't right:
That's evil, evil is goin' on wrong.
I am warning you, brother,
You better watch your happy home.
Well, long way from home, and can't sleep at all,
You know another mule is kicking in your stall:
That's evil, evil is goin' on wrong.
I am warning you, brother,
You better watch your happy home.
*   (instrumental break)*
—You better catch it—
—'cause something wrong—
—In your home—
Well, if you call her on the telephone, and she answers awful slow,
Grab the first train smoking, if you have to hobo:
That's evil, evil is goin' on wrong.
I am warning you, brother,
You better watch your happy home.

> *(instrumental break)*
> *If you make it to your house, knock on the front door,*
> *Run 'round to the back, you catch him just before he goes:*
> *That's evil, evil is goin' on.*
> *I am warning you, brother,*
> *You better watch your happy home.*
> (Willie Dixon, 1954)

"EVIL," a Chess recording from the 1950s, is both a song about men's anxieties about women and a lyric that constructs a community of listeners by addressing its audience, paradoxically, by addressing a single person. Like the Muddy Waters song that deals with a man not being able to satisfy his 19-year-old partner's sexual needs, Dixon writes of a man who is not able to satisfy his partner because he is a long way away. This lyric has a certain poignance, given the employment conditions under which black Americans of the era relocated to different areas of the country and took jobs, especially in menial labour (and, to a lesser extent, in the entertainment industry), that required being far from home for long periods.

As in Waters's song, Howlin' Wolf sings here both to an individual and to an entire audience in such a way as to blur any ironic distinctions between them: the song is certainly not written just for the one person who is having troubles with his woman, but Wolf draws the assembled audience into his performance exactly by his commitment in seeming actually to address a particular person at a particular moment. Interestingly, though, in Dixon's lyric each verse has both a rhetorical situation ("If you make it to your house, knock on the front door") and a suggested course of action to deal with it ("Run 'round to the back, you catch him just before he goes"). Then, the repeating verse comments on the overall situation and concludes with a warning that reaches beyond the specific situations described in each verse to a more general urgency ("That's evil, evil is goin' on. / I am warning you, brother, / You better watch your happy home"). The narrative itself progresses from the cuckolded man getting a feeling that something is wrong, to making a telephone call, being unsatisfied by the call, boarding a train home, and finally catching a man leaving his house by the back door.

However, Dixon's rhetorical strategy has the effect of lending this linear progression a sense of being a constantly occurring present. Even though things seem to be happening, they continue to be narrated only provisionally; perhaps nothing is actually happening at all. Overall, as far as what happens when these anxieties get aired within a community of listeners, this is a lyric where the threat itself is somehow deferred indefinitely by a rhetorical strategy that allows the performer, the individual being addressed, and the audience in general all to be both the potential victims of unfaithfulness and at the same time people removed far enough from the situation to be able to comment on it from outside. The idea that one in the audience could be totally implicated in the embarrassing predicament of having an unfaithful partner would no doubt be discomfiting, yet the song would not be compelling if it did not deal with an anxiety that many in the audience would share. It only hits home, I think, as both warning and entertainment at the same time if the perfidy in question does not ever quite materialize in full, even for the hypothetical man being addressed by the performer.

WORK CITED

Dixon, Willie. "Evil." *Willie Dixon: The Chess Box*. Chess CHD2–16500, 1988. Recorded Chicago, 25 May 1954. Vocals and harmonica Howlin' Wolf. Piano Otis Spann. Guitar Jody Williams and Hubert Sumlin. Bass Willie Dixon. Drums Earl Phillips. Originally released as Chess single 1575.

35 Blues Lyrics as Poetry Course

MEGAN EVANS

THE IRONY OF BEING A UNIVERSITY STUDENT is that most memories one has of the time spent in university have little to do with the time paid for by tuition fees. I am no exception to this rule, but I was fortunate enough to take Dr Stovel's English 483 class, Blues Lyrics as Poetry. I have a love-hate relationship with poetry. Reading between the lines of imagery and connecting the dots between metaphors and allusions leaves me irritated and confused. Dr Stovel's class was where I learned to appreciate the beauty of subjectivity.

Our weekly assignments involved transcribing a song from a particular era in blues history, then analyzing the content as if it were poetry. The quality of some recordings was terrible, and though my roommates may not have appreciated listening to the same Etta James recording for hours, each time I listened to the song I found something new. A different word, inflection, twang of the guitar—the track was on repeat, but the song didn't start again. It started anew.

The delight of interpreting the blues comes from the fact that listening to this music is never a matter of passive sound absorption. The meaning of a song is found in the fusion of the emotions exuded by both the performer and the audience. The relationship between performer and audience is enjoyed at its maximum potential when the performance is live, but is also felt at a lesser intensity if listening to a recording. Clapping, toe tapping, and exclamations can be an expression of enthusiasm or a way to signal agreement with the musician: "Mmmhmmm, I hear you baby!" or "Yeah, I'm feeling that"—as if, somehow, the musician struck the exact note to express what, until that moment, you were unable to.

Watching a professor who is impassioned by his subject matter is magic—lucky for me Dr Stovel favoured the blues and not quantum physics—and the student who sits in on the show each week cannot fail to learn or to be inspired.

I did not fall in love with the blues in English 483, but I began a mild flirtation. I cultivated an appreciation of the music that is my soundtrack for a rainy Sunday afternoon. I found the song to play when it's sunny outside but I can't quite manage a smile to match it ("'Taint Nobody's Bizness If I Do," by Bessie Smith). I discovered that the blues isn't just a feeling. It's any feeling to be found in the mixture of musician, instrument, and personal reflection. For some it's about enjoyment; for others it's a passion. I am thankful that I had the opportunity to learn this from Dr Stovel—a man who understood this better than most.

36 In the Pursuit of Art

Jane Austen, B.B. King, Kurt Browning,
and...Bruce Stovel

AMANDA LIM

WHEN I AM REMEMBERING BRUCE STOVEL, I can feel myself for-
mulating a question that sounds like the beginning of a corny joke—
not because there was anything even remotely corny or laughable about
Bruce, but because he was so multi-faceted and open to so many different things. What do Jane Austen, B.B. King, and Kurt Browning have
in common? The answer would be Bruce Stovel. Bruce was an expert on
all things Jane Austen, and he was a veteran of the blues music scene in
every sense—devoted fan, spectator, commentator, promoter, and radio
DJ. For many years, he co-hosted with his son Grant the popular show
Calling All Blues for the University of Alberta's campus radio station,
CJSR. He knew B.B. King *personally*. As for Kurt Browning, I really have
no idea whether Bruce knew him or not, but it would not be as big a
surprise as one might imagine. I have read only one book by Jane Austen
(*Emma*) and have only a very passing knowledge of B.B. King; I am, however, a huge figure-skating fan and was completely astounded to discover
that Bruce was as well.

My first encounter with Bruce came in my third year of undergraduate studies when I ended up in his Restoration drama class. Not only

did we read plays in the class, but we performed scenes from them. We were not exactly budding thespians (except for those of us who did have theatrical backgrounds or experience), but our play-acting, in all senses of the word, showed us that the text was not confined to the page, especially where drama was concerned. The class also had an online component, a discussion forum through which we could discuss the plays we studied. Posting in the off-topic section of the forum, I remember excitedly discussing figure skating with a fellow classmate, and these online conversations carried over into class. It was after class one day that Bruce suddenly said to me, "So you like figure skating?" Surprised, I said yes, after which I discovered that Bruce was also a fan of this beautiful, unpredictable sport. Bruce's question led to conversations about the new judging system that eliminated the perfect 6.0 score in favour of the "Code of Points" that added points rather than deducting for mistakes. We discussed which female figure skater was more well-rounded and deserved to win the world championship (Russia's Irina Slutskaya or America's Sasha Cohen), the knowledge of the skating commentators and their tendency to sometimes talk over and detract from the skater's performance, the value of the quad in men's skating, and other sundry and eclectic details about a winter sport close to Canada's heart and never far from controversy. I found an unlikely mutual figure-skating fan in Bruce, who did not seem like the "typical" skating fan to me—older man, English professor, Jane Austen lover. Jibes about the "femininity" of the sport—aimed toward the costuming, the music, and the skaters themselves—and criticisms about its political intrigues and judging scandals obviously did not discourage Bruce from loving it without reservation. But then, nothing about Bruce seemed typical or ordinary, as I discovered when I chose to take his blues class in my final undergraduate year.

It was probably one of Bruce's dream classes, and it turned out to be one of my most enjoyable. Bruce's stories about the vibrant blues music scene and the eclectic and legendary blues musicians he had come to know over the years peppered his spare, yet informative, lectures—which he always tried to keep to a minimum because they were, in his opinion, the most boring and least useful method of teaching or learning.

Instead, Bruce emphasized more interactive activities, such as group discussions and presentations, just as he had incorporated play-acting into our Restoration drama class. He would bring books or records from his own personal collection, and come to each class with new stories about blues musicians and gigs in famous Chicago clubs. He brought out of every song that we studied the balance of humour and sadness that is one of the characteristic trademarks of blues music, and illustrated how the blues influenced rock-and-roll music—which I greatly appreciated, being more a rock than a blues fan. Blues music involves storytelling and is nothing if not raw, honest feeling. It is about listening to the music not only as it is packaged as slick records, but also as it is performed live, with all the intensity, spontaneity, and emotion that are intended. Having been a veteran of the blues music scene for many years, Bruce obviously understood this, and so he invited blues musicians to perform for us at the end of every weekly class. These would range from local, little-known blues solo artists from Edmonton to fairly established bands from the States. One major highlight for me was the pleasure of watching Bruce's son, Grant, and his band play live, and I understood then how Bruce and Grant could make such a dynamic blues duo on the radio.

Our figure-skating conversations continued through the blues class as well—I remember enthusiastically relating Joannie Rochette's superlative skate to Igor Stravinsky's famous classical composition *The Firebird*, during the 2005 Canadian National Figure Skating Championships. Bruce had, unfortunately, missed seeing the performance, but had heard about the standing ovation that nearly drowned out the last twenty seconds of Joannie's winning program. When I was completing my master's degree the next year, I visited Joannie's official website, which included video clips of her performances, including her famous *Firebird* program. I emailed Bruce to let him know that he could download and watch the performance, and I can still remember the email he sent back with a big "thank you."

Bruce appreciated beauty and art in different ways, showing his receptiveness to different forms of art. He told me about his memorable *Stars on Ice* experience, having had the good fortune to sit next to the mother of Tara Lipinsky, the 1998 Olympics gold medalist. I still have not attended a *Stars on Ice* performance, but just watching video clips that skating fans have uploaded to the Internet reminds me of Bruce. I am sure that he would have enjoyed immensely this year's performances by Jeffrey Buttle and Joannie Rochette, the current Canadian men's and women's champions. Jeffrey, breaking loose from his usual introspective fare, sported a Mohawk, leather vest, chains, and ripped pants in his maverick skate to The Clash's "Should I Stay or Should I Go," while Joannie, also uncharacteristically, rocked out to Pat Benatar in a leather skirt and red bra under a black mesh shirt. Even knowing how unpredictable the world of figure skating can be, there are still surprises every once in a while.

Canadian pianist Glenn Gould once said, "The purpose of art is not the release of a momentary ejection of adrenaline but is, rather, the gradual, lifelong construction of a state of wonder and serenity" (qtd. in Bazzana). Fittingly, I discovered this quotation when Jeffrey Buttle revealed it as the inspiration for his 2005–2006 free skate program, a beautifully choreographed tribute to Gould and his artistic genius. Somehow, Gould's quotation seems well applied to Bruce, for, even though I knew Bruce only in my capacity as a student, his openness toward life and toward the people around him was inspiring and evident in everything that he did. I will miss the figure skating conversations and the lively blues music, but, most of all, I lament the fact that we all have one less artist amongst us.

WORKS CITED

Bazzana, Kevin. 2008. "Bio." *Glenn Gould* [website]. 2008. 27 September 2008
       <www.glenngould.com>.
Rochette, Joannie. "Video Clips." 2005. *Joannie Rochette* [website]. 27 September 2008
       <www.joannierochette.com/videos.htm>.

37 Blues for the Blues

JANNIE EDWARDS

Even the blind man can tell
When he walkin' in the sun.
(B.B. King, "Walking in the Sun")

What I would give
What I would give for a horn
in this lonely room
Give to get pulled
through the blue marrow of a climbing slide pitch its arc
perfectly
to your absence
What I would give to play the note that pulls you all the way in
To do for you what red
does for blue
Go deeper
Man, what I would give
for you.
So long gone
from this lonesome bed hot
with the midnight blues

38 "I've Known Rivers"

Langston Hughes's Blues Poetry

NADIA NIVEN RUSHDY

I've known rivers:
I've known rivers ancient as the world and older than the flow of
*   human blood in human veins.*
My soul has grown deep like the rivers.
(Hughes, "The Negro Speaks of Rivers" 634)

HOW DOES ONE SUM UP the life and work of a poet? Langston Hughes
was an African American who began writing during the 1920s, and was
in the forefront of the Harlem Renaissance movement: "Within a few
years of his first book [*The Weary Blues*], he was the poet laureate of his
people" (Meltzer x). He believed that localized, specific writing drawn
from everyday life became universal in import; he believed that poets
should write from their own experience, as he did: "We younger Negro
artists who create now intend to express our individual dark-skinned
selves without fear or shame....We build our temples for tomorrow,
strong as we know them, and we stand on top of the mountain, free
within ourselves" (qtd. in Davis 19).

He wrote about black culture and folklore, in the United States and
abroad. He also concerned himself with the racial tension between

black and white people in America. His poetry drew on the local speech of uneducated African Americans, as well as their blues music. Hughes's poetry is both an expression of his personal experience as an African American and a commentary on race relations in America, not previously satisfactorily addressed by African American poets or their literary contemporaries.

In one of his earliest poems, "When Sue Wears Red," Hughes's life-long poetic technique of including music in his poetry was already apparent:

> When Susanna Jones wears red
> Her face is like an ancient cameo
> Turned brown by the ages.
> Come with a blast of trumpets,
> Jesus! (1–5)

The simple simile is accentuated by the gospel-like intensity of the fourth and fifth lines. The inclusion of a plain refrain drawn from an established musical tradition is Hughes's most distinctive poetic technique. The figure of Susanna Jones is at once local and universal: she is at once Hughes's classmate and an eternal image of female beauty. Written when he was 17 years of age, "When Sue Wears Red" is a sign of his early maturity as a poet, and, according to Onwuchekwa Jemie, "The poem derives its power from its vision of eternity and from the holler and shout of religious enthusiasm (Come with a blast of trumpets / Jesus!)" (133). "When Sue Wears Red" incorporates two elements that are representative of Hughes's poetry: music and simplicity.

Hughes's love affair with blues poetry resulted in one of his most famous poems, "The Weary Blues," with the speaker commenting on the blues tradition itself. This poem is quite different from his others. Rather than being the performer, the speaker is a spectator at a blues performance:

> Swaying to and fro on his rickety stool
> He played that sad raggy tune like a musical fool.

Sweet Blues!
Coming from a black man's soul. (12–15)

Hughes's poetry is rarely written in any particular poetic form, but he makes use of rhyme and metre without being bound by them. In "The Weary Blues" he uses a straightforward *aab* rhyme scheme with multiple variations, and his skill is such that the reader may come away feeling as if there is a hidden rhyme scheme where there is none. Hughes also captures the musical form of most blues songs:

I got the Weary Blues
And I can't be satisfied.
Got the Weary Blues
And can't be satisfied —
I ain't happy no mo'
And I wish that I had died. (25–30)

The colloquial diction, rhythm, and rhyme scheme representative of African American blues and jazz music of the time are clearly captured in Hughes's verse. He preserves the spontaneous improvisation so central to blues and jazz; this improvisational tone permeates Hughes's poetry in general (Cullen 3). It is interesting to note, however, that, although "Hughes prided himself on being an impromptu and impressionistic writer of poetry...an analysis of some of his poems on economic and social class issues will reveal that much of his poetry was carefully and artfully crafted" (Barksdale, "Hughes" 96). "The Weary Blues" marked a change in Hughes's poetic direction: "by 1926 he was beginning to focus on scenes and settings and themes that were less than palatable to the self-appointed monitors of black cultural development during the twenties" (Barksdale, *Langston Hughes* 17). Countee Cullen, a fellow poet, expresses this view clearly in a review of Hughes's book of poetry, *The Weary Blues*, published in 1926: "in the light of reflection I wonder if jazz poems really belong to that dignified company, that select and austere circle of high literary expression which we call poetry" (4). It is a sign of Hughes's determination to represent the lives of the people he knew in his poetry that such reviews from his associates and fellow poets failed to deter him from writing in his unique poetic style and concerning himself with socially explosive subject matter.

One of Hughes's most controversial poems is "Christ in Alabama," which was published as part of a series of poems called "The Bible Belt." It was written in response to the Scottsboro case, in which eight young black men were summarily convicted of raping two white women after narrowly escaping a riot lynching (Berry 119, 129–30). They were subsequently executed in the electric chair. "Christ in Alabama" was first published in Hughes's play *Scottsboro Limited* in 1932: "Christ is a nigger, / Beaten and black: / Oh, bare your back!" (1–3). Hughes compares the eight men to a black figure of Christ who has been lynched. According to Jemie, "'Christ is a nigger' in two senses: in the historical sense as a brown-skinned Jew...and in the symbolic sense of Jesus as an alien presence" (113). Jemie goes on to state that both the figure of Christ and the black men function as scapegoats for society. Hughes's references to "Mammy of the South" (5) and Mary, as well as to "White Master above" (8) and God, create a dual metaphor. The religious connotations are clear, with the figure of Christ being Mary's son and also the son of God. These figures are then cast by Hughes into the roles of wealthy white Americans in the South. The figure of Christ represents the black men's eternal standing as heroes, but may also suggest the stigmatized (but nonetheless common) interracial mixing between white men and black women, and white women and black men. The simple rhyme scheme (*abb*) and the minimal metre (two or three feet to a line) lend credence to Hughes's image of Christ as an uneducated black man.

While "Christ in Alabama" may seem artless, Hughes has chosen his images, diction, and structure carefully in order to support his dual metaphors. His susceptibility to blues rhythm and style is present even here, where the third line in each stanza serves the same function as the third set of lines in a blues stanza. The refrain becomes half command, half chorus: "Oh bare your back! / ...Silence your mouth / ...Grant Him your love" (3–9). Hughes's attachment to African American folk idioms is evident. His choice of diction echoes specific words found in folk speech, such as "Mammy" (5), certain sentence structures, such as

"Nigger Christ" (12), and certain exclamations that recall gospel music when read in the context of the poem, such as "Oh" (3). The diction serves to solidify the connection between Hughes's dual metaphor of Christ in the religious sense and the figure of Christ in the social or political sense.

Hughes's unique poetic techniques, which incorporated African American blues and jazz music, colloquialism, rhythm and simplicity, all culminate in an often ironic, humorous exposition on the subject that occupied Hughes all his life: black folklore, and the subversive racial divide that perpetuates, in some form or another, the long-standing disunity between black people and white people. He demonstrated that "the local and the regional can—and do—become universal" (Meltzer 257). Langston Hughes passed away on 22 May 1967 (Meltzer 257). His writing, including his poetry, proves his determination to live his life as an author writing about his people.

WORKS CITED

Barksdale, Richard. "Hughes: His Times and His Humanistic Techniques." *Langston Hughes: Critical Perspectives Past and Present*. Ed. Henry Louis Gates Jr. and K.A. Appiah. Amistad Literary Series. New York: Amistad, 1993. 96.

——. *Langston Hughes: The Poet and His Critics*. Chicago: American Library, 1977.

Berry, Faith. *Langston Hughes Before and Beyond Harlem*. Westport: Lawrence Hill, 1983.

Cullen, Countee. "The Weary Blues." *Langston Hughes: Critical Perspectives Past and Present*. Ed. Henry Louis Gates Jr. and K.A. Appiah. Amistad Literary Series. New York: Amistad, 1993. 3–7.

Davis, Arthur P. "Langston Hughes: Cool Poet." *Langston Hughes, Black Genius: A Critical Evaluation*. Ed. Therman O'Daniel. New York: William Morrow, 1971. 19.

Elmann, Richard, and Robert O'Clair, eds. *The Norton Anthology of Modern Poetry*. 2nd ed. New York: W.W. Norton, 1988.

Hughes, Langston. "The Negro Speaks of Rivers." Elmann and O'Clair 647.

——. *Scottsboro Limited: Four Poems and a Play in Verse*. New York: Golden Stair, 1932.

——. "The Weary Blues." Elmann and O'Clair 647–48.

——. "When Sue Wears Red." *Poetry for Young People: Langston Hughes*. Ed. Arnold Rampersad and David Roessel. New York: Sterling, 2006. 15.

Jemie, Onwuchekwa. *Langston Hughes: An Introduction to the Poetry*. New York: Columbia UP, 1976.

Meltzer, Milton. *Langston Hughes: A Biography*. New York: Thomas Y. Crowell, 1968.

39 Blues for Bruce

MARTIN M. TWEEDALE

NOT MANY OF MY ACADEMIC FRIENDS could be found Friday nights weaving through the smoke-shrouded crowd at the Commercial, but as often as not I'd see Bruce standing off to the side taking in the performance, nodding to the beat. It was some time before I learned how knowledgeable about blues music he was and how committed he was to the success of its local practitioners. For a while I assumed that, like me, he listened to the sounds just for the connection they made with some part of the gut that received little exercise from the goings-on in the Humanities Centre, but without which one might shrivel up from within. I'm sure that was part of it, but gradually I discovered that, for Bruce, it was something more, something that fit into the academic side of his life more than it did into that side of mine. He used to give courses on blues lyrics and bring in local musicians to show the youngsters how it sounded. No one doubts there was some great poetry produced by blues songwriters, especially the earlier ones writing from their Delta roots. Still, it was unusual in academia to give that much attention to any song lyrics of the twentieth century. I never asked Bruce just what *he* thought about the educational value of the course; but I have thought about it myself, and Bruce might have had some sympathy for my line of thought.

You can call the blues, you can call the blues any old thing you please
You can call the blues any old thing you please
But the blues ain't nothing but the doggone heart disease
(Traditional)

What interests me here is the relevance of blues music and lyrics to the humanities. Musicologists have had their field day with the blues, and anthropologists of the folklore sort have been all over the geography of blues from the Delta to Memphis to St Louis and, of course, to "sweet home" Chicago. One could well think that those studies pretty well exhaust whatever significance the blues would have for academics *qua* academics, but Bruce would have dissented, and I do, too. I'd like to start this dissent not with the bizarre socio-economic arrangements of the Mississippi Delta in the early twentieth century, nor with the sophisticated rhythms that came over from West Africa, and not with twelve bars and flatted thirds—stuff I don't really understand and evidently never will—but with some reflections on the music's gut appeal.

Yes, I cried last night and I ain't gonna cry no more
Yes, I cried last night and I ain't gonna cry no more
But the good book tells us you got to reap just what you sow
(Charley Patton, "Pea Vine Blues")

First of all, contrary to what one might think from the name, blues is hardly ever sad—I mean sad in the way that tries to make you cry, like so much folk music from the Celtic tradition does. I heard the other day a well-known and very fine balladeer of Celtic music say that song after song just said, "I left her, and now she's dead and gone." There is in that music this overwhelming sense of supreme happiness and joy having been glimpsed and then missed, and now we are left with that sweet sense of the tragedy of our lives. Well, the blues is hardly ever like that. It's not that the originators of the style were unacquainted with tragedy and missed chances for happiness; it's just that their attitude toward all that is entirely different. I'm tempted here to say that, while there is recognition of tragedies, there is no tragic sense of life.

Instead, there is the sense that life is to be fully embraced, no matter what it brings, including all the pain and agony that comes when you don't try to protect yourself from pain and agony.

> *I'm lookin' for a woman who's lookin' for a low-down man*
> *I'm lookin' for a woman who's lookin' for a low-down man*
> *Ain't nobody in town get more low-down than I can*
> (Freddie Spruell, "Low-down Mississippi Bottom Man")

Everyone knows that sex is really dangerous, and I'm not talking about syphilis and AIDS. All human societies officially encourage a lot of repression of sexual passions and with good reason. Eros leads us down a path at the end of which is violence and Thanatos. Eros is about breaking the eggs to make the cake, and often the cake never gets made. The blues, we find, is endlessly about male-female relationships and all the stuff that goes on in them. Other traditions, of course, deal with them too, but it's usually with LOVE and all that sickly feeling that comes over you when you've got a real crush — and then often the crush is not returned in kind, and, oh, how that hurts, or she or he goes away, and the sun is gone forever from the Red River Valley. That's not the way the blues handles all this.

> *I'm gonna take my whip and whup her, I'm gonna shup her down to*
>   *the ground*
> *I'm gonna take my dirk and stab her, you know I'm gonna turn it round*
>   *and round*
> (Robert Lockwood, "Little Boy Blue")

> *I take a long look right smack down in your mind*
> *I take a long look right smack down in your mind*
> *And I see more women, all up and down the line*
> (Charlie Patton, "Mind Reader Blues")

The shade of blue of blues is not robin's egg or some other pastel; it is much darker, more like Prussian. The emotions that are stirred are the perilous ones, the ones that can lead to things really bad, like murder. Some Celtic folk songs deal with those, too. Among the most famous lovers of American song have got to be Frankie and Johnnie, and we all know what Frankie did to her wandering Johnnie. That's a sad and tragic ballad; you come away thinking, man, I'm never going to go there. If I've got a gal like Frankie, I'm sure going to stay away from all those other women. Not so the blues.

> Yeah I love my baby, just like I love myself
> O-o-o-oh, just like I love myself
> Well if she don't have me, she won't have nobody else
> (Son House, "Preachin' the Blues")

> I like to fuss and fight
> I like to fuss and fight
> Lord, and get sloppy drunk off a bottle and ball
> And walk the streets all night
> (Charley Patton, "Elder Green Blues")

To understand this you have to realize that the blues originated as party music down there in the Delta, where parties were a lot else besides boozing: like gambling, whoring, and fighting. Young men and women came to those parties to let loose after a week of working long hours in the fields and kitchens just to make a bare living. They knew the parties were bad—like sinful. There were preachers and church choirs aplenty to tell them that. What that party music did was give them *permission*: permission to feel all those perilous, erotic emotions that make life so intense. Protect yourself against these, and you seal yourself away from life: that's the message of the blues, if you want to think it has a message. The more the peril is recognized the more intense the experience. The songs are *not* saying, "Don't be afraid of Love, because it's really this beautiful thing that will inevitably enhance your life; just open your heart up to it and let the warm light in." That's Tin Pan Alley and Rogers and Hammerstein. The blues is giving you permission to feel something bad and very possibly destructive of your life and the lives of those closest to you. It knows the cold, dark side of Eros.

> Early this morning when you knocked upon my door
> Early this morning when you knocked upon my door
> I said, "Hello Satan, I believe it's time to go."
> Me and the Devil was walking side by side
> Me and the Devil was walking side by side
> I'm going to beat my woman until I get satisfied.
> (Robert Johnson, "Me and the Devil Blues")

At the extreme is a certain toying with the satanic. Robert Johnson promoted a legend about himself to the effect that he had made a sort of Faustian pact with the devil one night at a crossroads. It was the devil that had given him that way of making music that drew so many over to his darker side. Auburn "Pat" Hare wrote a song called "I'm Gonna Murder My Baby," and then went off some years later and did exactly that.

> I'm gonna buy me a Johnson machine gun and a carload of
>   explosion balls
> I'm gonna be a walkin' cyclone, from Saginaw to the Niagara Falls
> ....
> Now, little girl, the undertaker's been here, girl, and I gave him your
>   height and size
> Now if you don't be makin' whoopee with the Devil tomorrow this
>   time, baby,
> God knows you'll be surprised
> (Sunnyland Slim, "Johnson Machine Gun")

Blues music at the present time has few pretensions to that shade of blue; for the most part, it is fun party music in slightly risqué venues like the Commercial. But I recall listening to one of the musicians Bruce arranged to play at the Yardbird, Otis Taylor, and there was more than a hint of danger and bad stuff lurking in the background of his playing. We are being given permission to feel things most of us have firmly decided to repress; the blues, the really deep blues, invites us to crack that shell for once.

> Go look at the weather, I believe it's goin' to be a flood
> Go and look out at the weather, I believe it's goin' to be a flood
> I believe my baby gon' quit me, because I can feel it all in my blood
> (Muddy Waters, "Flood")

What has all this to do with the humanities? Those of us who have lived and worked in the "arts-and-letters" side of academia know how great is the temptation to take the goal of our work to be some quasi-scientific understanding of what has gone on and is still going on in human culture, and no doubt that is a goal; but, as Aristotle used to say, some of the things we do for their own sakes we also do for the sake of something else, and I think that is true of this particular goal. The thing it is for the sake of, I believe, is opening up the lives of students and readers (and hopefully even just friends and acquaintances) to what being human can mean, and doing this in a way that changes their ways of living. We know some things in a way that does not make them any sort of force in our lives; they are there, like the stars, and we know *about* them, and that's as far as it goes. Other things we know as powers to be reckoned with. Thoughts and ideas can be like that; but feelings, urges, and passions are often even more powerful and more difficult to integrate into life. The way of repression denies that the thought and feeling, whatever they may be, are really us, really human. The humanities teacher resists that way and says embrace it, deal with it, and in doing so enhance your life. To move students in that direction is *the* goal of the humanities, that which all else is for the sake of.

> Now I met the blues this mornin' walkin' just like a man
> O-o-o-oh, walkin' just like a man
> I said good mornin' blues, now give me your right hand
> (Son House, "Preachin' the Blues")

That, I suggest, is also the spirit of the blues on encountering those emotions talked about above, and that, I think, is why the blues are a gift to the humanities. They are giving us the permission that we and our students need. I don't know whether Bruce thought this way about why the blues had a place in the curriculum, but I would suggest that as he listened to the music he loved he would have joined with me (and Cicero) in approving that famous line from Terence: *nil humani alienum mihi puto*—nothing human seems alien to me.

WORKS CITED

Hare, Auburn "Pat." "I'm Gonna Murder My Baby." *Mystery Train*. Rounder, 1990.

House, Son [Edward James]. *Preachin' the Blues*. Paramount, 1930.

Johnson, Robert. "Me and the Devil Blues." *Me and the Devil Blues*. Universal, 2004.

Lockwood, Robert. "Little Boy Blue." *Robert Lockwood Plays Robert and Robert*. Evidence, 1993.

Patton, Charlie. "Elder Green Blues." *Charlie Patton: Complete Recordings, 1929–1934*. Disc 3. JSP, 2002.

———. "Mind Reader Blues." *Charlie Patton: Complete Recordings, 1929–1934*. Disc 5. JSP, 2002.

———. "Pea Vine Blues." *Charlie Patton: Complete Recordings, 1929–1934*. Disc 1. JSP, 2002.

Slim, Sunnyland. "Johnson Machine Gun." *Be Careful How You Vote*. Earwig, 1992.

Spruell, Freddie. "Low-down Mississippi Bottom Man." *Mississippi Bottom Blues*. Mamlish, 1973.

Waters, Muddy. "Flood." *The Chess Box*. Chess/MCA, 1989.

40 Montana Motel Blues

CHRISTOPHER WISEMAN

Big hot sun is slidin', drips like oil down through the sky.
That Montana sun is slidin', drips like oil down through the sky.
And I just can't get my thoughts right, no matter how I try.
The blues can mean you're broken, the blues can mean just sad.
You know the blues can mean you're broken or the blues can mean just sad.
But whatever blues I'm nursin', I ain't never felt this bad.
That old song has it right, motel ceiling stares you down.
I know that old song has it right, the motel ceiling stares you down.
I'm in a breeze-block prison in a nowhere breeze-block town.
Sheets smell kinda musty, towels are worn-out thin.
Yeah the sheets smell kinda musty, towels are worn-out thin.
The blues can mean you're broken, the blues can mean just sad.
Yeah the blues can mean you're broken, the blues can mean just sad.
But whatever blues I'm nursin', I ain't never felt this bad.
Moon over Montana, its light is shinin' down.
This moon over Montana, its light comes pourin' down.
Gonna leave tomorrow, don't look for me around.

Epilogue

A Tribute to Daddy

LAURA STOVEL

Laura Stovel gave this talk at the celebration for Bruce Stovel,
the week after his death.

THANKS TO EVERYONE FOR COMING from campus and further afield; our father would have been delighted. We have been extremely touched during this very difficult week by the outpouring of support we have felt from the people in this room. My father would be speechless to know you have all gathered here at this service in his name. For those of you who did not know my father and are here in support of my mother, my brother, or myself, or of each other, thank you for coming. My father would have been very grateful for that, too.

I am going to talk with you for a few moments about my father. I am going to share stories about him that are family favourites. They will be new to all of you except his family members. We hope that you recognize the man that you knew in each of them.

The story that I will tell was told to me many years ago by my grandmother, my father's mother. When my father was growing up, his family moved many times. According to my grandmother, at the time of this particular move, my father was three years old. Following the move into the new house, my grandmother mused aloud that she needed to hang her pictures on the walls. The next morning she awoke to sounds of banging coming from downstairs. When she went down to the living room she found that my father had just finished hanging all of the paintings and pictures side by side around the room, at a height of two feet off the floor. This story is so revelatory of my father: his energy, his earnestness, his disregard for obstacles, and his loving service to others. We have wonderful memories of my father. I would like to share a few.

When Grant and I were small, my family lived in Halifax. For a time, my mother taught ballet all afternoon on Saturdays, and my father would take us out on Sunday mornings to give her a well-deserved chance to sleep in. He decided that, on these mornings, we would visit every playground in Halifax in turn, until we had explored every one. On Sunday morning, he would get out his map of the city and locate that week's destination. We went to every one in the city until we had our favourite spots, which we returned to over and over. In this way, he had a gift for making things exciting and fun for us as children. He played tirelessly with us: spelling bees, Scrabble (he valued spelling), memory, Monopoly. He seemed to have an encyclopedic knowledge. There was no question we could pose that he couldn't answer, whether it had to do with historical events, geography, politics, etymologies, or, of course, literature. When Grant and I were a little older, Trivial Pursuit made its debut, and he vanquished all comers. My father was thrilled in 1983 when VCRs were invented, as this meant he could watch his favourite movies again, many for the first time since they had been released. He screened for us, at ages 12 and 8, and generally without my mother's knowledge or consent, a number of his favourites: *The Day of the Jackal, The Graduate, Five Easy Pieces, Missing, The Conversation, Monty Python and the Holy Grail, Klute, Dog Day Afternoon.*

My family moved to Edmonton in 1985, by which time I was 14 and Grant was 11. In our first years in Edmonton, we would come here, to the Faculty Club, for dinner on Friday nights, and then go home to watch a movie, all four of us squeezing onto my parents' king-size bed. Always torn between selections at the video store and unable to choose, my father would bring home three movies each Friday night, which we would "preview" for ten minutes each before settling on a pick for that evening. As Grant and I grew up, my father delighted in getting to know our friends, about whom, amazingly, he could remember every detail, even before he had met them. He took an interest in our interests. He was thrilled with my brother's interest in music, and followed his gigs devotedly. He embraced the Edmonton Folk Music Festival, and in our teenage years, he would pack a huge cooler with tuna-fish sandwiches and granola bars to sustain us all weekend. He continued to attend the Folkfest with enthusiasm every year. He could always be spotted in his wide-brimmed straw hat at the Blues Stage.

Through the years growing up, there was the Big Island, at his family's long-held property in Quebec, where we spent time every summer. No one enjoyed it more than he did. He had a cherished routine: always an early riser, he would take his morning dip at his preferred swimming spot, make breakfast for everyone, then retire with his coffee to read his book and watch the hummingbirds. In the evenings, he would read under the window that got the last light of the day, and then take his final swim. Afterwards, as the four members of my family sat talking after the light had gone, he would sometimes quietly fall asleep, though he never, ever admitted it. He was the heart of the place for us. Those were wonderful times.

We thought it would be in keeping with our father's nature, rather than talking about his many accomplishments, to speak about things he enjoyed. We are going to share a few with you.

My father loved teaching, and he was very fond of his students. He talked about them frequently, even after he retired last June. Grant and I can still recall the oft-mentioned names of particular students from Dalhousie and the University of Alberta who, though we never met them, were famous in our household. When my mother first began teaching at the Windsor School for Girls in Boston in the 1960s, my father would read her high-school students' essays for pleasure, and then would later astonish her students, when he met them, by remarking on how much he had enjoyed particular passages in their papers. About 12 years ago, we discovered a bag of candy hidden in one of our kitchen drawers, and thus uncovered one of his secrets: that when the weather was inclement, or when it was, he felt, a difficult or taxing week for his students, or if he was making them give oral presentations, he would bring a bag of candy to class, and give it out to his students. He always wondered to what extent this had contributed to his winning the Students' Union Teaching Award several years ago.

My father loved to read. He had an immense breadth of knowledge of literature, from the classics of Greece and Rome to the most contemporary novels. He could quote at length, seemingly from any source, and rejoiced in spontaneously breaking into *The Canterbury Tales*. He would read anything, and famously whizzed through books at the rate of one per day, often reading other people's Christmas presents before they had a chance to get to them, including occasions when he had been the one to bestow the present. We could detect this because, although he tried to be surreptitious, he could not help leaving his trademark crease down the middle of the spine of one's pristine new book. He also inspired the long-held tradition in our family of the "First Sentence," wherein the recipient of a new book at Christmas and birthdays must read the first sentence for the approval of the rest of the family. A particularly good first sentence would be greeted by my father with appreciative noises, a cry of "Pretty good!" and, when it had been especially superb, a request for the second sentence. Always a reader of expansive tastes, in recent years he developed an especial fondness for "chick lit," and we have several great photographs of him happily engrossed in books with bright pink and yellow covers.

My father loved conversation. Never able to keep a secret, he proclaimed his identification with the blues lyric "Don't start me to talking — I'll tell you everything I know." He was delighted when, a few years ago, he discovered a T-shirt that bore this line. When I would go to visit him at his office in the Humanities Centre at the University of Alberta, it was rare that I would have to go all the way to his office to find him. Usually I would discover him in one of the hallways or common spaces engaged in conversation with one of his students or colleagues. If he was in his office, he was usually on the phone.

My father loved animals. He would return from holidays with my mother full of stories about particular dogs who had been staying at the same hotel as my parents, with whom he had frolicked during his stay. Though I could not say that he unequivocally loved the several squirrels who, over the years, chose to make their homes in my parents' roof and attic, he had an affectionate respect and regard for their persistence at storing their pine cones in the crannies of our house, even as he pronounced them "pesky," which was one of his favourite words. When faced with the dilemma of how to deter the squirrels, he settled on a method that he felt would be least likely to be traumatic to them. He located a trap that would confine the squirrel without injuring it. Then, once he had trapped one of our invaders, he would drive it 45 minutes out of town to a particularly attractive stand of trees near Morinville, which he had chosen because he felt that the dispossessed squirrels would find it acceptable as a second home. He made many such runs over the last 15 years. The last time he did so, he got an $80 speeding ticket on the highway out to Morinville, which caused my mother to remark that that was the most expensive taxi ride that that squirrel was ever going to have.

He loved music, and he loved doing his radio show.

My father loved to be at home. As the chief cook in the household, he had an eclectic repertoire of dishes that he developed, including curry chicken, hash and mash, chili chicken, and stew. He took any opportunity to sneak a turkey into the oven, complete with his delicious gravy, stuffing, mashed potatoes, and cranberry sauce. The last time I saw him, on January 1st, he surprised us with a turkey, which he said was both festive and a little sad, as New Year's Day meant our Christmastime was over. He talked whimsically over the years about opening his own restaurant in his retirement, which he would call Bruce's Roadside Restaurant; it would be a honky-tonk kind of place where he would serve his dishes off a limited menu. While in the kitchen in the throes of creation, he would get caught up in conversation, and lean back against the stove; many a sweater bore singe marks and burn holes. He loved conversing over mealtimes, and he loved sitting together in our sunroom having tea or watching favourite movies. He also seemed to love retiring to his study to read or quietly washing dishes in the kitchen while the life of the house went on around him. Both his study and the kitchen are adjacent to the sunroom, where we spend most of our time, and so from his chair in his study and from the kitchen he could keep an eye on and an ear cocked for proceedings. He would frequently abandon his task to reappear and join in with us.

Finally, my father loved Edmonton. He lived in this city for the last 21 and a half years of his life, longer than he had lived anywhere before, and for him, it was home. He would often remark upon his return from a trip elsewhere that although other places might have things to recommend them, he did not desire to live anywhere else. What did he love about Edmonton? He loved the University of Alberta and the campus radio station, CJSR. He loved the river valley, and the festivals that were held there, the Folkfest and the Bluesfest. He loved the places he went to hear music: the Commercial Hotel, the Yardbird Suite, the Sidetrack, Festival Place, and the Arden Theatre. He loved the ballet, the opera, the symphony, and Edmonton's many theatre spaces. He loved the places my family gathered for birthday dinners and other celebrations: the High Level Diner, and in recent years, Bua Thai. Most of all, as you all know, he loved the people who bring each of these places to life. He would have loved to be here today to see all of you.

I would say that, as a rule, my father did not often offer unsolicited advice. There was one thing, though, which he would often say to me when I came home exhausted after being up all night writing a paper in university, after a set of exams in medical school, or after a draining week. He would say to me, "You have to let the well fill up." He meant that when you are tired and spent, you need to take some time to rest and recover before you can turn to another task. I think that is what we are all doing now: letting the well fill up when it feels most terribly empty. All of you are helping us with this, and we see that you are helping each other, too. Thank you very much for this. My father was the sweetest, most generous, and humblest of men. As my mother said earlier in this terrible week, we will miss him all day, every day.

In closing, I would like to read a passage from James Joyce's novella "The Dead." It is a story my father admired and loved. I read it first when I was 18, in a literature class at the University of Alberta. Although I thought it was intensely good, because I was 18, I had to complain about it nonetheless. I told my father that I thought it was good, but that nothing happened for the first 40 pages. He looked at me intently and said, "There is not a single unnecessary word in that story." Here is the final paragraph of "The Dead":

A few light taps upon the pane made him turn to the window. It had begun to snow again. He watched sleepily the flakes, silver and dark, falling obliquely against the lamplight. The time had come for him to set out on his journey westward. Yes, the newspapers were right: snow was general all over Ireland. It was falling on every part of the dark central plain, on the treeless hills, falling softly upon the Bog of Allen and, farther westward, softly falling into the dark mutinous Shannon waves. It was falling, too, upon every part of the lonely churchyard on the hill where Michael Furey lay buried. It lay thickly drifted on the crooked crosses and headstones, on the spears of the little gate, on the barren thorns. His soul swooned slowly as he heard the snow falling faintly through the universe and faintly falling, like the descent of their last end, upon all the living and the dead. (223–24)

WORK CITED

Joyce, James. "The Dead." *Dubliners.* New York: Viking Compass, 1967. 175–224.

Contributors

Book

AMANDA ASH is a graduate of the University of Alberta, where she attained her BA in English Honours. She currently works as a journalist and editor for a number of Canadian print and online publications.

ELAINE BANDER was born in New York in 1946, received her BA (1968) and PHD (1981) from McGill University, and has recently retired from the English Department of Dawson College in Montreal. She has published a number of articles on Jane Austen, Frances Burney, and English detective fiction, among other subjects, as well as poems in *Grain, Amethyst,* and *WLA: War, Literature and the Arts.* She currently serves on the editorial board of *Persuasions,* the journal of the Jane Austen Society of North America, and is the regional Coordinator of the Montreal–Quebec City region of JASNA.

DOUGLAS BARBOUR, Professor Emeritus of English, University of Alberta, has published many books of criticism and poetry, including *Fragmenting Body etc.* (2000), *Breath Takes* (2002), *A Flame on the Spanish Stairs* (2003), *Continuations,* with Sheila E. Murphy (2006), and *Wednesdays'* (2008). He was inaugurated into the City of Edmonton Cultural Hall of Fame in 2003.

LAURA CAPPELLO BROMLING is a native of Edmonton. She has an MA in English literature, and her special area of interest is the nineteenth-century British novel.

MARY M. CHAN is a PHD student in English at the University of Alberta. Her dissertation examines domestic interiors in eighteenth-century British novels. She has published on Austen in *Persuasions* and *Persuasions On-line*, and presented at conferences of the Jane Austen Society of North America.

INING TRACY CHAO is an educator specializing in educational technologies. She collaborates with faculty members to integrate technology into teaching. Her support for faculty has helped many re-think their teaching models and incorporate learner-centred approach in their practices. Her most recent challenge is educating her two young daughters who inspire her everyday.

MARGARET DRABBLE was born in Sheffield in 1939 and educated at Newnham College, Cambridge, where she studied English literature. She has published seventeen novels, most recently *The Sea Lady* (2006), and edited two editions of *The Oxford Companion to English Literature* (1985–2000). She is married to the biographer Michael Holroyd.

NATASHA DUQUETTE is an Assistant Professor at Biola University. She has published in *Mosaic, Notes and Queries*, and *Christianity and Literature* and has recently edited *Sublimer Aspects: Interfaces between Literature, Aesthetics, and Theology* (Cambridge Scholars, 2007). Her research on Mary Anne Schimmelpenninck is supported by a Chawton House Fellowship.

JANNIE EDWARDS has taught creative writing and English at Grant MacEwan College for over 25 years. She has published widely in literary journals and anthologies and is the author of two books of poetry–*The Possibilities of Thirst* (1997) and *Blood Opera: The Raven Tango Poems* (2006), the latter in collaboration with visual artist Paul Saturley. Her videopoem *Engrams: Reach and Seize Memory*, inspired by the work of Edmonton artist Darci Mallon, features Edwards's poetry translated into American Sign Language and performed by Deaf actor and translator Linda Cundy.

MEGAN EVANS graduated from the University of Alberta in 2005 with a double major in Drama and English. She has spent the past few years travelling and teaching ESL in Asia. When she is finished with her mis/adventures, she hopes to complete an MA in journalism—but for now it's all one day at a time.

KELSEY EVERTON graduated from the University of Alberta in 2007 with a BA in English and Psychology. She currently lives in Edmonton, and enjoys reading, editing, writing, and finding ways to procrastinate working on all of the above.

TOM FAULKNER collaborated with Bruce Stovel to raise undergraduate writing standards at Dalhousie University when they were both young professors. Faulkner is now Associate Professor of Church and Society in the Faculty of Theology of The University of Winnipeg. He studies academic freedom, combat ethics, healing miracles, and disaster management as theological issues. He also performs folk and country music, and is in awe of Bruce's mastery of the blues.

MELISSA FURROW is Professor of English at Dalhousie University, where her friend and colleague Bruce Stovel cheerfully took over her Middle English literature seminar as an unpaid overload during her maternity leave in 1983.

JEANNINE GREEN, Bruce Peel Special Collections Librarian, graduated from the University of Alberta with a BA SPEC. in 1977 and an MLS in 1980. After a brief foray into the world of corporate librarianship, she returned to the university to a position in the Undergraduate Library and Special Collections. She was appointed Head of Special Collections in 2005.

ISOBEL GRUNDY, FRSC, former Henry Marshall Tory Professor at the University of Alberta, is one of three editors of *Orlando: Women's Writing in the British Isles from the Beginnings to the Present*, published online by subscription, Cambridge University Press, 2006. She has published particularly on Austen, Johnson, and Lady Mary Wortley Montagu.

JONATHAN LOCKE HART (University of Alberta) has published books of poetry, including *Breath and Dust* (2000), *Dream China* (2002), and *Dream Salvage* (2003), plus scholarly books, most recently, *Interpreting Cultures* (2006) and *Empires and Colonies*. He has published poems in *Harvard Review*, *The Antigonish Review*, *Grain* and other literary magazines. A visiting fellow at Churchill College Cambridge, he has held visiting appointments at Toronto, Harvard, Princeton, and elsewhere.

HEIDI L.M. JACOBS has a BA (Hons) and MA in English from the University of Alberta and a PHD in English from the University of Nebraska-Lincoln. She is the English librarian at the University of Windsor's Leddy Library, where she finds particular joy in tending the Jane Austen collection.

HEIDI JANZ is a Post-Doctoral Researcher at the University of Manitoba and a visiting scholar with the University of Alberta's Dossetor Ethics Centre. In her "other life," Heidi is a writer/playwright. She's had plays produced at Fringe and Disability Arts Festivals. Her novel, *Sparrows on Wheels*, was published in 2004.

ROGER LEVESQUE is an Edmonton-based writer-broadcaster who has focussed his career on covering the sounds and personalities in jazz, blues, roots and world music. After joining CJSR Radio at the University of Alberta in the mid-1980s he eventually moved on to work for the CKUA Radio Network in 2005. His principal involvement in print media has been through the pages of the *Edmonton Journal*'s arts section since 1989.

AMANDA LIM was a student of Bruce Stovel during her Honours English degree at the University of Alberta. She is currently pursuing a doctorate degree at the University of Alberta in the field of contemporary Canadian poetry.

DAVID MARTIN recently completed an MA in English in Creative Writing from the University of Alberta and is currently writing and teaching in Calgary. His poems have appeared or are forthcoming in *The Fiddlehead*, *Event*, and *dANDelion*.

JULIET MCMASTER of the University of Alberta has taught and written on Austen for many years. Author of *Jane Austen on Love* and *Jane Austen the Novelist*, she is also co-editor with Edward Copeland of *The Cambridge Companion to Jane Austen* and co-editor with Bruce Stovel of *Jane Austen's Business*.

J.N. NODELMAN is currently Assistant Professor of English at the University of Winnipeg. He originally submitted his contribution to this volume as a student in one of Bruce Stovel's fondly remembered graduate courses in blues lyrics as lyric poetry at the University of Alberta.

PETER NORTH has been involved in the local regional roots music scene as a journalist in print, radio, and television and as a promoter of live music for the past 30 years. As a print journalist, North has been a columnist for 22 years, the last decade for the *Edmonton Journal*. His work in television included a six-year run co-producing the nationally broadcast music show *Country Beat*, on CBC. He was named Music Journalist of the Year in 1996 at the annual Canadian Music Industry Awards and named Media Person of the Year at the 2007 Western Canada Music Awards.

NADIA NIVEN RUSHDY graduated from the University of Alberta with a BA Honours in English in 2006. From Langston Hughes, she went on to study the role of African American women in various African American nationalist movements of the 1960s and in the gangsta rap music of the 1990s. Nadia is a founding member of the Jane Austen Fun [sic] Club of Edmonton.

PETER SABOR is Canada Research Chair in Eighteenth-Century Studies and Director of the Burney Centre at McGill University. His publications include (with Thomas Keymer) *Pamela in the Marketplace: Literary Controversy and Print Culture in Eighteenth-Century Britain and Ireland* (Cambridge University Press, 2005), and the *Juvenilia* volume in The Cambridge Edition of the Works of Jane Austen (2006).

KIM SOLGA teaches modern drama and performance theory at the University of Western Ontario. She is the author of *Witnessing Violence Against Women in Early Modern Performance: Invisible Acts* and co-editor of *Performance and the City*, both forthcoming from Palgrave MacMillan in 2009.

AMY STAFFORD took Dr Stovel's fantastic year-long course on the novel, early in her undergraduate degree. The class was such a joy that she took four more courses with him, and, due to his encouragement, she is currently working toward an MA in English at the University of Alberta under the supervision of Nora Foster Stovel. Her contribution was written as her undergraduate honours thesis, which Dr Stovel supervised.

BRUCE STOVEL retired in 2006 as Emeritus Professor from the University of Alberta Department of English, where he taught courses in the English novel and eighteenth-century literature. While he published numerous essays on fiction, his special interest was Jane Austen. He co-edited books on Austen and co-convened a Jane Austen conference.

LAURA STOVEL completed her BA in Honours English and her MD at the University of Alberta, where she also pursued her residency in psychiatry. She is Assistant Professor of Psychiatry in the University of Alberta Faculty of Medicine and Director of the Day Program in Psychiatry at the University of Alberta Hospital.

NORA FOSTER STOVEL is Professor of English at the University of Alberta, where she teaches twentieth-century literature. She has published books and articles on Jane Austen, D.H. Lawrence, Margaret Drabble, and Margaret Laurence. *Divining Margaret Laurence: A Study of Her Complete Writings* was published in 2008. She is currently composing *"Sparkling Subversion": Carol Shields's "Double Vision"* and is planning *Women with Wings*, a study of nineteenth-century Romantic ballets.

KERRY TAILLEFER graduated with distinction from the University of Alberta B ED program in 2006 with an English major in the Secondary route. She is currently completing an English major and Film Studies minor in the After-degree BA program and has plans to teach English overseas.

KARI TROGEN did her Honours BA in English at the University of Alberta in her hometown of Edmonton, and has a Creative Writing MA from UNB in Fredericton. She has written a play about the early life of L.M. Montgomery, and hopes to write and edit young adult fiction.

MARTIN M. TWEEDALE, Professor Emeritus of Philosophy at the University of Alberta, was born in New Jersey and got hooked on blues and jazz while a grad student at UCLA. He came to Alberta in 1988, after 15 years teaching in New Zealand, and retired in 2002.

JESSICA WALLACE graduated from the University of Alberta with an Honours After-degree in English Literature in 2007. She often writes for the Journalists for Human Rights' publication *Speak News* and plans to pursue a career in international journalism. Jessica enjoys any time she can write outdoors on her front step.

CHRISTOPHER WISEMAN taught English for 30 years at the University of Calgary, where he founded the Creative Writing Program. He now writes and edits full-time. He has published a study of Edwin Muir's poetry, and ten books of poetry, the most recent of which is *In John Updike's Room*.

Blues CD

A saxophonist who plays the tenor, alto, and baritone horns, Edmonton's DAVE BABCOCK is also a vocalist, producer, songwriter and bandleader who has played with luminaries like Taj Mahal, k.d. lang and Solomon Burke, and has recorded with the likes of Amos Garrett and Jay McShann. In addition to being a member of the Edmonton Folk Music Festival house band, Dave has also been spearheading groups of his own for many years, including the Jump Orchestra and Dave Babcock & the Nightkeepers.

The son of two English professors, Montreal's MICHAEL JEROME BROWNE is a multi-instrumentalist who is internationally known as a singer-songwriter, accompanist, producer, and student of many different North American roots music styles.

Sherwood Park, Alberta, native CHRIS BRZEZICKI is a versatile bassist whose past perfomance and/or recording credits include work with the Sean Carney Band, Big Time Sarah, the Rockin' Highliners, Carol Fran, Little Mike and the Tornadoes, Sue Foley, Big Jack Johnson, Rick Holmstrom, Sonny Rhodes, and Shirley Johnson.

A native of Cape Breton, BOBBY CAMERON is an Edmonton singer, song-writer, and guitar player who is at home in both electric and acoustic settings and in a variety of roots music styles. Over the course of his decades-long career in music, Bobby has garnered awards for his songwriting and his guitar playing from institutions as diverse as ARIA and MuchMusic, and has had his songs recorded by many different artists.

Edmonton's DAVID "CRAWDAD" CANTERA has been playing harmonica in a variety of musical settings from blues to country since the 1980s. In addition to performing with international acts such as Joe Beard, Mojo Buford, and Lazy Lester, David has been a part of Edmonton-based musical ensembles like Three Times the Blues, Jimmy and the Sleepers, and Come On In Our Kitchen.

KAT DANSER is an Edmonton-based singer-songwriter with several albums to her credit, as well as a degree in ethnomusicology from the University of Alberta. In addition to being a singer and songwriter, Kat plays an array of instruments, including acoustic, lap slide and resophonic guitars, as well as tack-head banjo and Zydeco scrub-board.

Known for his extensive involvement with the Chicago blues and R&B scene, B.J. EMERY has been a trombonist and featured vocalist with the Maurice John Vaughn Band for more than a quarter of a century. B.J. has toured the world playing music and has contributed trombone to albums by many different artists, including a solo disc of his own.

Born in Mississippi, LAFAYETTE "SHORTY" GILBERT is a legendary Chicago bluesman who has spent more than 20 years as a bass player and featured vocalist with the renowned group Eddie Shaw & the Wolf Gang, with whom he has toured all over the world and recorded several acclaimed albums.

GRAHAM GUEST is an Edmonton-based musician, singer, songwriter, producer and broadcaster. Within his wide spectrum of experiences in the music life, Graham has learned the blues music craft first-hand. A multi-faceted twenty-year association and friendship with Dr Bruce Stovel led to his involvement with this project.

A native of Manitoba, JIM GUIBOCHE has been an integral part of the Edmonton music scene since the early 1990s, playing guitar with a number of Alberta blues bands, as well as accompanying international artists like Lazy Lester, Larry Garner, Big Dave McLean, and Little Mike. Jim is also the leader of his own group, Edmonton-based Jimmy and the Sleepers.

Since leaving Osaka, Japan, in the mid 2000s for Edmonton, YUJI IHARA has delved deeply into the western Canadian blues and roots music scene, playing guitar for the likes of Donald Ray Johnson, Graham Guest, and the Boogie Patrol.

Grammy Award winner DONALD RAY JOHNSON is a native of Texas who has resided in Calgary since the 1980s. Donald is an accomplished drummer as well as being a singer and songwriter of international renown.

Hailing originally from Waterloo, Ontario, TIM LEE is an Edmonton-based musician who has spent many years fronting his group Tim Lee & the Revelators, and has also acted as an accompanist for many other blues artists, including Sonny Rhodes, Russell Jackson, and Mel Brown.

A singer, songwriter, and multi-instrumentalist, LARRY LEVER has been a major component of Edmonton's blues community since the 1980s. He first appeared on the scene as a member of the group Three Times the Blues, and was subsequently a member of the Oil City Sheiks for some years. Larry has since been fronting his own projects.

An accomplished and versatile guitar player and multi-instrumentalist, IAN MARTIN is also the owner/operator of a recording studio, the Twilight Living Room in Edmonton, where he has recorded and produced hundreds of artists. Ian is also a painter and a connoisseur of 1950s and 1960s pop culture, as well as an avid collector of musical instruments and recording equipment.

A blues harmonica devotee since childhood, SCOTT "SHADY" MCCRADY is a young Edmonton blues musician whose onstage credits include work with Big Dave McLean, Sonny Rhodes and Mojo Buford.

A recipient of the Maple Blues Awards' prestigious "Blues with a Feeling" Lifetime Achievement Award, Winnipeg's BIG DAVE MCLEAN is a legendary figure in the Canadian blues scene. He continues to tour and record prolifically, in acoustic and electric formats, both solo and with his band.

Edmonton bassist CLIFF MINCHAU has played electric and stand-up basses with a host of jazz, folk, pop, blues, and country music acts over a career that spans several decades, and which includes a lengthy stint spent performing and recording with Edmonton jazz and blues legend Big Miller.

Born in New York City, raised in the American Midwest and now residing in West Virginia, ANN RABSON first gained fame as a member of the W.C. Handy Award-winning group Saffire—The Uppity Blues Women, which she co-founded in 1987. A lifelong passion for blues music has also led to a highly successful solo career as a singer, songwriter, pianist, and guitar player.

The son of blues saxophone legend Eddie Shaw, Chicago's EDDIE "VAAN" SHAW was mentored in blues music since early childhood by artists like Howlin' Wolf, for whom Vaan's father acted as musical director for many years. Vaan has toured all over the world and recorded extensively, both as a solo artist and as a member of his father's group, Eddie Shaw & the Wolf Gang.

GRANT STOVEL is a drummer, producer, and radio host who lives in Edmonton. The son of Dr Bruce Stovel, Grant cherishes the years in which they enjoyed blues music together and co-hosted *Calling All Blues*, a weekly radio program on CJSR. His participation in this project is a continuation of his father's passions.

Born in Calgary, trumpeter and composer BOB TILDESLEY moved to Edmonton in the late 1970s, where he has worked with a wide variety of jazz, blues, and soul music artists. His recording credits include albums by Tommy Banks, P.J. Perry, Jay McShann, Mae Moore, and Long John Baldry. In addition to his many other projects, Bob also leads his own band, Bob Tildesley's Indigenous Aliens.

One of Chicago's best-loved and hardest-working blues bandleaders, MAURICE JOHN VAUGHN began his career as a saxophonist before taking up guitar, vocals, and keyboards. His career has seen him tour around the world many times over and issue several acclaimed albums, including *Dangerous Road*, *In the Shadow of the City*, and his landmark debut, *Generic Blues Album*.

TIM WILLIAMS is a Calgary-based singer, guitarist, and mandolinist who is active internationally in the musical and theatrical communities. He is also an acclaimed songwriter with a discography that spans several decades. In addition to creating his own records, Tim appears on numerous other recordings as a producer, a sideman, and a member of bands like Triple Threat and the Highwater Jug Band, as well as in a duo with Big Dave McLean.

CD Liner Notes

1. MAURICE JOHN VAUGHN — *Small Town Baby* (4:27)
   (Jimmy Walker)
   guitar and vocals: Maurice John Vaughn, trombone and background
   vocals: B.J. Emery

2. MICHAEL JEROME BROWNE — *It Takes Time* (4:19)
   (Otis Rush)
   guitar and vocals: Michael Jerome Browne, piano and organ: Graham Guest,
   bass: Ian Martin, drums: Grant Stovel

3. GRAHAM GUEST — *You've Got to Cry Out Loud (When the Sun Goes Down)* (4:31)
   (Graham Guest)
   piano, organ and vocals: Graham Guest, guitar: Eddie "Vaan" Shaw,
   bass: Lafayette "Shorty" Gilbert, drums: Grant Stovel

4. ANN RABSON — *Struttin' My Stuff* (3:28)
   (Lucille Bogan)
   acoustic guitar and vocals: Ann Rabson, piano: Graham Guest,
   drums: Grant Stovel

5. BIG DAVE MCLEAN — *Kind Hearted Woman Blues* (4:37)
   (Robert Johnson)
   Johnson resophonic guitar and vocals: Big Dave McLean,
   mandolin: Tim Williams

6.   DONALD RAY JOHNSON —*Alberta* (3:18)
   (public domain)
   vocals: Donald Ray Johnson, guitar: Yuji Ihara, harmonica: Scott McCrady,
   piano and organ: Graham Guest, bass: Chris Brzezicki, drums: Grant Stovel

7.   TIM WILLIAMS — *Let Your Shoe Leather Do The Talking* (2:56)
   (Tim Williams)
   acoustic guitar and vocals: Tim Williams, harmonica: Big Dave McLean

8.   TIM LEE —*(Is that Train) Heading West* (4:08)
   (Tim Lee)
   lead guitar and vocals: Tim Lee, organ and background vocals: Graham Guest,
   second guitar: Yuji Ihara, bass: Chris Brzezicki, drums: Grant Stovel,
   saxophones: Dave Babcock, trumpet: Bob Tildesley

9.   KAT DANSER —*(Notes from) The Other Side* (3:27)
   (Kat Danser)
   acoustic guitar and vocals: Kat Danser, twelve-string acoustic guitar and
   slide electric guitar: Michael Jerome Browne, upright bass: Cliff Minchau

10.   BOBBY CAMERON —*Cross Road Blues* (5:24)
    (Robert Johnson)
    guitar and vocals: Bobby Cameron, piano and organ: Graham Guest,
    bass: Chris Brzezicki, drums: Grant Stovel

11.   LARRY LEVER —*No Escape from the Blues* (6:26)
    (McKinley Morganfield)
    guitar and vocals: Larry Lever, lead guitar: Jim Guiboche, harmonica:
    David "Crawdad" Cantera, piano: Graham Guest, bass: Chris Brzezicki,
    drums: Grant Stovel

12.   EDDIE "VAAN" SHAW —*The Catfish Song* (9:00)
    (Eddie "Vaan" Shaw)
    acoustic guitar and vocals: Eddie "Vaan" Shaw, electric guitar: Yuji Ihara,
    piano: Graham Guest, upright bass: Cliff Minchau, drums: Grant Stovel

Recorded, mixed, and mastered by Ian Martin at Twilight Living Room Studios,
Edmonton, Alberta, Canada.

Index

adaptations and sequels, 178, 180

as "intelligent love stories," 165

authorship issues, 67–70

dancing in, 131–38, 167

height as characterization in, 73–82

introductions to, 178

juvenilia, 73–75, 140, 190

literary borrowing from, 187–89, 191

names, use of first and last, 173–75

novel reading in, 83–90

prayers, 13, 67–72, 93

publication and reception of, 42, 177–93

secrets, silence, and surprise in, 101–11

sublime and picturesque in, 91–100

women writers reading her works, 177–93

"Austen and 'The Advantage of Height'", 76

Austen-Leigh, James, 68, 180

Azania, Malcolm, xii

Babcock, Dave, xii, 259

Bacon, Francis, 145

Bander, Elaine, xv, 197–98, 253

Barbauld, Anna Laetitia Aiken, 86, 184

Barbour, Doug, xv, 113–14, 253

Bates, Miss (E), 78, 147–48, 162

Bates, Tony, 212

Bennet, Elizabeth (PP)

dancing in films (1995; 2005), 132–37

Darcy as father-husband for, 174–75

height as characterization, 74, 76–77

marriage and economic security, 156–58, 160–61

point of view in film (2005), 119–22

proposal scene (indoors vs. outdoors), 171–72

proposals to, 103–04, 107, 109

secrets, silence, surprise and, 102–10

spousal temperaments and, 168–71

views on picturesque and sublime, 91, 94–96

Bennet, Jane (PP), 103–06, 110, 120–22, 156–57, 169

Bennet, Kitty (PP), 120–22

Bennet, Lydia (PP), 104, 109–10, 120–22, 161–62, 175

Bennet, Mary (PP), 120, 134

Bennet, Mr (PP), 102, 121–22, 156–58, 168, 174

Bennet, Mrs (PP), 95, 102, 121–22, 156–58, 168, 171, 174

Benwick, Capt. (P), 75, 170

Bertram, Edmund (MP), 92, 96–97, 127, 157, 163, 169–70, 173–75, 179

Bertram, Julia (MP), 57, 79, 127–28

Bertram, Lady (MP), 127–28, 158

Bertram, Maria (MP), 57, 79, 128, 161–62, 171

Furrow, Melissa, xii, 255
  remembrance of B. Stovel, 15–16

Gardiner, Mr (PP), 110, 159
Gardiner, Mrs (PP), 106, 108, 159
Gilbert, Lafayette "Shorty," 260
Gilpin, Rev. William, 91, 93–96, 98
Girard, Rod, 4
Gould, Glenn, 226
Graham, Jean, 76–77
Grant, Anne, 184–87
Green, Jeannine, xvii, 42, 255
Green, Sarah, 84
Grey, Miss (SS), 161, 175
Grundy, Isobel, 255
  remembrance of B. Stovel, xii,
    11–14, 177
  on women writers reading JA's
    works, 177–93
Guest, Graham, xii, xv, xvii, 200,
    260
  remembrance of B. Stovel,
    47–49
Guiboche, Jim, xii, xv, 200, 260

Hall, Mrs, 166
Halliday, E.M., 105
Hamilton, Elizabeth, 184, 187
Hare, Auburn "Pat," 239
Hart, Jonathan Locke, xv, 55, 255
Harvard University, B. Stovel at,
    xvi, 3, 11, 44
Harville, Capt., 75
Hawkins, Augusta (E), 160
Hawkins, Laetitia Matilda, 185
Hayden, Cam, xviii

height as characterization in JA's
    works, 73–82
Hennelly, Mark, Jr., 76
High Level Diner, 250
Hoare, William, 62
Holland, Lady, 63
House, Son, 238, 240–41
Howlin' Wolf, xiv, 217–19
Hughes, Langston, 229–34
husbands in JA's works. See
    marriage in JA's works
Hutcheon, Linda, 87
Hutton, Catherine, 184

Ihara, Yuji, 260–61
"I'm Gonna Murder My Baby"
    (Hare), 239
Inchbald, Elizabeth, 184
Innes, Kathleen, 182
"Insignificant Dwarves and Scotch
    Giants" (Chan), 73–82
"Interrupted Friendships in Jane
    Austen's Emma" (Perry), 152
"In the Pursuit of Art" (Lim),
    223–26
"I Sing the Blues" (Guest), 47–49
"'I've Known Rivers'" (Rushdy),
    229–34

"JA Blues" (Barbour), 113–14
Jacobs, Heidi L.M., xii, 256
  remembrance of B. Stovel, 21–25
James, Etta, 221
James, P.D., 178
Jane Austen: A Students' Guide to
    the Later Manuscript Works
    (Southam), 71

as humourist, 15–16, 19, 23
as husband, 43
as interested in African
American culture, xiii–xv
as Jane Austen fan, xvi–xvii, 3–4,
13–14, 15–16, 20, 22–23, 39,
44, 165
as movie lover, 246–47
as music lover, 14, 44, 250
as neighbour, 7–9
as professor at Dalhousie
University, 3, 11, 15, 31, 246–
47
as professor at Yale University,
xvi, 3, 11, 44
as radio host, xii, xv, xvii–xviii,
4, 44, 200, 223, 225, 261
as reader, xvi, 22, 248
as student at Concordia
University, 3
as student at Harvard, xvi, 3, 11,
44
as student at McGill University,
xiv, xvi, 4
as student at University of
Cambridge, 3, 11
awards and honours, xvii, 4, 13,
43–44, 248
early life, xiii–xiv, xvi, 3–4, 43,
245–46
Edmonton Journal article on,
43–45
family life, xvi, 8, 11–12, 245–51
memorial celebrations, xi–xii,
xviii, 7–9, 11–14, 245–51
memorial half-mast flag at
U of A, xv, 43

memorial in special collections
library, xvii, 41–42, 53–54
memorial scholarship, xi, 4
overview of life of, 3–4, 258
retirement and passing, xi, 3–4,
43
student remembrances of, 17–
37, 73, 83, 91, 115–17, 221–26
Stovel, Joseph Bruce (Bruce),
studies with
blues as lyric poetry, 44, 201–26,
235–41
drama courses, 17–20, 27–30,
223–25
film studies, 115–17
JA's works, 22–23, 115–17
women novelists in 18th
century, 12–13, 177
Stovel, Joseph Bruce (Bruce), works
"Blues in the Academy," 201–15
"Emma's Search for a True
Friend," 139–53
overview of, 3–4, 13–14, 44
"Secrets, Silence, and Surprise
in *Pride and Prejudice*," 101–11
"'The Sentient Target of Death':
Jane Austen's Prayers," 13,
68–71
Stovel, Laura Elizabeth
family life, 8, 12, 245–51
life of, xi–xii, xiv, 24, 250–51,
258
on students of B. Stovel, 32
Stovel, Nora Foster
as ballet lover, 24, 246
as wife and mother, xiii–xiv,
11–12, 24–25, 43